The Insider-Outsider Theory of Employment and Unemployment

The Insider-Outsider Theory of Employment and Unemployment

Assar Lindbeck and
Dennis J. Snower

The MIT Press
Cambridge, Massachusetts
London, England

This book was set in Palatino by Asco Trade Typesetting Ltd., Hong Kong, and printed and bound by Halliday Lithograph in the United States of America.

Library of Congress Cataloging-in-Publication Data

Lindbeck, Assar.
 The insider-outsider theory of employment and unemployment.

 Bibliography: p.
 Includes index.
 1. Unemployment. 2. Wages. 3. Unemployed. 4. Labor turnover. 5. Job security.
I. Snower, Dennis J. II. Title.
HD5707.5.L56   1989   331.13'7   88-26079
ISBN 0-262-12139-5

To Dorothy and Judith

Contents

Foreword

The main part of this book consists of a number of articles that have been edited and amended to provide continuity and cohesion. The first and last chapters (chapters 1 and 11), however, have been written specially for the book. (Bibliographical information on the articles on which chapters 2–10 are based is given following this foreword.)

The book has been organized with a view to reconciling two potentially conflicting aims. On the one hand, the chapters are arranged in a sequence that is designed to convey a single, expositionally coherent account of the insider-outsider approach to wage, employment, and unemployment determination. Thus, those who read the book from cover to cover will, it is hoped, find a continuous line of argument. On the other hand, each chapter is self-contained, in the sense that the reader should be able to delve into separate chapters without reading the rest of the book. To reconcile these two objectives without being unduly repetitive, chapter 1 is meant to serve as an introduction, telling the reader enough about the terminology, assumptions, and implications of the insider-outsider approach to make each chapter independently comprehensible. In addition, each chapter is preceded by an overview, summarizing the main ideas of that chapter and relating them to the theme of the book.

The book has been written with the aim of making its main ideas accessible to a wide audience, without thereby sacrificing precision and rigor in our analysis. On one level, the book may be viewed as a contribution to basic research in macroeconomic theory and labor economics, and consequently some sections are rather technical. On another level, our basic message can be absorbed by undergraduates, nonspecialist economists, and policymakers. Accordingly, we have kept the introductory and concluding chapters (1 and 11) nontechnical, and the overviews to all the intervening chapters are of course easily digestible as well. The same may also be said of chapter 2 (which surveys current theories of unemployment) and chapter 4 (which surveys the insider-outsider theories of unemployment).

We are grateful to a number of colleagues who have read earlier drafts of individual chapters. In particular, we would like to thank David Begg, Alan Drazen, Niels Gottfries, Thorvaldur Gylfason, Ben Lockwood, Alan Manning, Torsten Persson, Carl Shapiro, Ron Smith, and Lars Svensson. Individual chapters have also been presented at seminars in various universities in Europe and the United States, including our home institutions, the Institute for International Economic Studies (IIES), Birkbeck College, and the Centre for Economic Policy Research (CEPR). Much of the work has been done at the IIES, whose research environment and facilities have been invaluable in conducting this research. The financial support of the Humanistic and Social Science Research Council of Sweden and the Economic and Social Research Council of the United Kingdom are gratefully acknowledged.

June 26, 1988

Assar Lindbeck
Institute for International Economic Studies
University of Stockholm

Dennis J. Snower
Birkbeck College
University of London
and CEPR

Articles on Which
Chapters 2–10 Are Based

Chapter 7: "Strike and Lock-Out Threats and Fiscal Policy," *Oxford Economic Papers*, 39, December 1987, 760–784. Copyright © 1987 Oxford University Press.
Previous version: "Strikes, Lock-Outs, and Fiscal Policy," Seminar Paper No. 309, Institute for International Economic Studies, University of Stockholm, Sweden, 1984.

Chapter 8: "Wage Rigidity, Union Activity, and Unemployment," in *Wage Rigidity and Unemployment* (ed. W. Beckerman), Duckworth and Johns Hopkins Press, 1986, pp. 97–125. Copyright © 1986 Johns Hopkins Press.
Previous version: "Involuntary Unemployment as an Insider-Outsider Dilemma," Seminar Paper No. 309, Institute for International Economic Studies, University of Stockholm, Sweden, 1984.

Chapter 9: "Union Activity, Unemployment Persistence, and Wage-Employment Ratchets," *European Economic Review*, 31, February 1987, 157–167. Copyright © 1987 Elsevier Science Publishers B.V. (North-Holland).

Chapter 10: "Long-Term Unemployment and Macroeconomic Policy," *American Economic Review*, 78(2), May 1988, 38–43. Copyright © 1988 The American Economic Association.

The Insider-Outsider Theory of Employment and Unemployment

1   Introduction

This is a book about "insiders" and "outsiders" in the labor market. Insiders are experienced incumbent employees whose positions are protected by various job-preserving measures that make it costly for firms to fire them and hire someone else in their place. The outsiders have no such protection; they are either unemployed or work at jobs in the "informal sector," which offer little, if any, job security. Insiders have more clout than outsiders. They participate in wage negotiations, either individually or through unions; they generally have an important influence on the work morale and productivity of their colleagues; they may cooperate with management in generating production, sales, and profits, or they may create strikes, work-to-rule actions, and absenteeism. Outsiders can do none of these things. This book analyzes how insiders get market power, what they do with that power, and how their activities affect the outsiders.

Of course, the outsiders can, and do, exert an indirect influence on the insiders' wages and job prospects. If the insiders demand too much compensation or call too many strikes or put too little effort into their jobs, then the employers may find it worthwhile to dismiss insiders and replace them by outsiders. The insiders know this and thus, in the conduct of their various activities, they try to ensure that they remain at least as profitable to their employers as the outsiders could be.

However, the outsiders' indirect influence is limited, for the simple reason that it is expensive for firms to replace insiders by outsiders. Before outsiders can truly take the place of insiders, the firm may have to to advertise for, screen, negotiate with, and train them—all costly, time-consuming activities that insiders clearly do not require in the same measure. Moreover, before insiders are dismissed, it may be necessary for the firm to implement costly firing procedures, engage in litigation, incur severance pay, run the risk of strikes, and create low morale in the remaining workforce. For these reasons, the insiders may face only limited competition from the outsiders.

Beyond that, the insiders may even be able to influence the outsiders' potential productivity and willingness to work. For instance, suppose that outsiders attempt to acquire jobs at the insiders' expense, by offering to work for less than the insiders' wages. Then the insiders may be able to protect themselves from such underbidding by refusing to cooperate with any new entrants in performing productive activities. Thereby the insiders may be able to reduce the marginal products of potential entrants sufficiently to discourage the firms from hiring these workers. Alternatively, the insiders may threaten to have unfriendly personal relations with newcomers who underbid (e.g., they may harass them), and they may thereby be able to raise the potential entrants' disutility of work sufficiently to discourage these workers from underbidding in the first place. In short, insiders may have some control over outsiders' potential profitability to the firm. The outsiders have no analogous influence.

As noted, there are two broad types of outsiders: unemployed workers and those employed in the "informal sector." For simplicity of exposition, this book (with the exception of the last chapter) deals almost exclusively with outsiders of the first type. In any event, it is worth noting that the distinction between the two types of outsiders may not always be sharp in practice, because unemployed workers often perform productive services in the "household sector" and sometimes even in the "underground sector" of the economy.

This book is concerned not just with the causes, but also with the micro- and macroeconomic consequences of insider market power. Perhaps the most important macroeconomic consequence is involuntary unemployment. In the first part of this book (chapters 2 and 3), we explore how the insider-outsider explanation for unemployment compares with the explanations offered by other theories. Another consequence of insider power is that temporary macroeconomic shocks may have persistent effects on wages, employment, and unemployment. This persistence phenomenon, sometimes called "hysteresis," is studied in chapters 9 and 10. The insider-outsider approach also provides a rationale for union activities, which are examined in chapters 6–9.

The next section of this introduction, section 1.1, describes the conceptual setup underlying the insider-outsider approach to the labor market. Section 1.2 summarizes some of the implications of this approach for wages and unemployment. Section 1.3 tries to clarify some potential misunderstandings of the insider-outsider theory. Section 1.4 outlines the structure of the book.

1.1 The Underlying Conceptual Setup

The insider-outsider approach focuses attention on one critical source of market power of incumbent workers: labor turnover costs. These include all the costs that arise when workers enter or leave a firm, and they come in many guises. Some may be set down by law, e.g., severance pay or advance notice of dismissal. Some are given by technological conditions, e.g., screening and training costs. Whereas all of these turnover costs are exogenous to the workers' decision making, others are endogenous, in the sense that they are the outcome of incumbents' rent-creating activities, such as the cooperation and harassment activities mentioned above. Yet other costs are introduced through various union activities (e.g., strikes or work-to-rule actions).

The insider-outsider theory divides workers into three groups, on the basis of the turnover costs above:

i. the "insiders," whose positions are protected by significant labor turnover costs,

ii. the "entrants," who have recently acquired jobs with a future prospect of gaining insider status, but whose current positions are not associated with significant turnover costs, and

iii. the "outsiders," defined above.

When an outsider is hired, he becomes an entrant to a firm. We assume that he retains his entrant status only for a limited period of time, which we call the "initiation period." During this span of time, the entrant acquires the productive and rent-creating skills of the insiders, gains job security through legal entitlement and possibly also union membership, and gets the opportunity to renegotiate his wage. (We assume that long-term wage contracts, whereby entrants can commit themselves to relinquishing their market power over their working lifetimes, are unenforceable.) Once the initiation period is over, the entrant turns into an insider.

The insider-outsider models in this book rest on five central assumptions:

A1: Insiders have some market power, arising from the economic rent that is generated by the labor turnover costs.

A2: Insiders use their power to pursue their interests in wage negotiations, without taking the entrants' and outsiders' interests fully into account.

A3: Outsiders and entrants have less market power than insiders.

A4: Entrants become insiders after a limited "initiation period," and insiders become outsiders immediately after losing their jobs.

A5: The present value of a firm's wage costs over a worker's remaining lifetime is positively related to the insider wage.

Each of these assumptions plays a crucial role in our analysis of wages, employment, and unemployment. If insiders had no market power (contrary to A1) or if they were no more powerful than the entrants and outsiders (contrary to A3), then they would be unable to drive their wages above the entrant wage and the outsiders' reservation wage. If insiders would pursue the outsiders' interests as diligently as their own (contrary to A2) or if dismissed insiders would retain their insider status in wage negotiations (contrary to A4), then the insiders would have little incentive to raise their wages above the market-clearing level. Finally, if firms' total wage costs per worker would not be positively related to the insider wage (contrary to A5), then the insiders' wage-augmenting activity would not lead to a fall in employment and a rise in unemployment (as discussed below).

The insiders' wages are assumed to be the outcome of negotiations between insiders and their firms. The insiders may bargain "individualistically" (each insider taking the wages and employment of all other insiders as given) or collusively (say, through a union). The employment decisions are assumed to be made unilaterally by the firms.

The wage, employment, and rent-creating decisions may be depicted as part of a two-stage decision-making sequence. In the first stage, wages are negotiated and insiders plan their rent-creating activities (if any), taking the employment response to these decisions into account. In the second stage, firms make the employment decisions, taking the wages of insiders and entrants as well as the rent-creating activities as given.

In exercising market power in the wage negotiation process, the insiders drive their wages above the minimum level at which entrants would be prepared to work. But, on account of the labor turnover costs, the firms may nevertheless have no incentive to replace their insiders by entrants. The greater the turnover costs, the greater the wage that the insiders can achieve without creating the threat of dismissal. For this reason, it may be in the insiders' interests to exert upward pressure on the turnover costs through their rent-creating activities or political lobbying.

In practice, of course, the distinction between insiders and entrants is generally one of degree rather than of kind. With the passage of time, workers tend gradually to gain more experience at their jobs, become better acquainted with their colleagues and bosses, and receive greater legal protection. As result, the costs of replacing this worker by an outsider rise gradually. In short, there may be many degrees of "insiderness," and our sharp distinction between insiders and entrants is made merely for simplicity. As will be discussed in the final chapter, there may also be many degrees of "outsiderness" in practice, since laid-off insiders may lose their insider status only gradually. The distinction between the short-term and long-term unemployed turns out to be important for various purposes.

1.2 Wages and Unemployment

To paint a clear and instructive picture of how insiders may exercise upward pressure on wages and thereby generate unemployment, let us make a convenient assumption: Suppose that each insider *sets* his wage individualistically (taking the wages and employment of all other insiders as given), with due consideration for the maximum wage the firm is willing to pay. Consequently, each insider sees himself as the marginal incumbent employee when setting his wage. Relative to the influence that insiders exert on wage negotiations in practice, this assumption clearly overstates the insiders' power in one respect, since they generally do not have unilateral control over their wages. However, it may understate it in another respect, since the insiders of a firm often negotiate in unison rather than individualistically. Nevertheless, the assumption is useful since it puts the insiders' role in wage and employment determination into sharp relief. It also serves as a reminder that the insider-outsider theory is not merely a theory of union activity, even though it provides a rationale for such activity.

Our assumption of individualistic wage setting implies that the insider wage will be set as high as possible, subject to two constraints:

i. the insider must remain profitable to the firm (the "absolute profitability constraint") and

ii. the insider must remain at least as profitable to the firm as the marginal entrant (the "relative profitability constraint").

The first condition implies that the insider wage must not exceed the marginal revenue product of the firm's incumbent workforce plus the marginal firing costs (since each insider views himself as the marginal incumbent). If this condition were not fulfilled, the firm would dismiss the insider. The second condition implies that the insider wage must not exceed the entrant wage plus the marginal hiring and firing costs. If this condition were violated, the firm would replace the insider by an outsider.

Under this setup, the level at which the insider wage will actually be set depends on the size of the firm's incumbent workforce. To illustrate why, let us assume that the firm's production technology is characterized by diminishing returns to labor. Thus, the larger is the firm's incumbent workforce, the lower the marginal revenue product of this workforce will be, and the lower the entrants' marginal revenue product will be as well.

When the firm's incumbent workforce is sufficiently large, the entrants' marginal revenue product (net of the marginal hiring costs) falls beneath their reservation wage, and consequently entrants are not profitable to the firm. Since entrants are then completely excluded from finding jobs in the firm, the insiders can disregard the relative profitability constraint and rather set their wage in accordance with the absolute profitability constraint. In short, the insider wage is set equal to the marginal revenue product of the incumbent workforce plus the marginal firing costs.

On the other hand, when the firm's incumbent workforce is sufficiently small, so that entrants' marginal revenue product (net of the marginal hiring costs) exceeds their reservation wage, then some entrants will be hired. The insiders are now in competition with the entrants, and thus they set their wage in accordance with the relative profitability constraint. In this case, the insider wage is a markup over the entrant wage, with the size of the markup determined by the sum of the marginal hiring and firing costs.

One important implication of this analysis is that the insider wage—and and therefore also the level of employment—depends on the size of the firm's incumbent workforce. The same may hold true on a macroeconomic level. In an economy populated by firms of the sort described above, the equilibrium levels of aggregate employment will be determined, in part, by the size of the aggregate incumbent workforce. This aggregate incumbent workforce, in turn, is historically given—its size depends on the size of the aggregate incumbent workforce in the previous period, the rate at which insiders retire or quit, and the number of entrants in the previous period. The number of entrants in the previous period depends, inter alia, on past macroeconomic shocks, which affected entrants' marginal revenue products. This economy does not contain a "natural rate of employment" since the equilibrium employment level is not uniquely given by the preferences, technologies, and endowments of agents, but also depends on the size of the initial incumbent workforce.

As mentioned above, the exercise of insider power may give rise to involuntary unemployment. To see how this can happen, we need to take a closer look at the labor turnover costs. Let us divide these costs into "production-related" and "rent-related" turnover costs. The former (which might be screening or training costs) are necessary to attract, train, motivate, and retain employees. The latter are not primarily required to secure productive services, but rather are the outcome of job security legislation or rent-creating activities. For example, legislation may determine severance pay, whereas rent-creating may (as we have seen) include insiders' refusal to cooperate with workers who gain their jobs through underbidding, or insiders' harassment of such underbidders.

Due to the rent-related turnover costs, insiders work under more favorable conditions than those that the outsiders must face in order to gain employment. In particular, for any given wage—normalized by productivity differences—the insider's chance of retaining his job exceeds the outsider's chance of finding a job.

The outsiders may be willing to work for a wage that falls short of the insider wage by an amount sufficient to compensate the firms for insider-outsider productivity differences and all production-related turnover costs, but the outsiders may nevertheless be unable to find jobs. The reason, obviously, is that the rent-related labor turnover costs may be sufficiently high to discourage firms from hiring the outsiders.

In short, the outsiders have a smaller choice set—in terms of wages received and productive services offered—than the insiders. It is job security legislation, union activity, and the structure of social relations between insiders and other workers that is responsible for the outsiders' restricted opportunities. Their unemployment is "involuntary" in the sense that they would like to be "in the shoes" of the current insiders, but are unable to find jobs on account of the *discrimination* they face in the labor market.

Our notion of involuntary unemployment captures what laymen often consider to be its most distinguishing feature: the social injustice of being unemployed due to unequal opportunities. This notion may be clarified by the following simple analogy:

A little old lady is accosted by a mugger, who proposes, "Your money or your life." The lady considers her options, chooses the former, and hands over her wallet.

Is this transaction voluntary? Some economists might wish to argue that it is, because the lady's action is the outcome of a voluntary choice. But most people would disagree, since the lady's choice set—through no fault of her own—is more limited than that of other, comparable agents. Our notion of involuntary unemployment follows the latter view. Outsiders are involuntarily unemployed when their choice sets—through no fault of their own—are more limited than those of the insiders.

On a different tack, some economists may argue that the outsiders described above are not really involuntarily unemployed because they may have the same expected stream of lifetime utility as the insiders, provided that the utility streams are evaluated at the beginning of the agents' respective working lifetimes. After all, every insider was once an entrant, and if every entrant receives his reservation wage (which is consistent with A4), he is indifferent between work and leisure over his lifetime. Consequently, by this argument, no outsider can be involuntarily unemployed. However, this is like arguing that the little old lady voluntarily gave the mugger her wallet because, when she was young, she decided not to move to a safer neighborhood. According to our definition, workers are involuntarily unemployed when they are unable to find work on the same terms as insiders—regardless of the relative magnitudes of their lifetime utilities. We want to capture the notion of inequality of opportunity over a period starting at a particular time, when some workers are insiders while others are entrants or outsiders.

Furthermore, it might be argued that the insiders' exercise of market power may not generate unemployment, because changes in the insider wage may not lead to changes in employment. To fix ideas, suppose that insiders find new rent-creating opportunities and consequently drive up the insider wage. As result, the reservation wage must fall (for the higher the wage that workers expect to receive in the future, the lower the wage they are willing to accept at present). Now suppose that entrants receive this reservation wage. Then the firm's present value of expected wage payments over a worker's remaining lifetime may remain unchanged, the higher wage that the worker receives as an insider being counterbalanced by the lower wage he receives as an entrant. In that event, the firm's employment may also be unchanged. If so, the insiders' influence over their wage would not create unemployment, but merely steepen the intertemporal wage profile.

Assumption A5—whereby a rise in the insider wage raises the firm's present value of wage costs per worker—excludes this possibility. Various rationales may be given for this assumption. For example, workers may have a higher rate of time discount than firms, and consequently a rise in the insider wage may not reduce the reservation wage sufficiently to keep the firm's present value of wage costs (under the firm's rate of time discount) from falling. Besides, the entrant wage may exceed the reservation wage because (a) the insiders (possibly operating through their unions) exert upward pressure on the entrant wage (in order to discourage under-bidding or new hiring) or (b) the entrant wage may be infeasible on account of credit restrictions or minimum wage laws. Yet whatever the reason, assumption A5 appears plausible: in practice, we do not find that entrants' wages fall whenever the insiders' wages rise.

As noted, our formal analysis is not concerned with the "secondary (informal) sector" of the economy, where there is little job security. Rather, we are primarily concerned with the "primary (formal) sector," where jobs are protected by significant labor turnover costs. Yet even though the secondary sector is often an important source of employment, it does not necessarily do away with involuntary unemployment. As will be explained in the final chapter of the book, workers in the secondary sector—like the unemployed—are "involuntarily" shut out of the primary sector if they would have preferred primary sector jobs. As outsiders cannot escape discrimination by accepting jobs in the secondary sector, it is reasonable to regard the jobless outsiders as involuntarily unemployed, even though they choose not to work in the secondary sector. After all, their choice set (in terms of labor services provided and wages received) is more limited than that of the insiders in the primary sector. It is perhaps due to considerations like these that work in low-paid, insecure jobs in the secondary sector has often come to be called "disguised unemployment."

1.3 Potential Misunderstandings

At this point it is important to clear up some potential misunderstandings of the insider-outsider theory. Here are four particularly tempting pitfalls.

First, the theory is *not* a variation on a theme established by the efficiency wage theory. As explained in chapter 3, the two theories rest on different assumptions and have different implications. As the efficiency wage theory focuses on firms' influence on wage determination whereas the insider-outsider theory focuses on workers' influence, the two theories may be viewed as complements, not substitutes.

Second, the insider-outsider theory is *not* primarily a contribution to the analysis of union behavior. Hiring and firing costs may well be present even when unions are not. The rents associated with these costs may be quite substantial even when workers bargain individualistically with their firms. Moreover, cooperation and harassment activities can be pursued within any small group of employees who work as a team; unions are not necessary here either. In many cases, these activities may, of course, be executed more effectively through union initiatives, but they often develop informally and do not necessarily need to be institutionalized through union activities.

Third, although the insider-outsider theory shows why the size of a union's membership can exert a strong influence on the union's objectives in wage negotiations, the theory aims to make a more fundamental contribution to the union literature: It provides a rationale for union activities by showing how unions can augment economic rent, which permits them to achieve higher wages for their members. It also explains how labor turnover costs give unions their clout. Finally, it examines how the magnitude of these turnover costs, along with threat credibility, can constrain the union in pursuing its wage-employment goals.

Fourth, the insider-outsider theory is *not* just about European labor markets, and in particular, it is *not* just designed to explain the persistence of unemployment in Europe during the 1980s. Rather, the theory is meant to apply to any labor markets in which labor turnover costs are significant and workers have some say in wage negotiations. Admittedly, turnover costs appear to be much more prominent in Europe than in the United States, and the theory does suggest that prolonged adverse shocks will have comparatively persistent effects in countries with comparatively high turnover costs. But the insider-outsider rationale for the persistence of European unemployment is just one of many implications, which are summarized in the final chapter of the book.

1.4 The Structure of the Book

The continuous tale running through the chapters of this book is illustrated in figure 1.1 and may be summarized briefly as follows:

Chapter 2, "Explanations of Unemployment," contains a nontechnical survey of recent theories of unemployment, written primarily for the "educated nonspecialist." It covers both voluntary and involuntary unemployment (shown in the second row of the figure), but focuses particular attention on the latter. It shows how different theories relate to one another and sets out criteria for assessing their strengths and weaknesses. We argue that two particularly important criteria for evaluating rival theories of involuntary unemployment are whether they explain (a) why involuntarily unemployed workers and layed-off workers are unwilling or unable to find jobs by underbidding the currently employed workers and (b) why firms do not capture all the rent associated with employment activities.

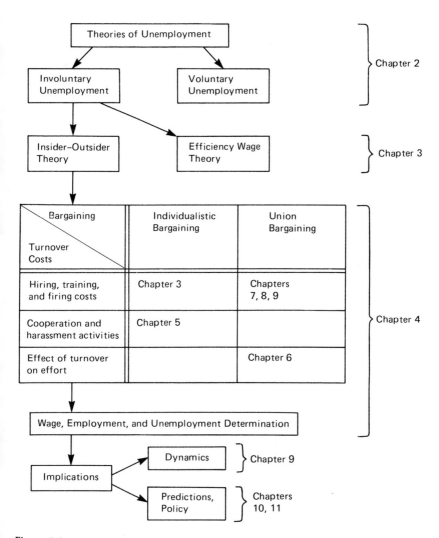

Figure 1.1
Organization of the book.

Chapter 3, "Efficiency Wages versus Insiders and Outsiders," takes a closer look at two theories that address these questions. This chapter attempts to provide a simple and concise overview of the formal structure of the efficiency wage theory and the insider-outsider theory and shows in what sense these theories are complementary. We describe how the incentive to keep wages above their market-clearing levels is ascribed to firms by the efficiency wage theory, and how it is ascribed to incumbent workers by the insider-outsider theory.

Chapter 3 indicates that there are many different types of labor turnover cost whereby insiders may gain market power, and there are many different types of wage negotiation in which this power may be exploited. To fix ideas, this book considers three important types of labor turnover cost:

hiring, training, and firing costs,

costs arising from insiders' cooperation and harassment activities, and

costs arising from the effect of job security on work effort.

We also consider two types of wage negotiation:

"individualistic bargaining," in which each insider bargains individually with his employer, taking the wages and employment of all other employees as given, and

"union bargaining," in which all insiders in a firm bargain jointly with their employer.

These varieties of labor turnover cost and of wage negotiation are illustrated by the matrix in the fourth row of figure 1.1. The formal analysis of chapter 3 rests on a particularly simple combination of them: Insiders derive their power from hiring, training, and firing costs, and they bargain individualistically (as shown in the first row and first column of the matrix).

In chapter 4, "Wage Setting, Unemployment, and Insider-Outsider Relations," the conceptual underpinnings are examined in greater depth. In particular, we show how the different types of labor turnover costs (described above) give insiders different levers for exerting influence on their wages. We discuss how involuntary unemployment can arise in each case. The chapter also provides an overview of the economic role of unions in the insider-outsider theory.

Whereas chapter 3 deals with hiring, training, and firing costs as the basis of insider activities in the labor market, chapters 5 and 6 are concerned with other types of labor turnover costs. In chapter 5, "Cooperation, Harassment, and Involuntary Unemployment" (shown in row 2, column 1 of the matrix in figure 1.1), we analyze how insiders may protect themselves against underbidding through cooperation and harassment activities, as discussed before, and how involuntary unemployment can arise as result.

In chapter 6, "Job Security, Work Incentives, and Unemployment" (shown in row 3, column 1 of the matrix in figure 1.1), we investigate the effects of labor turnover—and, more generally, job security—on work effort. In order for underbidding to take place, it may be necessary for firms to replace their high-wage insiders by low-wage outsiders. Yet such replacement may be costly to the firms because it may have an adverse effect on workers' effort. We examine how the resulting turnover cost affects wage and employment determination and may generate involuntary unemployment.

To show that insiders may have an important role to play even in labor markets that do not contain unions, chapters 3–6 assume that insiders bargain individualistically over their wages. By contrast, chapters 7–9 provide economic rationales for union activities and examine how these may affect wages, employment, and unemployment. Although any of the turnover costs analyzed in chapters 3–6 could serve as a source of union power, for simplicity, our formal analysis focuses attention on hiring, training, and firing costs. We concentrate on two important union activities: striking and working to rule.

In chapter 7, "Strike and Lockout Threats and Fiscal Policy," the union's strike threat is seen as a "wage-preserving device," in the sense that the firm's rejection of the union's wage proposal provokes a strike. In addition, we analyze a rather common response by firms to strikes: the lockout. In this context, we argue that the traditional model of union behavior—in which the union's utility function is maximized subject to a labor demand function or an isoprofit function—must be amended to take account of two constraints on a union's wage setting: (i) the "union punch constraint," which reflects the amount of damage that the union can potentially inflict on the firm, and (ii) the "credibility constraint," which describes the wage demands under which the strike threat remains credible. We show that the effect of fiscal policy on wages depends on which of these constraints is binding.

In chapter 8, "Wage Rigidity, Union Activity, and Unemployment," the strike threat is depicted as a "job-preserving device," since the firm's decision to fire a union member triggers the strike. We provide an economic rationale for a union's work-to-rule threat. Furthermore, we show how insider wages respond to changes in entrant productivity, hiring-training-firing costs, and the probability that the strike will persist.

Chapters 9 and 10 deal with some macroeconomic implications of the insider-outsider theory. In chapter 9, we show how insider power over wage setting may make a labor market less "resilient." In particular, the exercise of insider power may perpetuate the effects of unforeseen, transient labor demand shocks on unemployment. We identify two types of unemployment persistence: "symmetric persistence," whereby the fall in unemployment from a favorable shock is just as large as the rise in unemployment from an unfavorable shock of equal magnitude, and "asymmetric persistence," whereby the favorable shocks reduce unemployment by less than the unfavorable shocks increase it. We believe that the current discussions of the "hysteresis" phenomenon in the labor market could benefit from these distinctions.

Chapter 10 analyzes unemployment persistence from foreseen shocks and examines the implications for macroeconomic policy. We argue that when insiders have some power in wage determination, the notion of a natural rate of unemployment loses much of its usefulness. Furthermore, the associated effectiveness of demand-management policies on wages and employment is shown to depend significantly on the supply-side effects of these policies.

Finally, chapter 11 discusses the predictions of the insider-outsider theory regarding a number of phenomena that it was not originally designed to explain: the persistence of temporary macroeconomic shocks; the variability in employment over time; the existence of dual labor markets; the level, duration, and composition of unemployment; the wage-employment trade-off; and the interindustry wage structure. The chapter concludes with a discussion of some of the theory's policy implications.

2   Explanations of Unemployment

Overview

This chapter surveys various theories of unemployment, examines the relations among them, and attempts to evaluate their comparative strengths and weaknesses. We accord special attention to the most recent theories of involuntary unemployment. These aim to provide microeconomic rationales for some workers' persistent failure to find jobs even in the absence of government or union impediments to wage adjustment. Thereby the chapter also provides the backdrop against which the insider-outsider theory of unemployment is to be understood and evaluated.

A fundamental distinction among the various explanations of unemployment is that between the market-clearing and non-market-clearing approaches. The various Keynesian and "Classical" theories, as well as more recent contributions, fall into either one or the other category.

The pre-Keynesian theories of unemployment were non-market-clearing, at least in the labor market: unemployment was portrayed as the outcome of government wage regulations and other artifical impediments to trade, such as minimum wage laws, or sluggish labor market adjustments to changing economic conditions. Thus, unemployment was regarded either as a temporary phenomenon ("frictional unemployment") or as a problem that can be solved by reducing government or union interference in the labor market.

The Keynesian theories also dealt with a nonclearing labor market, but the diagnosis of the unemployment problem and the associated policy implications were quite different. Two dominant models of unemployment emerged from the literature built on Keynes's General Theory*: In one model, the labor market fails to clear on account of nominal wage rigidities, whereas prices adjust to clear the product market. Here, unemployment is associated with an excessive real wage, as in the pre-Keynesian analysis. But in contrast to that analysis, the problem could be rectified through expansionary fiscal or monetary policies, which raise prices* relative to nominal wages and thereby reduce the real wage and increase employment. In the other Keynesian model, both the nominal wage and the price level is rigid and there is excess supply in both the labor and product markets. Here the demand for labor is derived from the demand for products, so that unemployment is associated with deficient product demand, rather than with an excessive real wage. Expansionary macroeconomic policies lead to a chain reaction of demand increases in the labor and product markets, as described by the Keynesian multiplier.

The New Classical Macroeconomics, by constrast, has pursued the market-clearing approach. This literature is concerned more with explaining fluctuations in output and employment than with explaining unemployment; however, as the variations in employment considered by these theories are commonly accompanied by variations in leisure, it is often argued that "voluntary unemployment" is analyzed. In one strand of this literature, fluctuations in employment simply reflect intertemporal substitution of labor on the supply or demand side in connection with anticipated wage changes through time. In another version, agents may make their labor demand and supply decisions on the basis of incorrect (albeit rational) expectations. Here, unemployment may arise in the sense that agents decide to work less than they would have done under correct expectations.

Despite their obvious differences, the Keynesian theory and the New Classical Macroeconomics suffer from some similar deficiencies. The failure of wages and prices to clear their respective markets (in the Keynesian models) and the failure of agents to engage in information acquisition (in the New Classical Macroeconomics) are each responsible for unexploited gains from trade, and neither theory explains why agents do not to exploit them. Furthermore, both theories generally rest on the assumption of wage- and price-taking, which can be rationalized by supposing that each market contains many agents, each of whom has perfect information and can buy and sell as much as he wants at the prevailing wages and prices. However, when markets do not clear or when information is imperfect, agents generally become imperfectly competitive wage and price setters.

These deficiencies (and others) have been addressed by more recent theories of unemployment. In the market-clearing tradition, the following (partially overlapping) approaches have been particularly significant:

• In the implicit contract theories, wage-employment contracts serve not only to remunerate workers for their productive services but also to provide insurance against income fluctuations. These contracts are set before business conditions are known, and thus adverse shocks may give rise to unemployment.

• In the imperfectly competitive macroeconomics, there is a division of responsibility over price and quantity decisions. For example, sellers may set prices *while buyers may determine the quantity transacted. This division of responsibility may be Pareto inefficient, and thus the resulting level of employment may fall short of the socially desirable level.*

• *In the* customer market theory, *variations in relative prices induce agents to engage in a costly search process. Agents are willing to pay a premium for stable prices, which obviate the need for search. Applied to the labor market, this theory suggests that workers may be willing to work at a discount for employers who keep their wages sufficiently stable to make job search unnecessary. If firms make employment decisions unilaterally, then such wage stability in a business downturn may give rise to unemployment.*

• *The recent literature on* inventories and delivery lags *also has applications to the labor market. When firms face significant costs of hiring, training, and firing, their employment decisions must take account of their "inventories" of incumbent workers and "delivery lags" for new workers. The implications of these considerations for unemployment remain largely unexplored, although some have been taken up by the insider-outsider theory.*

• *The* multiple-equilibrium theories *show that there may be "low-employment" as well as "high-employment" equilibria, on account of the shapes of the labor demand and supply functions, externalities of search by both workers and employers, and expectations of future market conditions.*

The non-market-clearing approach to unemployment has given rise to a different set of recent developments:

• *In* adjustment cost theories, *the real wage may not adjust to clear the labor market due to costs of wage and price changes. Administrative wage-price adjustment costs have received some attention, but are unlikely to be sufficiently large to explain observed fluctuations in unemployment rates. Goodwill considerations, costs of oligopolistic retaliation, and costs of formulating collective bargaining agreements may be much more important in explaining wage-price sluggishness, but these remain largely unexplored.*

• *In* labor union theories, *the union is assumed to have some market power in the labor market and the exercise of this power may give rise to a wage that exceeds the market-clearing wage. The resulting unemployment is "union-voluntary" (since the union is responsible for the supracompetitive wage) but may be "membership-involuntary" (e.g., if the unemployed members could be made better off by abolishing the union). The shortcoming of these theories is that they generally do not explain what gives the unions their clout (i.e., why nonunionized workers are not able to underbid the wage negotiated by the union), why unions do not represent the interests of the unemployed workers, and why the unemployed unionized workers do not engage in underbidding.*

• *The unemployment theory centering on* increasing returns to scale *aims to show why involuntarily unemployed workers may be unable to start new firms and thereby create jobs for themselves. The reason is that under increasing returns to scale and imperfect competition in the product market, new firms must be large but the entry of large new firms may significantly depress product prices.*

• *In the* efficiency wage theory *(which is described more fully in chapter 3), wages are positively correlated with the productivity of their employees or negatively with the training costs. Thus firms may have an incentive to keep wages above the market-clearing level.*

• *In the* insider-outsider theory *(to be covered in greater detail by the rest of this book), the jobs of incumbent workers are protected through the existence of labor turnover costs, and thus the incumbent workers are able to drive their wages above the level at which the unemployed workers would be willing to perform their jobs.*

In the final part of this chapter, we formulate criteria for evaluating rival theories of involuntary unemployment. In particular, we require that a successful theory should be able to explain

• *why involuntarily unemployed workers and laid-off workers are unwilling or unable to underbid the current employees,*

• *why firms are unwilling or unable to capture all the economic rent associated with employment activities,*

• *why the involuntarily unemployed workers do not employ themselves by starting new firms,*

• *why the involuntarily unemployed workers do not form coalitions with firms and/or their employees in order to exploit all the relevant potential gains from trade, and*

• *why the involuntarily unemployed workers are unwilling or unable to engage in job sharing with their employed counterparts.*

The theories above are then evaluated with reference to these criteria. We argue that the efficiency wage theory and the insider-outsider theory come closest to satisfying these criteria. We present a simple analytical comparison of these two theories in the next chapter.

Economists commonly distinguish between two sorts of unemployment. Roughly speaking, the "involuntarily unemployed" workers are unwillingly out of work (i.e., they feel that they would be better off with jobs). On the other hand, the "voluntarily unemployed" workers prefer to be out of work (for any of a wide variety of reasons—e.g., because they are searching or training for a job or because they choose leisure over work).

This chapter attempts a selective evaluation of what appear to be particularly noted or fruitful contributions to the literature on this subject, especially the most recent. The emphasis is primarily on involuntary unemployment.

Our ultimate concern lies with theoretical explanations of involuntary unemployment; empirical studies lie outside our purview. Strange as it may seem to the layman, economists have found it difficult to agree on what should be meant by involuntary unemployment and to pose coherent arguments that show why people who are willing and able to work at the prevailing wages in market economies cannot find jobs when they seek them. Thus, an evaluation of the theoretical explanations—even without consideration of empirical testing—turns out to be quite a challenge in its own right. Besides, some of the most intriguing explanations in the running are too recent in origin to have received significant empirical attention.

The chapter is organized as follows. Sections 2.1–2.3 provide an overview of "early" (pre-1970s) and recent contributions to the literature. The purpose is to isolate the salient strengths and weaknesses of rival explanations, thereby reducing the field to a few interesting contenders, which are to be considered in greater detail later. Section 2.4 attempts to clarify what economists commonly mean by the term "involuntary unemployment" and proposes several criteria that successful explanations of involuntary unemployment might satisfy. The few chosen contenders are evaluated in this light.

2.1 Early Contributions

As noted, economists have had a difficult time explaining how involuntary unemployment comes about and why it may persist for substantial periods of time. They appear to have gone through all the various behaviors that doctors exhibit in the face of unresponsive patients: skepticism, diagnosis, refinement of the diagnosis, finding reasons for doubt, retracting the diagnosis, pronouncing the problem nonexistent, formulating a new diagnosis, and so on.

Until the mid-thirties, the conventional economic wisdom was that unregulated market economies can overcome the problem of involuntary unemployment automatically, though temporary unemployment spells may occur. The standard story ran as follows. Changing economic conditions —arising out of, say, new tastes, technologies, patterns of world trade—

mean shifting business fortunes, and the workers who happen to find themselves in the declining sectors may be put out of work. Naturally, they then seek work elsewhere and, if they do not find it reasonably promptly, they reduce their wage demands. This process continues until the unemployed have either found jobs or are no longer willing to work. Whatever the outcome, involuntary unemployment disappears, provided that wages are not regulated by government or strong unions.

The Great Depression of the thirties and the less severe (but nonetheless painful) recessions since then appear to have put the lie to this tale. Even if we accept that government and union controls may be responsible for some unemployment, it is farfetched to suppose that *swings* of the unemployment rate in major capitalist countries between, say, 2 and 10% in the postwar period (or between 5 and 20% in the interwar period) have depended on *changes* in such controls.

Thus, we are forced to reopen the question of why market economies are periodically unable to provide all the jobs that people look for. The answers to this question are of critical practical importance, since they suggest economic policies needed to alleviate the problem.

2.1.1 The Early Keynesian and "Classical" Diagnoses

Keynes's (1936) diagnosis in the thirties attributed unemployment to a deficient demand for goods. Unemployment persists because the deficient goods demand arises from unemployment itself: Firms employ too little labour because their customers buy too few goods. And the reason for the customers' deficient demand is their limited purchasing power, which, in turn, is due to the circumstances that a proportion of them is unemployed. Thus, the vicious macroeconomic circle is closed.

One way to break it is through government demand-management policies. A rise in government spending induces firms to employ more labor, which raises purchasing power, and thereby leads to increased private-sector spending (which induces firms to employ even more labor, and so on). In general, a rise in the aggregate demand for goods (regardless of whether it arises from government expenditure increases, tax reductions, export increases, etc.) leads to a fall in unemployment and (if firms' production capacity thereby becomes exhausted) possibly also to inflation. This was the basic diagnosis-treatment combination that the Keynesians refined throughout the fifties and much of the sixties.

The early Keynesians have been opposed by economists who believe that economic activity in every unregulated market has an inherent tendency to reach its "natural," market-clearing rate. Moreover, during the last two decades, divergences of actual activity from this "natural rate" have been regarded as primarily due to errors in wage-price expectations. This latter hypothesis is known as the "natural rate hypothesis," and we shall call its proponents the "natural rate theorists" (which include some Keynesian as well as non-Keynesian economists). Needless to say, the natural rate hypothesis is testable only in conjunction with a theory of expectations formation, which tells us how the errors in wage-price expectations arise. The early contributors to the natural rate hypothesis assumed theories of expectation formation that allowed systematic errors to occur. By contrast, many descendants of this group believe that such systematic errors do not occur, i.e., that expectations are "rational." The proponents of this view are known as "New Classical Macroeconomists."

The natural rate theorists indicated that the Keynesian diagnosis was not in accord with the then accepted body of microeconomic theory (e.g. Friedman 1968) or with the actual movement of inflation and unemployment, particularly in the late sixties and early seventies (e.g., Flanagan, 1973; Gordon, 1972; Wachter, 1976). The microeconomic theory presupposed that economic agents buy and sell all that they wish to demand and supply at the prevailing wages and prices. In other words, markets were assumed to clear, so that full employment prevails. Moreover, the empirical evidence appeared to suggest that fluctuations in aggregate demand were not consistently driving inflation and unemployment in opposite directions.

Accordingly, the natural rate theorists proposed a different diagnosis, whereby unemployment was viewed as the outcome of errors in people's wage-price expectations and/or government regulations. The expectational errors are due to people's inability to predict economic events accurately, and one source of these errors may be unanticipated changes in government policies. The unemployment-inducing government interventions may be not only wage-price controls, but also a wide variety of other regulations: High unemployment benefits and high marginal tax rates may create voluntary unemployment reducing people's incentive to work at low-paying jobs; rent-control and government provision of housing may reduce mobility of labor and thereby give rise to frictional unemployment; government regulations restricting the entry of new firms may also create frictional unemployment.

Thus, according to the natural rate theorists, unemployment could be viewed as either voluntary ex ante (since the expectations are formulated freely, though errors are regretted once they come to light) or straightforwardly curable (by eliminating the relevant government interventions). Of these two explanations, the one concerning expectational errors received the lion's share of attention. It was consistent with market clearing: regardless of what people's *expected* wages and prices may be, the *actual* wages and prices would move to bring demand and supply into equality in each market.

2.1.2 The Reappraisal of Keynes

Throughout the seventies, these two broad stands of thinking about unemployment—the Keynesian and the natural rate—were elaborated and reinterpreted in virtual mutual disregard.

The Keynesian camp attempted to develop microeconomic foundations for its macroeconomic unemployment theory (see for example, Barro and Grossman, 1976; Benassy, 1975; Dreze, 1975; Malinvaud, 1977; Muellbauer and Portes, 1978). This line of research has come to be called the "Reappraisal of Keynes." Here, economic agents pursue the same objectives under the same constraints as in the natural-rate world, except that they now take into account the possibility of being rationed. An economic agent is "rationed" whenever his preferences, technology, and endowments lead him to demand or supply more than he is able to buy or sell at the prevailing wages and prices. For example, under involuntary unemployment, workers are rationed, so that the prevailing wages and prices induce them to supply more labor than they are able to sell.

In the natural-rate world, such rationing could not persist because wages and prices are assumed not only to be responsive to surpluses and shortages, but capable of eliminating them. The wage-price adjustment process continues until demand and supply in each market are identical. In the Reappraisal of Keynes world, involuntary unemployment persists because wages (and possibly also prices) are not viewed as responsive in this sense. Instead, they are assumed to be "rigid" at levels that are incompatible with full employment. The "rigidity" lasts at least long enough for agents to make their demand and supply decisions compatible with the rations they face. Thus, the reason why involuntary unemployment was seen to arise from deficient demand for goods is that wages failed to clear the labor market. Under rigid wages, firms may have no incentive to hire unemployed workers, since these workers would produce goods that the firms may be unable to sell.

This was a departure from Keynes's own position. Keynes did not make his explanation of unemployment entirely dependent on the assumption of wage-price rigidity. Rather, he argued that even if they were responsive to excess supplies and demands, involuntary unemployment would nevertheless refuse to disappear. In other words, once the vicious circle of unemployment and deficient goods demand was in place, it would take more than wage-price deflation to get rid of it. Thus, there was no need to look very closely at the hows and whys of wage-price rigidity.

One difficulty with this argument lay in the "real balance effect": when wages and price fall, the real values of monetary assets held by the private sector may rise, thereby stimulating private sector spending and reducing unemployment. The real balance effect was debated as early as the 1930s, when Pigou offered it as a challenge to Keynes. Despite considerable (albeit sporadic) attention, the debate is still unresolved. Keynesian economists have argued that the monetary assets in question are not significantly large, that the effect of a rise in real balances on private sector spending is small, and that even if this effect were large, there are equally large counterveiling effects at work when the economy suffers from involuntary unemployment and deflation (e.g., expectations of further deflation in the future). Yet the empirical evidence is inconclusive.

It was only by assuming that wages (and sometimes also prices) were fixed that the Reappraisal of Keynes microfoundations could be constructed. Economic agents accept the prevailing wages and prices—together with the resulting rations—as given and formulate their demands and supplies on this basis. But not only do rations influence demands and supplies but—since one agent's purchases are another agent's sales—these demands and supplies also influence the rations. A major job in the Reappraisal of Keynes was to describe the circumstances under which all the rations are "consistent" with each other, in the sense that a particular set of rations gives rise to a particular set of demands and supplies, which, in turn, gives rise to the original rations.

For example, when firms' sales are rationed, they demand a limited amount of labor. The limited labor demand gives rise to job rationing. And when jobs are rationed, workers demand a limited amount of goods. This limited goods demand leads to a rationing of firms' sales. The big question is whether this sales rationing is the same as that with which we started out. If so, then the firms' sales rations are "consistent" with the workers' job rations. The Keynesian "multiplier" is a portrayal of how this happens. For example, when government expenditures rise, firms employ more labor and thereby raise workers' job rations. As a result, the workers buy more goods and the sales rations rise to become consistent with the previous job rations. But more sales call for more employment, and thus the job rations must rise to become consistent with the previous sales rations. At the end of this multiplier process, the two sets of rations are mutually consistent.

Wages (and possibly also prices) in this theory remain fixed long enough for ration-consistency to be achieved. The question that remains open is why. The Reappraisal of Keynes provided no answer. Early contributors suggested that since wages and prices could not be expected to clear their markets completely and instantaneously—and massive swings in unemployment as well as inventory and order-backlog statistics bear this out—it is reasonable to suppose that they are "rigid." But such rationalization is unsatisfactory. It is one thing to agree that wages and prices do not clear respective markets; it is quite another to suppose that they remain unaffected by the entire process in which rations become consistent.

Thus, there is a hole in the logic of the Reappraisal of Keynes theory: The assumption of wage-price rigidity was not rationalized in terms of agents' objectives and constraints. This is a serious drawback, since the Keynesian policy prescriptions are generally not independent of the prevailing wage and price levels. If government policies (such as changes in taxes and transfers) and their private sector repercussions do indeed affect wages and prices—and it would be a strange world in which they did not—then the Reappraisal of Keynes theory ceases to provide reliable guidelines for dealing with problems such as involuntary unemployment.

The only sort of economy that the Reappraisal of Keynes can cover in a logically consistent manner is one with a comprehensive system of wage controls (and perhaps also price controls). This may be a reasonable approximation of some centrally planned economies, but it is certainly a long way away from the market economies that had been the focus of Keynes's attention.

Nevertheless, since Keynes's time, most capitalist countries have evolved a variety of wage restrictions, as governments tried (effectively or ineffectively) to keep their citizens from falling beneath particular minimum standards of living. There have been minimum wage laws, public sector pay scales, and various other government regulations regarding labor remuneration. Could it be argued that these are responsible for involuntary unemployment of the Keynesian variety? Paradoxically enough, this would imply that the Keynesian explanation of involuntary unemployment is the *same* as that suggested by the pre-Keynesian economists.

The underlying argument is straightforward: If the legal minimum wage is greater than the wage required to clear the labor market, then labor supply will exceed labor demand. But at second glance, things become more complicated. If employers have monopsony power in an unregulated labor market, the imposition of a minimum wage may *raise* the level of employment, since it prevents the exercise of this monopsony power (e.g., Maurice, 1974; Stigler, 1946). When the minimum wage has incomplete coverage, its imposition merely drives labor from the covered into the uncovered sectors (Gramlich, 1976; Mincer, 1976; Welch, 1974). The empirical evidence is that the effect of the minimum wage on unemployment is not overwhelming (e.g. Moore, 1971; Lovell, 1972; Ragan, 1977; Brown, Gilroy, and Kohen, 1982). The volatile statistics of wage inflation from year to year do not give the impression that there are rigid institutional forces fixing the levels or rates of change of wages.

2.1.3 The Natural-Rate Hypothesis and the New Classical Macroeconomics

Meanwhile, as the Reappraisal of Keynes developed in the seventies, the natural-rate camp refined its analysis of how expectational errors can cause swings in the unemployment, employment, and production. A variety of microeconomic rationales were adduced for the natural-rate hypothesis.

In the "misperceived real wage approach" (related to the work of Friedman, 1968, 1976 and others), the real wage relevant to firms is the nominal wage they pay in terms of the product price they receive and the firms are assumed to have reasonably accurate perceptions of both elements. On the other hand, the real wage relevant to workers is the nominal wage they receive in terms of the expected consumer good prices they pay and they may misperceive the later element (i.e., the prices). The greater the expected price level relative to the actual one, the smaller the real wage perceived by the workers relative to that perceived by the firms. As a result, the lower is the level of employment. The difference between the full-information level of employment and the actual employment level (above) is often called voluntary unemployment.

The upshot of the argument is this. If the price level falls unexpectedly while the nominal wage clears the labor market, firms reduce their labor demand (since the real wage rises for any given amount of employment) and workers reduce their labor supply (since their expected real wage falls for any given amount of employment, due to a fall in the nominal rate). Thus, the greater the difference between the expected and actual price levels, the greater the rate of voluntary unemployment, in the sense mentioned above.

In the "misperceived interest rate approach" (inspired by Lucas and Rapping, 1970; Weiss, 1972; and others), workers misperceive real interest rates. The greater the expected rate of inflation relative to the actual inflation rate, the smaller the perceived real interest rate relative to the actual one. If workers respond to a fall in the real interest rate by reducing their current labor supply (since current work yields less purchasing power in the future), then employment falls. Here, the greater the difference between the expected and actual inflation rate, the greater is the rate of voluntary unemployment.

In the "capital gain approach" of Lucas (1975), economic agents know the current price level, but they can observe neither the money balances transferred by the "young" generation to itself when it becomes "old" nor the distribution of the population between "young" and "old." A low current price level may be due to either a low money transfer or a large "young" generation (which is assumed to produce all the goods). Since the "young" people do not know which is the case, they suppose that each of them is possible. The smaller the current price relative to the expected future price, the greater the capital loss on the intergenerational money transfer anticipated by the "young" people (since they ascribe a low current price, in part, to a large "young" cohort). Consequently, employment falls. Once again, we find that the difference between expected and actual prices is positively related to the voluntary unemployment rate.

In the "job search approach" (Alchian, 1970; Gronau, 1971; MacCall, 1970; Mortensen, 1970; Parsons, 1973; Siven, 1974; and many others), workers may misperceive the distribution of wages that they face. On the basis of their perceived wage distribution, they are viewed as calculating the marginal benefits and marginal costs of being unemployed while searching for a job. (Here the explanation of unemployment rests on the assumption that job search can be performed only while unemployed). The greater the workers' expected wages relative to the actual wages they face, the greater the marginal benefits of job search relative to the associated marginal costs. Consequently, the greater is the amount of job search, the greater is the level of search unemployment.

Finally, the "wage setting approach" of Phelps (1970a) goes far beyond the standard conceptual confines of the natural rate hypothesis. It explicitly recognizes that when workers have imperfect information about wage offers, firms gain monopsony power in the labor market. Phelps assumes that the greater the unemployment rate and the lower a firm's vacancy rate, the lower the firm will set its wage relative to what it perceives the average market wage to be. Given that unemployment and vacancies are inversely related, there is a unique "natural" rate of unemployment, at which each firm sets its wage equal to its perceived average market wage. Moreover, the lower the unemployment rate, the greater the difference between each firm's set wage and its perceived average market wage (and consequently the faster the average market wage rises). Note that, unlike the other approaches to the natural-rate hypothesis, unemployment is not necessarily voluntary here; i.e., the analysis does not rely on the assumption that the labor market clears. This is also true of Phelp's paper (1967), which provided the first formal statement of the natural rate hypothesis.

Mortensen (1970) adopts a similar approach, except that he assumes firms choose their profit-maximizing wage-employment combinations from a sequence of short-run labor supply curves. Due to workers' imperfect information about wage offers, a "high" wage generates an increasing supply of labor to the firm (at that wage) and a "low" wage generates a shrinking supply. Since workers are not off their labor supply curves, whatever unemployment there is may be considered voluntary ex ante (i.e., voluntary, given workers' imperfect information).

Another related strand of labor market-clearing literature is concerned with the "intertemporal substitution hypothesis" (see Barro 1976); Brunner, Cukierman, and Meltzer, 1980; Grossman and Weiss, 1982; Lucas and Rapping, 1969; Lucas, 1972; and many others). According to this hypothesis, temporary changes in the real wage and the real interest rate lead households to change their intertemporal allocation of work and leisure. In particular, a fall in the current real wage and the current interest rate induce a fall in the current labor supply and hence also in the level of employment. Of course, firms may also engage in intertemporal substitution of labor demand for other factors or for inventories. Note that this is a theory about fluctuations in employment, not unemployment.

The next influential development was the "rational expectations hypothesis" (see, for example, Muth, 1961; Walters, 1972; Lucas, 1976). Economic agents are assumed to avoid predictable errors in expectations. What is "predictable" depends on the particular economic model we have in mind. With reference to such a model, agents' expectations are "rational" whenever they coincide with the predictions of the model itself, contingent on the information the agents are assumed to have.

In the so-called "New Classical Macroeconomics," the rational expectations hypothesis is combined with the natural-rate hypothesis to yield dramatic implications for the nature of unemployment. Whatever the expectational errors are that generate unemployment (in accordance with the natural-rate hypothesis), they must be unpredictable (in accordance with the rational expectations hypothesis). Consequently, all unemployment is not only voluntary ex ante, but also quite transient; it can last only as long as the unpredictable errors (and their repercussions) do. If the natural rate of unemployment does not change much through time, then the actual unemployment rate must move as randomly as the unpredictable errors that generate it (see, for example, Barro, 1976; Lucas, 1972; McCallum, 1980; Sargent and Wallace, 1975; Shiller, 1978).

This line of thinking ran into some severe difficulties. In empirical studies using any of the standard macroeconometric models of major market economies, the movement of the unemployment rate through time certainly does *not* appear to be predominantly random (e.g., Hall, 1975). Consequently, a number of economists (e.g., Lucas, 1973; Sargent, 1976) have argued that the natural rate of unemployment moves cyclically and thereby explains the cyclical movement of the actual unemployment rate. Yet the suggested rationales for such activity (e.g., a prompt investment response to swings in wage-price expectations) are not obvious. Moreover, it would of course be absurd to argue that the massive unemployment of the thirties, accompanied by the misery and sometimes even homelessness and starvation of the unemployed workers, was the result of their desire to choose more leisure or to engage in more job search on account of a change in their expectations about real wage rates or interest rates.

Recall that what is considered "random" (viz., unpredictable) depends on the reference model, and the appropriate reference model, in turn, depends on the economic information that economic agents possess. But how do we find out what economic agents know? In would be a logically and practically hopeless task to find out by asking them directly. Thus, it is difficult to see how the rational expectations hypothesis could be falsified. A stopgap strategy would be to develop a theory of information acquisition and this theory could then be tested conjointly with the rational expectations hypothesis. To date, however, little has happened in this area.

In practice, this problem is commonly sidestepped by simply assuming that the public always knows the structure of the macroeconomic model used by the author of each successive article on this subject. Usually any disagreement between the public and the author is ascribed to the supposition that the public's economic statistics are one year (or one quarter) out of date. There is something rather curious about the view that households and firms in every country always change their perception of the world whenever a new rational-expectations macro model is constructed.

2.1.4 The Standoff

At this point in the development of Keynesian and New Classical macro-economic thinking, the controversy over the causes of unemployment seemed to have stalled. The Keynesian economists had three major objections to the New Classical research program. First, they regarded the Neoclassical assumption of clearing markets as blatantly counterfactual. They found it impossible to believe that the unemployment of, say, the 1930s depression or the 1978–1982 recession was largely voluntary.

Second, they had overwhelming doubts that errors in wage-price expectations could be large enough to account for the magnitude and length of witnessed fluctuations in unemployment. It seemed implausible that these errors should have such a powerful impact on workers' labor supply, that the unemployment rate could frequently double or halve in the course of a single year. It seemed even more implausible that these errors—occurring largely because macroeconomic data is not available to the people who need them—should be unavoidable for time periods long enough to explain the persistence of recessions. Yet if this objection is granted and thus (in accordance with the natural-rate hypothesis) unemployment fluctuations are attributed mainly to swings in the natural rate of unemployment, there is another difficulty. The natural rate of unemployment depends solely on the tastes, technologies, and endowments of an economy and these are quite unlikely sources of cyclical macroeconomic activity.

Third, the New Classical economists provided no microeconomic reason for why the public does not acquire those pieces of information that it needs to avoid its expectational errors. (Why is it that newspapers, government statistical bureaus, and economic consulting agencies do not publish them?) Of course, there are costs of information acquisition and dissemination, but little attempt has been made thus far to show that these costs are sufficiently large to account for the costs of periodic recessions.

On the other side of the barricades, the New Classical macroeconomists pointed out that the Reappraisal of Keynes theory was incomplete in its scope, defective in its logic, and misleading in its policy implications.

As already noted, the quantities demanded and supplied in each market are formulated in accordance with agents' objectives and constraints, but prices are not explained in this way. Prices are neither set by individual agents, nor driven by market forces. A macroeconomic theory that covers quantity determination but not price determination—even though quantities demanded and supplied do, in general, depend on prices—must be incomplete.

Furthermore, when markets fail to clear, agents face unexploited gains from trade: By changing the prices and quantities at which they trade, some agents could be made better off without any others being made worse off. For example, when there is involuntary unemployment, the marginal product of labor (which underlies the market-clearing labor demand) falls short of the marginal value of workers' time (which underlies the market-clearing labor supply). Thus, by employing additional workers, producing additional output, and selling this output to consumers, the agents could succeed in generating goods whose value—in terms of labor time—is greater than its cost. These are the sorts of gains from trade that agents in market economies have obvious incentive to exploit. Yet in the Reappraisal of Keynes world, these gains are exploited only through quantity adjustments, not through price adjustments. This theory does not explain why Pareto-improving changes are blocked.

Finally, although the Reappraisal of Keynes theory implies that the way in which government policies affect unemployment depends (in part) on wage and price levels, the theory does not tell us how these wage and price levels respond to the government policies. In fact, wages and prices are assumed impervious to policy influence. Now, if this assumption turns out in fact to be false, then the theory provides no way of assessing what the effectiveness of government policies is.

Thus the Keynesians and New Classical macroeconomists had reached a standoff. The most convincing arguments of the contestants seemed to be their criticisms of each other.

It is interesting to observe that the weaknesses of the two positions are in fact quite similar. The failure of agents to acquire information that would enable them to avoid expectational errors, and the failure to adjust prices when in the agents' interests to do so—these both are potential instances of unexploited gains from trade.

Another weakness (which has received somewhat less attention) concerns the assumption that agents accept the prevailing wages and prices as beyond their control. This assumption is standard both in the Reappraisal of Keynes and in the New Classical Macroeconomics, but it does not sit well in either. Price-taking is usually associated with perfect competition, which arises out of two conditions:

a. there are many well-informed buyers and sellers in a market, each responsible for only a negligible proportion of the transactions in the market, and

b. each agent (with given tastes, technologies, and endowments) can buy or sell as much as he wishes to demand or supply under prevailing wages and prices.

These conditions imply that when a seller raises the price of his commodity above the prevailing market price, he loses all his buyers; and when the price is reduced, he gains more buyers then he can satisfy. (Similarly also for price-setting buyers.)

But when markets do not clear—as they do not in the Reappraisal of Keynes—the second condition does not hold. For example, when there is involuntary unemployment, workers are unable to sell all the labor they wish to supply. In that case, they are generally able to influence their employment rations (e.g., their places in job queues or their amount of part-time work) by adjusting their wages. Similarly, when there is deficient demand for goods, firms are unable to sell all the output they wish to supply, but they may well be able to influence their sales rations by adjusting their prices. Under these circumstances the incentive to be a price-taker disappears. However, the macroeconomic activity—and, in particular, the unemployment—which arises from price-setting behavior (e.g., Hart, 1982; and Snower, 1983a) is quite different from that described by the Reappraisal of Keynes.

In the same vein, when agents do not have perfect information about the wages and prices they face—as they do not in the New Classical Macroeconomies—the first condition does not hold. A firm that raises the price of its product above the prevailing market price does not lose all its customers, because some customers will not be aware that firm's product is overpriced. Similarly, a firm that reduces its wage payments beneath the prevailing wage does not lose its entire workforce, because some workers will not realize that they can get higher pay elsewhere. Once again, agents gain some latitude in setting their prices and price-taking behavior disappears. Phelps (1970a,b) and Mortensen (1970) are among the few who recognized the inconsistency of assuming that the agents have imperfect information *and* that they are price-takers. Apart from their work, little has been done to explore the macroeconomic implications of price setting within the New Classical framework of thought.

In this light, it would appear eminently sensible to investigate explanations of involuntary unemployment that recognize the existence of both imperfect information and price-setting behavior. Indeed, this has been the thrust of many recent contributions to the unemployment literature. But the joint assumptions of imperfect information and price setting do not go well the market-clearing foundations on which the New Classical Macro-economics is built.

When price setters are imperfectly informed about their economic environment, there is no guarantee that the set prices will eliminate all surpluses and shortages. (For example, a monopolist who does not know precisely what demand curve he faces may offer to sell his output at a price that results in undesired inventories or delivery backlogs.) Furthermore, when the price setters have less information about their products than the price takers (on the other side of the market), then prices may be set so as to influence product quality. As shown below (under the heading of the "efficiency wage hypothesis," section 2.3.4), this setup may also be incompatible with market clearing. Consequently, it is not surprising that many recent contributions to the unemployment literature have moved away from the presumption that all markets clear or have rested on new concepts of what "market clearing" means.

2.2 Recent Contributions in the Market-Clearing Tradition

Starting in the mid-seventies, both sides in the debate on the causes of unemployment began to address the criticisms they faced. By this time, loyalties to past schools of thought had faded, so that economists studying nonclearing markets no longer automatically considered themselves "Keynesian" and those exploring clearing markets were no longer always called "New Classical." Nevertheless, the divergent lines of research remained.

On the market-clearing side, there were several significant developments, of which the following perhaps deserve special attention.

2.2.1 Implicit Contracts

In their simplest guises, the "implicit contract theories" (e.g., Azariadis, 1975, 1979; Azariadis and Stiglitz, 1983; Bailey, 1974; Gordon, 1974; Grossman and Hart, 1981, 1983; Hart, 1983) combine three perceptions of labor markets:

a. workers are more risk averse than firms,

b. workers have less access to capital markets than firms, and

c. workers are imperfectly mobile among firms.

The first two elements imply that efficient wage-employment contracts involve an insurance package by firms to workers. The third implies that both the firms and the workers must decide in advance whom to employ, at what wage, and under which circumstances.

One aim of this analytical setup was to show that, under unpredictable, adverse business conditions, workers may be laid off in accordance with their previously agreed contracts. Here the underlying concept of "market clearing" is different from that of the natural-rate hypothesis.

In the latter, agents formulate their demands and supplies on the basis of their wage-price expectations and then actual wages and prices adjust so as to bring demand and supply into equality in each market. Thus, the market clears in the following ex ante sense: For the given expectations (which may or may not be mistaken), the offers to buy are matched by offers to sell. Yet ex post (when agents have discovered whether their expectations were mistaken), the market participants may conclude that it would have been better to have made different offers. But the past cannot be undone and, at every moment in time, demand and supply are equal.

By contrast, in the implicit contract theories, contingent trading agreements are made before the corresponding transactions take place and thus the market clears in a different ex ante sense: Given the agents' expectations, the contingent agreements are efficient (in that it is impossible to make one party better off without making another worse off). Yet ex post (when the agreements are put into effect on the basis of the contingencies that occur), it may turn out that offers to buy may not be matched by offers to sell. For example, labor demand may fall short of labor supply. In that event, the workers who turn out to be unemployed may wish to renegotiate their labor contracts, but do not have the opportunity to do so.

Whether such unemployment is called *"ex ante voluntary"* or *"ex post involuntary"* is a semantic issue. At any rate, the persistence of this unemployment now depends not merely on the survival of unavoidable expectational errors (as in the New Classical Macroeconomics), but also on workers' imperfect ability to move among firms and to renegotiate their labor contracts.

2.2.2 Imperfect Competition

This line of research (e.g., Blanchard and Kiyotaki, 1987; Hart, 1982; Layard and Nickell, 1984; Snower, 1983a) explores how imperfectly competitive behavior may generate suboptimally low employment—quite independently of any other impediments to trade (such as costs of information acquisition or costs of price change). Sellers are assumed to have some market power, whereas buyers have none. Thus, there is a division of responsibility over price and quantity decisions. In the product markets, firms set prices and workers decide how much of the goods to buy; in the labor markets, workers (say, through their unions) set nominal wages and firms make the employment decisions. The firms face product demand curves and the workers face labor demand curves. Moreover, the demand curves that firms and workers perceive may or may not coincide with the ones they actually face; viz., they may be "conjectures." In this sense, Hahn's work (1977, 1978) on "conjectural equilibria" fits into this framework as well.

At first glance, one may be tempted to consider the sellers to be "rationed," in the sense that their decisions are constrained by the demand curves they face. However this is a quite different concept of rationing from the one used in the Reappraisal of Keynes. Workers who freely and unanimously set their wages—knowing full well what the resulting levels of employment will be—can scarcely be called involuntarily unemployed.

The above division of responsibility over price and quantity decisions may be inefficient (in that a benevolent and omniscient dictator who determines wages and prices could make some agents better off without making others worse off). In particular, employment may be less when competition is imperfect than when it is perfect. In that event, employment may be called suboptimally low.

2.2.3 Customer Markets

Another line of research combines imperfectly competitive behavior with the observation that, in some markets, customers compare the relative prices of similar products mainly when they perceive these prices to be unstable through time. This product search behavior may induce the sellers to stabilize their prices, viz., not to adjust their prices completely and instantaneously to demand and supply shocks.

Okun (1976, 1981) distinguishes between "auction markets" (which always clear) and "customer markets" (where product search may occur). In the latter, product search is costly to the customers, and thus they are willing to pay a premium to sellers who keep their prices sufficiently stable to obviate the need for search. In practice, Okun suggests, this means that sellers may adjust their prices to permanent changes in cost, technologies, or overall demand, but not to transient ones (and particularly not ones that affect sellers in the same market differently). In other words, these sellers may be induced to keep their long-run markup (of prices over costs) roughly constant through time.

In principle, these ideas could also be applied to "customer labor markets," where workers find job search costly and are willing to work at a discount for employers who keep their wages sufficiently stable to make job search unnecessary. Yet, to date, there has been no methodical, detailed statement of this principle.

Moreover, the entire microeconomic rationale for customer markets remains incompletely explored. Given a customer's costs of product search, why should his search decision depend on the stability of a product price relative to the long-run costs of producing that product, rather than on the marginal benefits of search (which is related to the probability of finding a cheaper product)? If the latter is the case, then the stability of price relative to long-run costs is entirely irrelevant; all that matters is whether a product price is above or below the "acceptance price" (at which the marginal costs and benefits from search are equal).

2.2.4 Inventories and Delivery Lags

Another reason why prices may be sluggish in response to demand and supply shocks is that it may be profitable to adjust inventory levels and delivery lags as well (see, for example, Blinder, 1980, 1981; Carlton, 1978, 1979). Consider, for example, a profit-maximizing firm deciding on inventory holdings of its finished goods. Its output is such that its marginal cost of production equals the shadow value of inventories; its sales equate the shadow value of inventories with its marginal revenue. (Naturally, the difference between output and sales represents changes in the inventory stock.) A temporary increase in demand (reflected in marginal revenue) has little effect on the shadow value of inventories (which depends primarily on long-run considerations), and thus sales rise while production remains sluggish. Consequently, inventories must decline. Similarly, a temporary increase in marginal costs reduces production relative to sales, causing inventories to fall as well. These inventory responses to demand and supply shocks mean that the associated price adjustments are more moderate than they otherwise would have been. An analogous story can be told regarding delivery lags.

Yet although inventories and delivery lags can explain price sluggishness, this does not in turn explain the existence of unemployment. In the Reappraisal-of-Keynes models, temporary policy shocks have a smaller short-term impact on unemployment when inventories and delivery lags adjust than when they do not. In the New Classical models, unexpected policy shocks give rise to inventory movements, and thus their effect on employment lasts beyond the time during which expectations are in error.

Yet to explain unemployment, the logic of inventory holdings and delivery lags must be applied to the labor market itself. When there are significant costs of hiring, firing, and training, the profit-maximizing firm operates on several margins. In its hiring decision, it sets the marginal revenue product of inexperienced labor against the wage minus hiring and training costs. In its firing decision, it compares the marginal revenue product of experienced labor with the wage minus firing costs. And to find how much of its current labor to use (rather than to employ), it sets the relevant marginal revenue product against the wage. This general framework could explain unemployment, as well as labor hoarding, and vacancies. Elements of this have been taken up by insider-outsider analysis, but otherwise little attention has been devoted to this area. Ehrenbert (1971), Epstein (1982), Nickell (1978, 1984), Mortensen (1973), and others have examined employment decisions when the firm faces adjustment costs, but they do not explore how these generate unemployment.

2.2.5 Multiple Equilibria

According to this line of research, the labor market may be characterized by multiple equilibria, so that there may be "low-employment" as well as "high-employment" equilibria. There are various reasons why this may be so.

First, there may be externalities in the process of job search. These externalities may originate on both sides of the labor market: When a worker decides to search for a job, other workers' chances of finding a job are reduced and the firms' chances of filling their vacancies are increased through this decision (*ceteris paribus*). When a firm decides to search for an employee, other firms' chances of filling their vacancies are reduced and workers' chances of finding jobs are increased through this decision (*ceteris paribus*). (See, for example, Drazen, 1985ab; Howitt, 1986; Mortensen, 1988).

Second, multiple equilibria may exist due to the market participants' expectations of future market conditions. These future conditions are relevant to current labor demand and supply decisions because, for example, lags in the production process mean that firms' current employment decisions are made with a view to future sales. Alternatively, households' current labor supply decisions are based on a comparison of current and future wages, as shown in the intertemporal substitution hypothesis.

Third, there is the obvious possibility that, independently of the reasons above, firms' profit-maximizing and households' utility-maximizing behavior patterns may be such that the aggregate labor demand curve crosses the aggregate labor supply curve more than once in wage-employment space. A well-known example of this phenomenon arises in the case of a downward-sloping labor demand curve and a backward-bending labor supply curve.

Of these ideas, which lie (on the whole) in the market-clearing traditions, some (viz., the approaches concerned with customer markets and with inventories and delivery lags) are not sufficiently developed for critical appraisal; the imperfect competition approach deals with suboptimal employment arising from inefficiencies due to the exercise of market power, whereas the literature on multiple labor market equilibria analyzes the possibility of getting stuck in a low-employment equilibrium, and the implicit contract theories describe unemployment that is voluntary when labor contracts are signed, but may be involuntary once these contracts are in operation. Only the implicit contract approach contains a new insight into the causes of involuntary unemployment, and so it is this approach that will be taken up in section 2.4.

2.3 Recent Contributions in the Non-Market-Clearing Tradition

The investigators in the non-market-clearing tradition have endeavoured to meet the original neoclassical criticisms. Their research has proceeded along several distinct routes.

2.3.1 Adjustment Costs

The rigidity of wages and prices can be rationalized on the basis of wage-price adjustment costs (i.e., costs of wage or price changes). Whenever these costs exceed the associated benefits from setting wages and prices at their market-clearing levels, markets will fail to clear without leaving agents with unexploited gains from trade. In this context, the administrative costs of price changes (e.g., writing new price tags, printing new catalogs) has commanded some attention (e.g., Barro, 1972; Sheshinski and Weiss, 1977), although it was soon noted that such costs are quite unlikely to be large in comparison to the costs of forgone production during recessions.

However, the wage-price adjustment costs may also include a wide variety of negotiation costs (e.g., employers' and workers' costs of formulating new collective-bargaining agreements, the expected costs of retaliation in oligopolistic and oligopsonistic markets) and these appear to be far more substantial. Yet these latter costs have not, as yet, been incorporated, in formal macroeconomic models, where their impact on unemployment can be conceptualized.

The recent literature on "menu costs" (originated by Akerlof and Yellen, 1985; Manikiw, 1985) is concerned not so much with the sources of wage-price adjustment costs as with the magnitude they need to attain in order to be responsible for significant macroeconomic fluctuations. In particular, this literature shows that even in the presence of small adjustment costs, variations in aggregate demand or in the money supply may lead to large swings in output and employment.

For example, consider an imperfectly competitive economy in an initial equilibrium in which firms make the pricing, employment, and production decisions so as to maximize their profits subject to their production functions and product demand functions, while households (perhaps via unions) make wage-setting and product purchase decisions so as to maximize their utility subject to their budget constraints and labor demand functions. All price and quantity variables are assumed to be at levels that would be optimal in the absence of menu costs. Thereupon a contractionary monetary shock occurs. As result, firms face an inward shift in their product demand functions and, given that their production functions are characterized by diminishing returns to labor, they thereby gain an incentive to change their prices and labor demands. Similarly, workers face an inward shift in their labor demand functions and, given that their utility functions are characterized by diminishing utility of leisure, they thereby gain an incentive to change their wages and product demands.

In this context, it can be shown that the costs of wage and price adjustment are of second order; i.e., as the initiating shock tends to zero, the optimal wage-price adjustment tends to zero as well. However, the shock has first-order effects on firms' and households' objectives. Consequently, in the presence of menu costs and a small initiating shock, firms and households will not adjust their prices and wages, but will adjust their quantities. In this way, contractionary shocks may lead to reduced employment.

This is an interesting new development in the non-market-clearing literature, but it leaves some problems unresolved. First, the shocks that are actually responsible for severe recessions are large, whereas the argument above holds for small shocks. In the case of large shocks, it is conceivable that the second-order effects may be larger than the first-order ones.

Second, if agents do not in fact adjust wages and prices in response to shocks, then it is not reasonable to assume that, in the initial equilibrium (before the initiating shock occurs), all these adjustments have taken place. But the argument above does not necessarily hold if the initiating shock occurs when all the price and quantity variables are *not* at the levels that would be optimal in the absence of menu costs.

Third, in an inflationary environment, agents do in fact change wages and price regularly. Then, presumably the menu-cost argument must be amended to explain why these wage-price adjustments are not sufficiently large to obviate the need for significant quantity adjustments. But it is not apparent how such an explanation would run, especially since it does not appear to be much more costly to change wages and prices by large amounts than by small amounts.

Fourth, even if the menu costs are sufficient to ensure that a contractionary monetary shock reduces aggregate sales and production, that does not necessarily mean than employment will fall as well. In the face of this contractionary shock, firms may find it comparatively cheap to reduce sales and production simply by running up inventories or hoarding labor. But reducing employment may be comparatively expensive, not only on account of firing costs, but also on account of the expected hiring and training costs that will have to be incurred once the shock is over. In short, the contractionary shock will reduce employment only if we assume the menu costs of wage-price change to be large relative to the costs of hiring, training, and firing labor. This appears to be a rather implausible assumption.

2.3.2 Union Activity

In this approach (e.g., McDonald and Solow, 1981; Oswald, 1982; Gylfason and Lindbeck, 1984; Calmfors and Horn, 1985), workers are assumed to belong to unions, whose objective is given by a weighted average of their employed and unemployed members' welfare. If the union is "utilitarian," then the weights are the *numbers* of employed and unemployed members, respectively. Here the union is concerned with the *sum of* its members' welfares. On the other hand, if the union's objective is "expected utility," then the weights are the *proportions* of employed and unemployed members (respectively) to the total membership. The rationale for these objectives is that each union member is indifferent to risk and has an equal chance (over each period of time) to occupy the jobs at the union's disposal, in which case the weights may be interpreted as the probabilities of being employed and unemployed, respectively. (For constant membership, these two objectives yield the same wage-employment outcomes.)

Now suppose that the union sets the wage and the firms decide how much labor to employ at that wage. The resulting wage-employment combination is that point on the labor demand curve that maximizes the union's objective. In general, there will be some unemployment. If the union members are really risk-indifferent and have an equal chance at the available jobs, then this unemployment will be in each member's best interest. Otherwise there must be a conflict of interest between the union and its members and the unemployment will be "union-voluntary" and "membership-involuntary" (Corden, 1981).

It can be shown that the wage-employment combination above is inefficient, in the sense that the union could be made even better off without any sacrifice of firms' profits (see, for example, Leontief, 1946; McDonald and Solow, 1981). Efficient bargains involve maximizing the union's objective subject to the firms' achievement of some minimum level of profit. Here, too, the upshot will generally be some unemployment, which may or may not be voluntary from the members' viewpoint.

The problem with this explanation of unemployment is that it is not complete. First, recognizing that union members are usually *not* risk-indifferent and do *not* stand an equal chance at the available work, why do unions not represent their members' interests? Why is the available work not shared out equally among the members (through part-time labor arrangements or job rotation)? If unions do this (as in Snower, 1983), then involuntary unemployment would disappear (with the possible exception of the voluntary sort, due to inefficiency associated with the exercise of monopoly power).

Second, why do firms enter into agreements with the unions in the first place? Why do they not turn to nonunionized workers instead? If they could do so, the unions would lose their bargaining power and wages would fall to their market-clearing level.

This is not to say that the questions above are unanswerable, but merely that economists have not given them much attention. The second group, however, is tackled explicitly in the recent work on insider-outsider analysis (discussed below).

2.3.3 Increasing Returns to Scale

Weitzman (1982) considers a market economy characterized by increasing returns and imperfect competition and aims to show how the interaction of these two elements may be responsible for involuntary unemployment.

In particular, the increasing returns apply to labor and arise out of fixed costs (i.e., the greater the firm's workforce, the lower its fixed costs per unit of output). The imperfect competition is of the Chamberlinian (1933) monopolistic variety: Each firm produces a different product and there are sufficiently many firms, so that each firm can be assured that its activity has a negligible influence on its rivals.

For simplicity, all firms are assumed to be alike. Each makes its pricing, production, and employment decisions unilaterally, maximizing its profit subject to its product demand curve. When there are positive profits to be made, new firms are born; when profits are negative, some firms die. In the long run, the number of firms is such that profits are zero. Not surprisingly, it turns out that this number depends inversely on each firm's fixed costs and positively on aggregate demand (which, in turn, is inversely related to the unemployment rate).

All households are also assumed to be alike, except for their employment status. They can be either fully employed or completely unemployed (i.e., part-time work is ruled out). Their tastes are such that all firms' products are equally popular, at equal prices. The lower a product price, the higher the associated demand. Each product has substitutes, in the sense that if one product's price rises, then the demand for some other products rises as well. Every household devotes its income exclusively to the consumption of the product of its choice.

In the long-run equilibrium there are no incentives for change. Not only are profits zero, but the firms set their respective prices, production, and employment so that their marginal costs are equal to their marginal revenues, and the households find all the available jobs and buy the firms' products with the resulting purchasing power. It can be shown that each firm sets its price by a proportional markup depending (strangely enough) *inversely* on aggregate demand (Weitzman, 1982, p. 800). In other words, through its price-setting the firm determines the real wage (which is the inverse of the price-wage markup). The greater the level of aggregate demand, the greater the real wage.

Weitzman contends that the long-run equilibrium may be compatible with involuntary unemployment. An unemployed worker does not have the option of starting his own, one-man firm, because there are increasing returns to labor. Even if a group of workers should combine their efforts to take advantage of the increasing returns, creating a new firm would depress the market price (given the prevailing level of aggregate demand) and thereby generate negative profit.

Only through stimulation of aggregate demand—say, due to government pump-priming—can the number of firms be increased and, with it, overall purchasing power and the level of employment. The individual unemployed workers are helpless in creating jobs, but the government need not be.

2.3.4 Efficiency Wages

The efficiency wage theories start from the premise that employers have less information about the productivities of their individual workers than those workers do. The inability to monitor productivity perfectly is reflected in most employment contracts, which do not provide precise specifications of productivity. In time-rate contracts, work effort is rarely (if ever) defined and prescribed accurately; in piece-rate, time-rate and other types of contracts, the exact standards according to which output is to be produced are not given either. Such practice may be explained in terms of "bounded rationality" (e.g., Simon, 1979; Williamson, Wachter, and Harris, 1975), or the impossibility (or prohibitive expense) of observing productivity objectively (e.g., Alchian and Demsetz, 1972; Malcolmson, 1981). In practice, worker productivity does not depend solely on abilities that can be revealed by straightforward performance tests (of the sort described by Guash and Weiss, 1980). Thus, employment contracts usually specify only those attributes of a job that can be monitored cheaply and objectively.

The next step in constructing the efficiency wage theories is to assume that firms make the wage and employment decisions unilaterally. Moreover, since their monitoring of workers' productivities is imperfect, they may use the wage offer as a screening device for productivity. The main substance of efficiency wage theories lies in providing reasons why firms may wish to do this and to investigate the consequences for employment and unemployment.

The economic problems arising when product quality is assessed through the product price have been studied in the context of many markets (e.g., Akerlof, 1970; Arrow, 1963), not just the labor market. They take two forms:

• adverse selection (in which product characteristics are imperfectly monitored) and

• moral hazard (in which activities of agents are imperfectly monitored).

In the same vein, the efficiency wage theories may be divided into these two categories.

In the adverse selection approach, the productivity of individual workers is not monitored perfectly. It comes in several guises. In the *"productivity differential models"* (e.g., Weiss, 1980; Malcomson, 1981), the firm cannot distinguish between high-productivity and low-productivity workers. Workers skills are not entirely firm specific. Thus, the higher the firm's wage offer, the higher the quality of workers (on average) that is attracted. In the *"turnover models"* (e.g., Stiglitz, 1985), the "quitters" among the firm's workforce cannot be distinguished ex ante from "stayers." Some of the costs associated with quitting (especially training costs) are borne by the firm. The higher the wage, the more workers can be induced to stay with the firm and the lower the firm's quit-associated costs. [A moral-hazard version of this idea exists as well. Here each individual worker is less likely to leave his firm, the greater his wage relative to wages of other, comparable jobs and to the level of unemployment benefits (see also Salop, 1979).]

The moral hazard approach supposes that workers' productivities depend on their effort on the job, which the firm cannot observe directly. This relation can take various forms. In the *"shirking models"* (e.g., Calvo and Wellisz, 1978; Shapiro and Stiglitz, 1984), a worker who is caught "shirking" (i.e., devoting little effort to his job) is suspended or fired. Clearly, the punishment for shirking depends (at least in part) on the difference between the firm's wage offer and the income upon suspension or expulsion. By raising the wage, the firm increases the magnitude of this punishment and thereby induces more work effort. In the *"search models"* (Snower, 1983b), effort depends inversely on the amount of on-the-job search performed by the worker. When the firm increases its wage offer, it makes search less worthwhile and thus raises worker productivity on the current job. In the *"sociological models"* (Akerlof, 1982), effort depends on whether workers believe that they are being treated "fairly." By offering the workers a "gift" above the required minimum, the firm can raise group work norms above the required minimum.

In all these adverse selection and moral hazard theories, a rise in a firm's wage offer increases the average profitability of its employees. This gain to the firm must be set against the labor cost. The profit-maximizing wage—at which the marginal revenue from a wage increase is equated with the associated marginal cost—may be compatible with involuntary unemployment. The unemployed may be willing to work for less pay than the incumbents, but firms who hired them on those terms would find that their marginal revenue would decline more than their marginal cost.

2.3.5 Insider-Outsider Theories

Whereas the efficiency wage theories place labor market power (regarding wage and employment decisions) entirely in the hands of the firms, the insider-outsider theories assume that it lies at least partially with the workers.

The latter theories' point of departure is the observation that, in general, a firm finds it costly to exchange its current, full-fledged employees (the "insiders") for workers outside the firm (the "outsiders"). The process of turning outsiders into insiders takes time. The length of this "initiation period" depends on technological, administrative and legal considerations (e.g., how long it takes to train, to acquire legal job security requirements as well as rent-creating skills, and to renegotiate the wage contract). Workers going through this process are "entrants" to the firm. The turnover cost generates economic rent, in that the firm would be willing to pay something to avoid a given level of turnover. The insiders are assumed to have enough bargaining power to capture some of this rent when they make their wage demands (see, for example, Aoki, 1980, Lindbeck and Snower, 1984a,c, 1985; Shaked and Sutton, 1984). In particular, they raise their wage above the entrant wage, but not by more than the relevant turnover cost. By implication, workers must be able to renegotiate their wage contracts periodically, for otherwise the insiders could be prevented from gaining the wage increases above.

Furthermore, entrants might be in an analogous position vis-à-vis the outsiders, and thus the entrant wage could be greater than the reservation wage. There are several reasons why this may be so:

• Entrants may have some rent to exploit (e.g., because the firm may already have expended advertising, screening, and some training costs on them and may incur even further costs to fire them).

• The insider wage is sufficiently high to make the reservation wage negative, but entrants have limited access to credit and thus they cannot receive this reservation wage.

• Firms may have an incentive to set the entrant wage above their reservation wage due to efficiency wage considerations.

The upshot of this story is that the firms may be unable to capture all the rent inherent in their employment activities.

Under these circumstances, the economy may get stuck in an equilibrium with involuntary unemployment. Here, the relative bargaining power of the firms and workers gives rise to a wage structure in which the insider wage exceeds the entrant wage, which, in turn, may exceed the reservation wage. Consequently, workers prefer being employed to being unemployed. Yet there may nevertheless be unemployed workers whom no firm has an incentive to hire. The reason is that the wage differentials between insiders, entrants, and outsiders do not exceed the associated turnover costs for the firm.

Clearly, the practical importance of this phenomenon hinges on the magnitude of these turnover costs. Different insider-outsider theories have focused on different forms of these costs.

First, in Lindbeck and Snower (1984a,b) and Solow (1985), there are straightforward hiring, firing, and training costs. The hiring costs cover the expense of advertising, screening, and negotiating conditions of employment. The firing costs include severance pay and costs of negotiation, litigation, and implementation of legally mandated firing procedures. The training costs cover not only the expense of running explicit training programs but also the diverse forms of on-the-job training. [Oi (1962) examines how such costs can turn labor into a "quasi-fixed factor of production."] Note that the division of these costs between the firm and its workers cannot be specified a priori; in the absence of the insider-outsider considerations, the firm might be able to shift all these costs to its workers simply by reducing its wage offers. Yet since the workers have some market power, they can prevent this from happening—and this is the situation with which the insider-outsider models are concerned. (Note that many of the training and firing costs accrue gradually over a worker's tenure with a firm and, through the exercise of market power in an insider-outsider context, may generate wage scales within the firm.)

Second, in Lindbeck and Snower (1984c), firms have imperfect information about individual employees' effort and future productivity is stochastically related to current effort. In response, each firm offers a remuneration package containing (a) a "time-rate" component (in which current productivity, and thereby past effort, is rewarded), and (b) a cutoff productivity (below which the worker is not retained). The higher the cutoff productivity (other things being equal), the greater the rate of labor turnover and thus the smaller the expected future reward for current effort. Consequently (if the substitution effect of turnover on effort exceeds the associated income effect), workers' effort declines.

The same point can be made more generally. Firms with high rates of labor turnover usually offer low job security, little opportunity for advancement, and little incentive for workers to build reputations. As a result, productivity may be low—and this is another cost of labor turnover.

Third, Linbeck and Snower (1985a) recognize that employees in a firm are generally able to cooperate with and harass one another, and consequently their productivities and disutilities of work become interdependent. When insiders feel that their positions are threatened, they may refuse to cooperate with entrants, and the resulting productivity differential constitutes the cost of an insider-outsider exchange. Besides, the insiders may protect themselves by harassing would-be entrants. As a result, outsiders may be unable and unwilling to replace insiders, even though the two groups of workers may have the same job characteristics.

Moreover, in Shaked and Sutton (1984), the firm is assumed to conduct wage negotiations with the insiders before it can turn to the outsiders. Furthermore, the bargaining process takes time and the negotiators have positive rates of time discount. Here the firm's cost of exchanging insiders for outsiders lies in the value of time that negotiating this exchange entails.

Due to these various costs, insiders have an inherent advantage over outsiders, one they can put to use in the wage negotiations with their employers. In this context, unions have an important role to play. Through them, workers may be able to amplify the costs of hiring, firing, and training (e.g., by imposing expensive hiring and firing procedures, insisting on lengthy training periods, and raising severance pay) and to expand workers' possibilities of cooperation and harassment. In addition, unions expand their members' bargaining power and create further costs by means of two potent tools: the strike and the work-to-rule (see Lindbeck and Snower, 1984a,b).

In this manner, the insider-outsider theories provide a solution to a difficulty inherent in the "union activity approach" (above) to unemployment: Why is it that firms do not ignore unions and deal with nonunionized workers instead? Yet the proposed answer has novel implications for the determination of wages and employment. No longer do these depend solely on fulfillment of union objectives subject to a labor-demand constraint or a minimum profit constraint, but the costs that the unions can credibly impose on firms become significant as well.

Out of the above approaches to involuntary unemployment, the "adjustment cost approach" remains rather unexplored and the "union activity approach" is open to some questions that are partially answered by the insider-outsider theories. So they will not be examined explicitly in the next section. Rather, the "efficiency wage theories," the "increasing returns to scale approach," and the "insider-outsider theories" (along with the "implicit contract theories" in the market-clearing tradition) are the salient explanations of involuntary unemployment that we now attempt to evaluate.

2.4 Evaluating Explanations of Involuntary Unemployment

We conduct our evaluation in three straightforward steps. First, we try to specify what, exactly, economists mean by the term "involuntary unemployment." Second, we propose several criteria that explanations of involuntary unemployment ought to fulfil. And finally, we assess the contenders above with regard to these criteria.

2.4.1 What Is "Involuntary Unemployment"?

It is not an easy matter to nail down what politicians and journalists (not to speak of the man in the street) mean by this term. But perhaps a reasonably common understanding of it may be encapsulated as follows. It exists whenever workers are willing to work at less than the prevailing wages for jobs that they could usefully fulfill, but are unable to find such jobs. In the conventional wisdom, involuntary unemployment is frequently associated with a perception of social injustice, namely, that among people of comparable labor endowments, some are not able to gain employment on the terms offered to others.

Yet this broad framework leaves much room for maneuver. For our purposes here, it is convenient to specify three independent definitions, each compatible with the popular conception above:

1. **Type 1 Unemployment** (U1): At the prevailing current wages and expected future wages (normalized for productivity differences), the unemployed workers would be better off being employed than remaining unemployed, but they are unable to find jobs.

2. **Type 2 Unemployment** (U2): At the prevailing current wages and expected future wages (normalized for productivity differences), some workers are unsuccessful in finding jobs because they face a more limited choice set between work and remuneration than incumbent employees face.

3. **Type 3 Unemployment** (U3): Workers unsuccessfully seek work at real wages that fall short of their potential contribution to society (given the appropriate, feasible government intervention).

The "involuntariness" of unemployment is a private phenomenon in the first two definitions and a social phenomenon in the third. Under U1 and U2, the unemployed workers unsuccessfully seek jobs on the same terms as the current job holders. U1 represents the involuntarily unemployed as workers who are jobless even though they have an incentive to work at the prevailing wages. U2 captures the idea that the involuntarily unemployed are jobless because they are discriminated against, in the sense that they face less favorable conditions of work than their employed counterparts. Under U3, unemployment is socially inefficient in the sense that, if the unemployed workers were employed, some agents in the economy would be better off without any others becoming worse off.

The first definition is narrower than the second: If the unemployed workers seek jobs at the prevailing wages (normalized for productivity differences) but are unable to find such jobs, then these unemployed workers must have a more limited choice set than current holders. On the other hand, U2 does not imply U1 because, given the more limited choice set of the unemployed workers, they may have no incentive to seek jobs. Moreover, the first two definitions are logically independent of the third.

None of the three definitions however, coincides with the definitions underlying the unemployment statistics of capitalist countries. Broadly speaking, people enter these statistics whenever they (a) are of "working age," (b) are out of work, and (c) submit acceptable evidence of having looked for a job in the recent past. What constitutes acceptable evidence varies from country to country (e.g., it may involve collecting unemployment benefits or merely assuring a government official that work has been sought). Of course, it is possible for a person to be included in such unemployment statistics, but nevertheless to be less qualified than the incumbents with whom he competes (thereby falling outside U1 and U2) and to demand a real wage in excess of his potential contribution to society (thereby falling outside U3). Conversely, it is also possible for someone to be U1-, U2-, or U3-unemployed but not to enter the official unemployment statistics.

2.4.2 Criteria for Evaluating Rival Explanations

In the light of these definitions and of the commonly recognized symptoms of involuntary unemployment, we now pose a number of questions that a macroeconomic theory should be able to answer in order to qualify as a successful explanation of why workers can be involuntarily unemployed in market economies:

A. Why are involuntarily unemployed workers unwilling or unable to underbid their employed counterparts?

Since involuntarily unemployed workers would prefer holding jobs (with the prevailing job characteristics) to being unemployed, why do they not offer to work for less than the incumbents' wages? If they do so, why do firms not accept these lower wage offers?

In the market-clearing macroeconomic theories of the New Classical schools, the workers above have an incentive to underbid and the firms have an incentive to accept the underbidding, and thus involuntary unemployment cannot persist. Either or both of these incentives must be absent if the problem is not to be solved automatically through the process of voluntary exchange in market economies.

At first glance, it may appear that whenever workers seek jobs with the prevailing job characteristics, they must be willing to underbid. After all, they seek jobs because they strictly prefer employment at the going wages to unemployment, and thus they must also prefer employment at something less than the going wages to unemployment. Yet this does not necessarily follow. If the process of underbidding itself has an adverse influence on the prevailing job characteristics (as in the harrassment version of the insider-outsider theories), then the unemployed may not be willing to underbid even though they would like to trade places with the incumbents.

Also, it may appear that whenever firms seek to maximize profits, they must be willing to accept the lowest wage bids. Yet if a drop in wages reduces not only labor costs, but productivity as well (as in the efficiency wage theories), then firms may lack this incentive.

B. Why do employed workers accept being laid off rather than take reductions in their wages?

Usually layoffs and hiring of previously unemployed workers play a much larger role in accounting for fluctuations in aggregate unemployment than do retirements and hiring of new entrants into the labor force. Consequently, a successful explanation of involuntary unemployment should tell us why layoffs are not avoided through wage cuts.

In many respects, the laid-off workers are in an analogous position to the unemployed. For example, in macro models where markets clear at all times, both types of workers have an incentive to underbid the incumbents and the firms have an incentive to take advantage of their wage bids. Yet insofar as the laid-off workers have more job training than their

unemployed counterparts, on average, they have an advantage in competing for jobs, and thus their underbidding need not proceed as far.

On the other hand, as the implicit contract theories assume, the laid-off
workers may be temporarily immobile among firms (or, at least, less mobile
than the longer-term unemployed), and thus they may be unable to underbid for a limited span of time. Moreover, a worker who loses his job may
find it impossible to regain it by accepting a wage cut, because the act of
underbidding would induce his colleagues to harrass him or to withdraw
their cooperation in production (as in some insider-outsider theories).
Finally, even if the laid-off workers do underbid, firms may be unresponsive
for efficiency-wage reasons.

C. **Why are firms unwilling or unable to capture all the economic
   rent associated with employment activities (e.g., through "long-
   term" wage contracts or "entry fees" or "exit fees")?**

While Questions (A) and (B) focus on the wage offers for workers, this
question is concerned with those of firms. By definition, if firms would
capture all rent from employment, then workers would be left indifferent
between work and leisure, and thus it may be argued that involuntary
unemployment would disappear. The firms may be able to do so in various
ways, of which the following are especially prominent:

"Long-term" wage contracts, whereby an entrant agrees to a particular
wage trajectory covering his entire period of employment at his firm. The
complete wage package offered over the whole employment period could
be such that each entrant is just as well off with work (over that period) as
he would be without it. [Since only the present value of wages is relevant
here, it remains for the firm to decide how to divide the complete wage
package among the various pay days. The firm could use this degree of
freedom to influence the workers' choice concerning the length of their
employment period, as in Lazear (1981).]

"Entry fees," whereby an entrant pays his firm a particular lump sum for
the privilege of receiving employment. In practice, these fees need not be
explicit in the wage contract; instead, they could take the form of lower
wages to entrants than to senior employees. Regardless of what wages the
senior employees receive, there is always an entrant wage that is sufficiently low so that the entrant is indifferent between work and leisure over
the span of the prospective employment period. In that event, the entry fee
is sufficiently large so that the firm captures all the rent from employing the
workers.

"Exit fees," whereby an employee pays his firm a particular lump sum if he leaves the firm prior to retirement (for reasons other than physical incapacity). For example, entrants could post bonds that would be forfeited when they quit their firms or were fired "with cause." In this way the firm can extract rent from the "quitters," but not the "stayers," in its workforce. If no worker knows in advance whether he would be a quitter or a stayer at a particular firm (e.g., because it is impossible for him to predict his future personal circumstances), then a rise in the firm's exit fee reduces the expected reward for work relative to that of leisure. Under these conditions, it is possible for the firm to set the exit fee sufficiently high so that an entrant becomes indifferent between the prospects of employment and unemployment.

D. **Why are the involuntarily unemployed workers unwilling or unable to employ themselves by starting new firms?**

If workers were always able to achieve self-employment, then there could be no involuntary unemployment. Whoever could not work for someone else, would work for himself.

In principle, it is probably always possible to find *some* form of self-employment; e.g., most people have the option of going fishing, picking berries, or selling flowers from an improvised stand off the road. Yet the available forms of self-employment may not match the unemployed workers' abilities. A nuclear physicist who, after having been laid off, prefers leisure to selling flowers, would not generally be classified as voluntarily unemployed.

The question remains, however, why workers are usually unable to start new firms with jobs similar to those they are seeking.

E. **Why do the involuntarily unemployed workers not form coalitions with firms and their employees in order to exploit all the relevant potential gains from trade?**

Involuntary unemployment U2 is an inefficient state. Eliminating it could make some people better off without making others worse off. In effect, the involuntarily unemployed workers could "bribe" the firms and the employed workers to create jobs and still be left better off than they were originally.

The question is why the inhabitants of market economies do not take advantage of such opportunities without government intervention. Wherein does the externality lie that makes the private benefits from coalition-formation smaller than the social benefits?

On the other hand, involuntary unemployment of type U1 may be efficient, in which case there are no potential gains from trade to be exploited. For example, the process of coalition-formation may involve costs (e.g., those associated with the dissemination and acquisition of information) or there may be adjustment costs of providing jobs for the involuntarily unemployed. In that event, agents in market economies have no incentives to form coalitions that eliminate involuntary unemployment, nor is it socially desirable to do so.

F. **Why are the involuntarily unemployed workers unwilling or unable to engage in job sharing with their employed counterparts (e.g., through job rotation or part-time work arrangements)?**

Although workers are sometimes put on short work weeks when business conditions turn adverse, layoffs and dismissals are nevertheless common. Besides, firms rarely rotate individuals between employment and unemployment.

If workers are risk averse, they would generally prefer job sharing (and thereby receive a comparatively steady stream of income) to the prospect of being employed at some times and unemployed at others. Why do firms not satisfy this preference?

2.4.3 Evaluating the Contenders

Let us now return to the contending theories of unemployment that we chose above and examine what form of involuntary unemployment they explain and how they tackle these questions.

Implicit Contract Theories
As noted, these theories assume that firms and workers commit themselves in advance to wage-employment contracts that are contingent on some unpredictable future events. Whether such contracts can generate unemployment—voluntary or involuntary—depends on who can observe and verify these events after they have recurred.

If the events are observable and verifiable by both the firms and their workers (i.e., in the case of "symmetric information"), then the implicit contracts create no unemployment (see, for example, Akerlof and Miyazaki, 1980; Azariadis and Stiglitz, 1983). Perhaps the simplest way of understanding this is to consider the production and insurance components of the contracts separately. In particular, suppose that a firm first offers its workers a wage-employment contract that brings its demand for labor into equality with its available labor supply. Then it offers another contract that subsidizes its workers' incomes under adverse conditions and correspondingly reduces these incomes under favorable conditions. When the two contracts are offerred in conjunction, employment remains at its market-clearing levels, while wages fluctuate less than their market-clearing counterparts. In other words, unemployment is completely absent.

Now suppose that the government provides unemployment insurance that is not "actuarily fair," in the sense that there would be excess demand for insurance under a symmetric information and perfect competition. Suppose furthermore that this unemployment insurance is not wholly subsidized by the firms whose workers benefit from it. Under these conditions, the firms and their workers will take advantage of the government handouts by agreeing to layoffs when worker productivities are sufficiently low. Here the unemployment is "ex ante voluntary" (since parties agreed to the contract before the state of productivity was known) and "ex post involuntary" (in the U1 and U2, but not the U3, sense).

Yet questions (A)–(F) are handled either through ad hoc assumptions or not at all. Recall the workers are simply assumed to be (a) unable to renegotiate their wage-employment contracts once they have been made and (b) immobile among firms throughout the contract period. It follows immediately that the laid-off workers cannot engage in underbidding. This is an implication from rather arbitrary premises. For the same reason, the firms are unable to capture economic rent that emerges after the signing of contracts. No rationale is given for the two assumptions above, and thus there is no answer to the question why efficient coalitions cannot be formed subsequent to the contracts. The questions concerning self-employment and job-sharing remain unanswered as well.

Now suppose that the "good" and "bad" states of productivity (on which the implicit contract is contingent) are observable to the firm, but not to its workers. Since workers are risk averse and have limited access to capital markets, they desire stable incomes, while their labor input varies in tandem with the good and bad states. Under these circumstances, the firm has no incentive to tell the truth about the states: By announcing a good state to its workers, it can get more labor for the same wage bill. In other words, the implicit contract is not "incentive compatible." In order to rectify this difficulty, the contract must be changed: Whenever the firm announces a good state, it must employ more labor than previously (so that in the good state the revenue from the extra output exceeds the cost of the extra labor, but in the bad state the reverse is the case).

Although this new type of contract does restore incentive compatibility, it has two unattractive features for our purposes. First, it rationalizes over-employment in good states rather than unemployment in bad states and, second, it implies that workers are better off in the bad states than in the good.

If unemployment in the bad states is to be explained, then it becomes necessary to assume that the firms are more risk averse than their workers. In this case, the workers have an incentive to provide insurance to the firms.

The "Increasing Returns" Approach

This approach is designed specifically to address the self-employment question (D). When there are increasing returns to labor and imperfect competition, the involuntarily unemployed workers may be unable to start new firms with jobs that are substitutes for the ones they are vainly seeking. The reason is

• Due to increasing returns to labor, a worker operating in isolation is less productive than a group of workers operating in conjunction. Thus, a single person firm would make losses when multiperson firms are drawing even. The involuntarily unemployed are unable to find a sufficient number of comrades to operate a firm at the requisite scale. If this were the only problem that the economy faced, then the level of unemployment would always be less than the workforce of a firm of minimum efficient size. (Of course, imperfect information about where the unemployed are to be found and geographic and occupational immobilities could allow unemployment to rise above the level.)

• Due to imperfect competition among sellers of goods, creation of a new firm in equilibrium involves glutting the market. If aggregate demand is given, the consumers' purchasing power is now spread more thinly among firms. If profits were initially at their equilibrium level of zero, they now turn negative. Thus, even if the unemployed are sufficiently numerous to start a firm as large as the existing ones, imperfect competition may make it unprofitable for them to do so. The crucial assumption behind this argument is that aggregate demand is given: The creation of a new firm does not generate enough purchasing power to have a significant influence on the firm's product demand.

One suspects that, in practice, increasing returns to labor are not the main reason why unemployed workers find it difficult to start new firms.

Increasing returns to capital are probably even more important. But the question why the unemployed workers cannot borrow enough funds to purchase this capital is not answered within Weitzman's analysis. Credit rationing can be explained through efficiency interest theories (e.g., Stiglitz and Weiss 1981) or loan-service risk (Lindbeck, 1963) rather than increasing returns per se.

Moreover, the process of starting firms requires organisational abilities that some workers may possess to a lesser degree than others. Perhaps on this account self-employed business people tend to be less prone to unemployment than employees in subordinate positions within organizational hierarchies.

Be that as it may, the "increasing returns approach" offers no answers to our acid-test questions other than (D). The involuntarily unemployed workers have every incentive to underbid their employed counterparts, and so we must presume that they do so in Weitzman's world. In response, Weitzman argues that if the nominal wages faced by all firms were to fall proportionately simultaneously, then each firm would have an incentive to reduce its product price proportionately as well. Thus, real wages would remain unchanged, and—in the absence of a real balance effect—aggregate demand and employment would stay constant as well.

Recall that the firms in this economy set their prices by a markup over wages, and this markup depends primarily on aggregate demand. Thus, in effect, the price-setting activity of firms determines the real wages. When firms realize that all nominal wages are falling in tandem (and that their market share would shrink if they held their prices constant), their profit-maximizing objectives induce them to generate real wages that are compatible with involuntary unemployment. Even so, there remains no economic rent for the firms to exploit.

The difficulty with this analysis is apparent. In practice, we do not in fact observe massive bouts of deflation whenever there is involuntary unemployment. Underbidding simply does not occur, and this phenomenon deserves explanation.

Moreover, the analysis provides no reason why efficient coalitions are not formed or why there is no job sharing.

Efficiency Wage Theories
In a sense, these theories may be seen as complements to the increasing returns approach—they are logically compatible with it, but the questions they address are different. The efficiency wage theories are not concerned with question (D) (why there are inadequate opportunities for

self-employment). Nor do they have much to say regarding question (E) (about coalition formation).

Although question (F) (about job sharing) has not received general scrutiny either, the efficiency wage theories are not incapable of addressing it. Once it is recognized that hours of work per person can play a different role in the firm's productive process from numbers of people employed, then the efficiency wage is set so that the marginal cost of a wage increase is equal to the associated marginal revenue per person and per hour. The firm chooses the size of the workforce and the length of the working day on profit-maximizing grounds. Part-time work will not be offered whenever it significantly discourages high-productivity job applicants, reduces effort in current employees, or prevents the exploitation of time-scale economies. Job rotation can be analyzed in the same way. However, as noted, this matter has not as yet been subject to detailed investigation, and thus it is impossible to tell whether these factors can account for the limited amount of part-time work and job rotation that we find in practice.

Be that as it may, the efficiency wage theories are designed primarily to provide a response to questions (A)–(C). Workers who are involuntarily unemployed or laid off may be willing to underbid their employed counterparts, but firms have no incentive to accept their bids, since doing so would reduce the average profitability of the workforce by more than the wage costs. The same principle explains why firms do not capture all the rent from their employees. The firms could do so if they wished, but it would not be profitable.

The weakness of this response to questions (A)–(C) is that it rests on a tenuous implicit assumption, namely, that all employees with a firm—junior and senior ones—receive the same remuneration. Thus, a firm that accepts underbidding offers a lower wage not only to its entrants but to its existing employees as well. In response, incumbents may quit (increasing the firm's turnover costs and—if the incumbents are of above average ability—reducing the overall productivity of the workforce) or they may shirk. Yet the assumption of uniform remuneration sidesteps the question of why firms do not capture rent through entry and exit fees or through long-term contracts with variable wages.

The turnover and shirking models are open to this criticism. By imposing entry fees, the firms can reduce not only their rates of turnover and shirking but also their labor costs. Thus, they have an incentive to raise these fees up to the point at which the *unemployed* workers are indifferent between employment and unemployment. Consequently, involuntary unemployment of the U1 type disappears. Long-term wage contracts function in the same way (e.g., Lazear, 1981). Note, however, that U2 unemployment remains: The unemployed workers face a more limited choice set than the incumbent workers, since the former face entry fees, whereas the latter need not.

Exit fees can also reduce turnover and shirking as well as the quitters' labor costs. The firms could raise them until the *incumbents* are indifferent between employment and unemployment. Would this eliminate involuntary unemployment? Clearly, those unemployed workers who are at least as prone to quitting as the incumbents would no longer prefer work to leisure. The rest—the unemployed stayers—would be willing to underbid, and, furthermore, the firms would have an incentive to accept these bids, since lower wages would not induce them to quit or shirk. (Here *low* wages act as a self-selection device for workers of high profitability.) The process of underbidding could continue until the involuntary unemployment of the U1 type disappears. Moreover, U2 unemployment disappears as well, since all workers face the same exit fees once they have gained employment.

Of course, it may be impracticable to levy entry and exit fees because the workers who are credit-rationed may not be able to pay them. Another problem is that firms might take unfair advantage of them. In particular, firms may declare workers to be shirking (and dismiss them) in order to collect the associated fees. Since the workers cannot protect themselves against this moral-hazard problem, the dismissal decisions would cease to operate as punishment for shirking. The same sort of problem is present under long-term wage contracts. (If effort were observable by both the workers and their firms, then the workers could protect themselves; but in that case, wages could be made contingent on effort and then there would be no need to set efficiency wages in the first place.) On the other hand, it may be true that some firms have reputations to defend and thus can be relied on not to pronounce anyone a shirker without cause.

The productivity-differential, search, and sociological models are less vulnerable to these limitations. Here any drop in labor remuneration from one firm relative to the other firms—regardless of whether it takes the form of entry or exit fees or long-term wage reductions—reduces the profitability of the firm's workforce, because (a) it reduces the firm's ability to attract high-productivity workers; (b) it increases the amount of on-the-job search done by the firm's current employees and thereby reduces their productivity; or (c) it leads workers to believe that they are being treated unfairly and thus reduces group work norms.

In short, the efficiency wage theories aim to show why neither the firms nor the unemployed or laid-off workers reduce their wage offers in the presence of involuntary unemployment. Some, but by no means all, of these theories do not deal with the issue of intertemporal remuneration schemes that permit underbidding to occur without any associated fall in productivity or rise in labor costs.

Insider-Outsider Theories

Broadly speaking, although the insider-outsider theories address the same questions as the efficiency wage theories, the proposed answers are radically different, as are their policy implications. Whereas the efficiency wage theories ascribe the existence of involuntary unemployment to firms' profit-maximizing wage decisions under asymmetric information, the insider-outsider theories ascribe it to the market power of the employees. The efficiency wage theories hang on the assumption that workers' profitability is imperfectly monitored by firms, and thus the firms do not find it worthwhile to exploit all the rent from their employment activities. By contrast, the insider-outsider theories rest on the premise that it is costly to interchange employed and unemployed workers in the process of production and the current employees are able to exploit some of the resulting rent. In the former context, involuntary unemployment is reduced when firms gain more (verifiable) information about their employees' profitability; in the latter, the unemployment falls when employees lose market power (due to either a weakening of their bargaining positions or a fall in turnover costs).

The insider-outsider theories are not aimed at question (D) (about self-employment) or question (E) (about coalition formation). They do, however, offer an explanation for why job-sharing is not a pervasive response to involuntary unemployment [question (F)]. Job-sharing (in the form of part-time work for both the currently employed and unemployed, or job rotation among these workers) is favored by *all* risk-averse workers only if they all face the same risk of being unemployed. Yet when there are costs of labor turnover for the employed workers to exploit, these workers find themselves with a much higher chance of retaining their jobs than the unemployed workers have in finding them. Under these circumstances, job-sharing benefits the outsiders at the expense of the insiders; and the insiders use their market power to prevent this from happening. This is perhaps a more convincing answer to question (F) than one that rests on the productivity disincentives of job-sharing.

The insider-outsider responses to questions (A)–(C) runs as follows:

a. Firms may have no incentive to accept underbidding because the act of underbidding may drive the marginal product of the newly hired workers below their marginal cost (either because the insiders may refuse to co-operate with the underbidders in the process of production or because a rise in the firm's rate of labor turnover may reduce work effort).

b. Outsiders may have no incentive to engage in underbidding because the act of underbidding would raise the reservation wages of the under-bidders above their marginal product (because the insiders may "harass" the underbidders).

c. Underbidding may be unsuccessful on account of rent-related labor turnover costs. In particular, the outsiders may be willing to work for less than the insider wages minus the production-related turnover costs (which account for the insider-outsider productivity differences), but the outsiders may nevertheless remain jobless because they are *not* willing to work for less than the insider wages minus the production- *and* rent-related turnover costs.

d. Credit constraints may prevent the outsiders from gaining employment even though they prefer being employed to remaining unemployed. Note that the greater the insider wage, the smaller the entrants' reservation wage. Now suppose that the insiders drive their wages up sufficiently to make the entrants' reservation wage substantially negative. Then entrants may have to borrow in order to receive their reservation wage. Yet credit constraints may make such borrowing impossible. In that event, firms are unable to extract all rent from the entrants, even if these entrants have no market power.

e. Firms may be unable to capture all the economic rent associated with employment activities because they do not have sufficient market power to do so. Since insiders wield some market power, the insiders' wage will exceed the insiders' reservation wage. Furthermore, even if entrants have no market power, it may be in the insiders' interests to drive the entrant wage above the entrants' reservation wage. (For example, the higher the entrant wage, the fewer entrants are hired, and thus—under diminishing returns to labor—the larger the marginal product of the insiders and the larger the insider wage.) As result, firms may be unable to provide a remuneration package that makes any of its workers' indifferent between work and leisure.

Observe that each of these responses provides a rationale for involuntary unemployment of type U2: The effect of underbidding on the productivity and reservation wage of the underbidders, the existence of rent-related turnover costs, the operation of credit constraints, or the exercise of market power by insiders may all ensure that the outsiders face a more limited choice set than the insiders. Moreover, responses (d) and (e) also provide a rationale for U1 unemployment: Even in the presence of their more limited choice set, the outsiders may nevertheless seek jobs and be unable to find them, because the operation of credit constraints or exercise of insider power may prevent outsiders from offering to work at their reservation wage.

Note, however, that the insider-outsider theories share some of the same limitations as the efficiency wage theories. In particular, they do not explain why workers may prefer to be unemployed rather than to start new firms. Nor do they rationalize fully why potential gains from trade remain unexploited through wage-employment packages that provide incentives for the creation of new jobs without reducing firms' profits or insiders' wage incomes (e.g., profit sharing contracts and two-tier wage agreements). Finally, some variants of both the insider-outsider and efficiency wage theories do not explain why firms do not exploit profitable employment opportunities through the use of entry and exit fees.

2.5 Concluding Remarks

From the various explanations of involuntary unemployment examined above, three appear to be particularly promising: the increasing returns approach, the efficiency wage theories, and the insider-outsider theories. The first is concerned primarily with why opportunities for self-employment are limited; the second and third show why the unemployed and laid-off workers do not underbid and why the firms do not capture all rent from their employment activities. In this sense, the two groups of explanations complement each other. However, they have yet to be brought together within a single, logically consistent framework of thought.

Although the efficiency wage and insider-outsider theories point to quite distinct sources of involuntary unemployment, they are not incompatible with one another. The insider-outsider theories may suggest why insiders receive significantly higher wages than entrants, while the efficiency wage theories may explain why entrants do not receive their reservation wages. Moreover, even when labor market power does not lie entirely with the firms, the efficiency wage theories do not become irrelevant. Rather, they can be used to determine the lower bounds for wages that are negotiated in accordance with the insider-outsider theories. In other words, the amount of involuntary unemployment may depend on both what firms are willing to give and what workers are able to get. To date, however, the interaction between the efficiency wage and insider-outsider theories remains unexplored.

3

Efficiency Wages versus Insiders and Outsiders

Overview

Having discussed rival theories of unemployment on the basis of the criteria presented in the previous chapter, we now take a closer look at two of them that explicitly address the issue of why there is no underbidding and why firms do not capture all the rent associated with employment activity. These are the efficiency wage and the insider-outsider theories. Both theories seek to explain persistent involuntary unemployment on the basis of optimizing microeconomic activities. Moreover, they complement one another in an obvious way: In the efficiency wage theory firms have an incentive to set wages above their full-employment levels, whereas in the insider-outsider theory workers have such an incentive.

Whenever there is involuntary unemployment, there must be workers who have no jobs even though they prefer to be employed at the wages (normalized for productivity differences) that the current employees receive. Consequently, these workers must have an incentive to gain employment by offering to work for less than the prevailing wages. In order for the involuntary unemployment to be persistent, there must be some other *agents who are both motivated and able to prevent such underbidding. The government may do so through, say, minimum wage laws; but involuntary unemployment appears to exist even without such government intervention. The obvious candidates in the private sector who may have an incentive to prevent underbidding are the firms and the employed workers. The efficiency wage and insider-outsider theories each consider one of these groups. In the efficiency wage theory, it is in the firms' interest to prevent the underbidding, whereas in the insider-outsider theory, this is in the interest of the incumbent workers.*

The efficiency wage theory rests on two fundamental assumptions:

i. *Firms exert market power in the wage setting process.*

ii. *Firms have imperfect information about the profitability of their employees.*

Consequently, these firms use their wage offers as a screening device for employee profitability. In particular, each firm observes that the greater its wage offer, ceteris paribus, the greater the average productivity of its workforce. The reason is that a higher wage stimulates effort (in the moral-hazard versions of the efficiency wage theory), encourages more able workers to apply for vacant positions (in the adverse-selection versions of the theory), and discourages trained workers from quitting (in both versions). Although the firm has imperfect information about the effort, ability, and quit propensity of individual workers, it nevertheless is able to observe a positive relation between its wage offer and the average productivity of its workforce and/or a negative relation between its wage offer and its average training cost per worker.

The firm sets its wage offer at the profit-maximizing level, i.e., the level at which the marginal cost (including average training costs) of a wage increase is just equal to the marginal revenue (via productivity improvements) of that wage increase. If this profit-maximizing wage exceeds the market-clearing wage, then there is involuntary unemployment. Each firm finds it unprofitable to accept underbidding by the involuntarily unemployed workers, because this would reduce the productivity of the workforce and raise training costs by more than it would reduce the firm's wage costs.

By contrast, the insider-outsider theory focuses attention on the incentive of incumbent workers to keep the prevailing wages from falling. This theory also rests on two fundamental assumptions:

i. Incumbent workers ("insiders") exert market power in the wage setting process on account of labor turnover costs.

ii. The insiders exercise this power to their own advantage, without taking full account of other workers.

The labor turnover costs give the insiders power because firms are not able to pass on these costs entirely to their employees in the form of wage reductions. Thus, firms may be willing to retain their insiders even when their wages are substantially higher than those necessary to attract, motivate, and retain new recruits. Moreover, turnover costs often can be influenced by the insiders themselves, who are assumed to exercise this influence with a view to exploiting their market power.

As we shall show in chapter 4, there exist many different kinds of turnover costs. In this chapter we consider the simplest and most obvious of these: costs of hiring, training, and firing. Chapter 5 analyzes turnover costs arising from insiders' cooperation and harassment activities. Chapter 6 deals with turnover costs that are due to employees' effort responses to job security.

The costs of hiring, training, and firing are diverse. For firms, the hiring and training costs cover the entire sequence of events that firms must follow to find workers, check their skills, and make them qualified for the jobs they are to perform. The firing costs may include severance pay, the implementation of legally and socially acceptable firing procedures, the preparation for and possibly conduct of litigation, and "bad will" on the part of the remaining employees (commonly manifested in their productivity).

It is useful to divide these costs into two categories:

a. "production-related turnover costs" (e.g., search and screening costs), which are necessary for the production of goods and services, and

b. "rent-related turnover costs" (e.g., severance payments), which are not primarily production costs and which may be the outcome of rent-creating activities.

In general, hiring, training, and firing costs each fall into both categories, but, as a rule, hiring and training costs tend to be predominantly production-related, whereas firing costs are frequently rent-related.

The rent-related turnover costs play a crucial role in the insider-outsider explanation of involuntary unemployment. Since the insiders are assumed to use their power to further their own interests, they drive their wages above the market-clearing level. Whenever the differential between the insider wage and the outsiders' reservation wage exceeds the insider-outsider productivity differential, we classify the unemployment as "involuntary," in the sense that outsiders face a more limited choice set (in terms of labor services offered and remuneration received) than that of the insiders.

The reason why the insiders may be able to drive their wage up sufficiently for the insider-outsider wage differential to exceed the insider-outsider productivity differential—without giving the outsiders an incentive to underbid or the firms to accept such underbidding—is to be found in the rent-related turnover costs. On account of these costs, the insider-outsider wage differential may fall short of total turnover costs (i.e., production- and rent-related turnover costs), and thus firms do not find it worthwhile to replace insiders. Moreover, although the outsiders may be willing to work for less than the insider wage by an amount sufficient to cover the insider-outsider productivity differential plus production-related turnover costs, they may not be willing to work for less than the insider wage minus total turnover costs. In short, on account of the rent-related turnover costs, the outsiders face less favorable employment opportunities than the insiders. Thus, the outsiders are the victims of discrimination in the labor market.

In this context, it is instructive to see the involuntary unemployment above as the outcome of the interactions among three groups of agents: the firms, the insiders, and the outsiders. If the unemployment is to be reduced, then the firms and the outsiders must find a way to "bribe" the insiders to reduce the labor turnover costs or to exploit these costs less in their own favor. These bribes might *take the form of profit-sharing (whereby insiders are rewarded for the revenue earned by new entrants) or two-tier wage schemes (which ensure that insider wages do not fall when the workforce is expanded). Such wage contracts are indeed important in some occupations and industries. However, it is also readily understandable, in the context of the insider-outsider theory, why such arrangements are not ubiquitous: profit-sharing schemes may impose significant costs of monitoring and risk on the insiders, while permanent two-tier wage schemes may be time inconsistent (since they may induce firms to fire the current insiders once the new entrants have been trained).*

When comparing the practical applicability of the efficiency wage theory and the insider-outsider theory, it is important to examine whether firms' imperfect information or workers' market power is more important in explaining persistent involuntary unemployment in market economies.

3.1 Introduction

This chapter aims to evaluate two competing microeconomic foundations of involuntary unemployment: the efficiency-wage theory and the insider-outsider theory. These theories compete not by being mutually exclusive, but by identifying different microeconomic sources of involuntary unemployment.

In the efficiency-wage theory, the source is firms' imperfect information about the profitability of their employees. Under this condition, firms may have an incentive to use the wage as a screening device for employees' profitability, implying that an increase in the wage raises not only the marginal labor cost (per unit of time) but the marginal revenue product (net of training costs) of labor as well. Then when wages are set at their profit-maximizing levels, aggregate labor demand may fall short of aggregate labor supply.

In the insider-outsider theory, the source of the unemployment lies in (a) an explicit labor turnover cost and (b) the ability of the full-fledged employees ("insiders") to exercise influence over their wages, without taking full account of the interests of the fledgling employees ("entrants") or the unemployed workers ("outsiders"). The insiders' market power arises from the turnover cost, and this power may also be devoted to augmenting that cost. Due to this cost, the insiders are able to raise their wage above the minimal level required to induce workers to become entrants, but firms nevertheless have no incentive to hire outsiders. For this reason, aggregate labor supply may exceed aggregate labor demand.

Both theories deal with employees who capture economic rent from being employed but whose wages are not underbid by the involuntarily unemployed workers. However, in the efficiency wage theory, underbidding does not occur because lower wages do not appeal to the firms, whereas in the insider-outsider theory the insiders use their market power to prevent wages from falling. The existence of involuntary unemployment is related to labor turnover costs in some versions of the efficiency wage theory and in all versions of the insider-outsider theory. However, in the former, the unemployment arises because firms set wages with a view to manipulating the turnover costs under imperfect information, whereas in the latter theory the turnover costs give insiders market power that permits them to drive wages above their market-clearing levels.

The two theories may be interpreted as alternative microfoundations for macroeconomic models of unemployment, where there is deficient demand for labor although the product market clears [viz., the boundary between the "Keynesian" and "Classical" regimes in the models of Barro and Grossman (1976) and Malinvaud (1977)]. In particular, the theories provide explanations for why the labor market does not clear, and these explanations do not rest on a failure of the product market to clear.

Broadly speaking, we define involuntary unemployment as a state in which there are workers without jobs, even though it is possible to find a wage, less than prevailing wages, that would induce them to work, provided that these workers could be employed under identical conditions of work as the incumbent workers. It is important to emphasize that this type of unemployment is quite distinct from the notion of *suboptimal* (inefficiently low) production and employment, relative to a hypothetical Walrasian equilibrium, in models with imperfect competition, as developed by Benassy (1977) and Negishi (1977), or models with search activity of employees depending on that of employers and vice versa, as developed by Drazen (1985b), related to the analysis of Diamond (1982).

To explain the existence of involuntary unemployment as defined in this chapter, it is necessary to show why there is no underbidding. By "underbidding" we mean, quite generally, any wage agreement among the actual and potential parties to a labor contract, whereby unemployed workers are enabled to find jobs at wages that make them less costly (to the firms) than the incumbent employees.

3.2 The Efficiency-Wage Theory

As mentioned, the centerpiece of the efficiency-wage theory is that wage increases may raise a firm's profit by having

- a positive effect on the average productivity of its workforce and/or
- a negative effect on the average labor cost per time unit.

Let $Q = f(e \cdot L)$ be the firm's production function, where Q is output, L is the number of employees, e is the average labor productivity per employee, and $f' > 0$, $f'' < 0$. Furthermore, let W be the firm's wage offer and T its costs of training its employees. Then the effects above may be expressed as

$$e = e(W), \qquad e' > 0,$$
$$T = T(W), \qquad T' < (0). \tag{1}$$

[In addition, e and T may also depend on other variables (such as the wage offered by other firms and the level of unemployment), but, for simplicity, we ignore these here.] Various rationales for these effects were discussed in chapter 2.

A particularly simple way of formalizing the firm's wage and employment decisions in this analytical context is

$$\underset{W, \lambda}{\text{Maximize}} \ \pi = P \cdot f(\lambda) - (\lambda/e) \cdot [W + T], \tag{2}$$

where $\lambda = e \cdot L$ is the firm's workforce in efficiency units and P is the exogenously given price of its product.[1] (We assume that the wage W and the training cost T refer to the same time period.) The first-order conditions for an interior optimum may be expressed as

$$\partial \pi / \partial W = -\lambda \cdot [\partial \phi / \partial W] = 0, \tag{3a}$$

$$\partial \pi / \partial \lambda = P \cdot f'(\lambda) - \phi = 0, \tag{3b}$$

where $\phi = (W + T)/e$ may be called the "efficiency labor cost." By condition (3a) (illustrated in figure 3.1a), which implies $\partial \phi / \partial W = 0$, and assuming $\partial^2 \phi / \partial W^2 > 0$, the wage ($W^*$) is set so that the efficiency labor cost is minimized. By condition (3b) (illustrated in figure 3.1b), the level of employment in efficiency units (λ^*) is such that the marginal value product of labor (in efficiency units) is equal to the efficiency labor cost.

Suppose that the economy contains a fixed number (F) of identical firms. Then the aggregate level of labor demand is $N_D = F \cdot (\lambda^*/e(W^*))$ as illustrated in figure 3.1c. Furthermore, suppose that the aggregate labor supply is positively related to (or independent of) the real wage: $N_S = N_S(W/P)$, $N'_S \geqslant 0$, as illustrated in figure 3.1d (for a given price). At the prevailing wage W^*, the aggregate labor supply may exceed the aggregate labor demand and the difference is the level of unemployment: $u^* = N_S^* - N_D^*$.

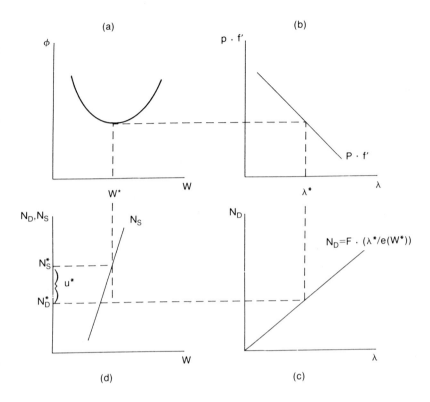

Figure 3.1
Unemployment in the efficiency wage theory.

The unemployment above may be *involuntary* by our definition—
namely, unemployed workers receive no jobs even though there exists a
wage, an effort level, and a training cost at which they would prefer
employment to unemployment and at which their efficiency labor cost is
less than that of the current employees. However, the unemployed workers
cannot precommit themselves to such an effort level (e) and such a training
cost (T) borne by the firm, because the firms cannot monitor e and T
directly and the workers would be unwilling or unable to keep such a
commitment of their own accord.

3.3 The Insider-Outsider Theory

The crux of the insider-outsider theory, as suggested in the introduction, is
that an "insider" in a firm faces more favorable conditions of work than an
"entrant" (*ceteris paribus*). The reason is that insiders can exploit and mani-

pulate labor turnover costs for the purpose of raising their wage rates. Various sources of these costs have been suggested. For example:

a. *Hiring, training and firing activities* whose implications are analyzed in this chapter. It is frequently the case that workers become entrants only after advertising, screening, and negotiation costs have been incurred; entrants may turn into insiders only after the absorption of training expenses; and the dismissal of insiders may require severance payments and the implementation of costly firing procedures.

b. *Cooperation and harassment activities*, which are examined in chapter 5. To boost their wage claims and prevent underbidding, insiders may choose to "cooperate" with each other (individually or by collective action) in the process of production but not to cooperate with undesired entrants, thereby creating an insider-entrant productivity differential. For the same reasons, insiders may "harass" entrants but not each other (i.e., have worse personal relations with entrants who underbid than with each other), thereby raising the entrants' disutility of work above their own.

c. *Effort response to labor turnover*, which is considered in chapter 6. If current labor remuneration is related to workers' past effort performance, then a rise in a firm's rate of labor turnover reduces its employees' expected future effort reward. This reduction in the effort reward has a negative substitution effect and a positive income effect on effort. If the substitution effect dominates, then a rise in the turnover rate leads to a fall in effort, and thus the firm bears an effort-related cost of labor turnover.

The distinction between "insiders" and "entrants" rests on such labor turnover costs (and not merely on seniority). The insider-outsider theory presumes not only that these costs exist but also that the insiders may influence them and that firms cannot entirely pass them on to their employees in the form of wage reductions. The main reason is that the insiders have market power (as individuals or collectively, although we shall not consider the latter possibility here). Thus, an insider receives a higher wage than an entrant (*ceteris paribus*), but since the firm bears some of the labor turnover costs, it may nevertheless have no incentive to replace the insider by the entrant. (Insofar as the entrant has market power as well, the wage that he receives will exceed his reservation wage.) In this context, the insider-outsider theory provides a rationale for unionization, since unions may help insiders to raise the firm's labor turnover costs (see chapters 7 and 8).

For simplicity, it may be convenient to conceive of outsiders, entrants, and insiders as homogeneous groups. When an outsider is hired, he becomes an entrant. The replacement of an entrant is associated with no (or "low") turnover costs. After passing through an "initiation period" at the firm, the entrant turns into an insider, whose replacement would require "high" turnover costs.

Let L_I and L_E be the number of insiders and entrants, respectively, employed by a particular firm. W_I and W_E are their respective wages. The firm's production function is $Q = f(L_I + L_E)$, where $f' > 0$, $f'' < 0$. The "incumbent workforce" is m (i.e., the number of insiders carried forward from the previous time period). Then, $L_I \leqslant m$. As noted, this chapter focuses attention on one particular type of labor turnover costs, namely, the costs of hiring, training, and firing. The firm's cost of dismissing insiders is $C_I(m - L_I)$ with the following properties: $C_I(0) = 0$ and, for $L_I < m$, $C_I' > 0$ and $\lim_{L_I \to m} C_I' = \tilde{c}_I$, where $\tilde{c}_I$ is a positive constant. (In other words, the dismissal costs are finitely large for all L_I less than m.) Furthermore, the firm's cost of hiring and training entrants is $C_E(L_E)$ with the following properties: $C_E(0) = 0$ and, for $L_E > 0$, $C_E' > 0$ and $\lim_{L_E \to 0} C_E' = \tilde{c}_E$, where $\tilde{c}_E$ is a positive constant. (In other words, the labor acquisition costs are finitely large for all positive L_E.)

To fix ideas, let the entrant wage (W_E) be a constant (say, equal to the reservation wage) and let the insider wage (W_I) be generated by bargaining between the firm and its insiders. Let the insiders bargain "individualistically" (i.e., each insider assumes the wage and employment of all other insiders to be exogenously given) and let them have "complete market power" (i.e., each insider sets his wage as high as possible consistent with his continued employment). (This strong assumption is a convenient simplification but is not necessary for the subsequent analysis. It would be sufficient to assume that the insiders receive some part of the rent generated by the turnover costs and that the greater these costs, the greater are their wages.) By implication, the insider wage is $W_I = \min[(f'(m) + \tilde{c}_I), (W_E + \tilde{c}_I + \tilde{c}_E)]$; i.e., the insider wage is the smaller of the insider marginal product (net of firing costs) and the sum of the entrant wage and the marginal turnover costs.

With W_E, W_I, and m exogenously given to the firm, the employment decision may be expressed as the solution to the following profit-maximization problem:

$$\text{Maximize } \pi = P \cdot f(L_I + L_E) - W_I \cdot L_I - W_E \cdot L_E$$
$$\phantom{\text{Maximize } \pi =} - C_I(m - L_I) - C_E(L_E). \tag{4}$$

Let the optimal solution be (L_I^*, L_E^*). Then supposing that $L_I^* > 0$, the first-order conditions are

$$\partial\pi/\partial L_I = P \cdot f' - W_I + C_I' \geqslant 0, \qquad (\partial\pi/\partial L_I^*) \cdot (m - L_I^*) = 0, \qquad (5a)$$

$$\partial\pi/\partial L_E = P \cdot f' - W_E - C_E' \leqslant 0, \qquad (\partial\pi/\partial L_E^*) \cdot L_E^* = 0. \qquad (5b)$$

Combining (5a) and (5b) we obtain

$$W_I - W_E \leqslant C_I' + C_E'. \qquad (6)$$

These conditions are illustrated in figure 3.2a, where the equilibrium locus of (W_I, L) points is given by the boldface curve. While (5a) and (5b) define the demand functions for insiders and entrants, respectively, (6) tells us that the insider wage cannot exceed the entrant wage by more than the sum of the marginal hiring, training and firing costs of labor.

As shown in figure 3.2a, if the firm has an incumbent workforce of $\hat{m}$, the insider wage is $\hat{W}_I$, all incumbents are employed ($L_I^* = \hat{m}$), and the firm does not find it profitable to hire any entrants [$L_E^* = 0$, by condition (5b)]. Moreover, for an economy with F identical firms, aggregate labor demand is then $\hat{N}_D = F \cdot (L_I + L_E)$ (illustrated in figure 3.2b). Let the number of workers in the economy be N_S ($> \hat{N}_D$). Then the level of unemployment is $u = N_S - \hat{N}_D$.

Is this unemployment involuntary? According to one common definition, involuntary unemployment exists when, at the prevailing wage, workers unsuccessfully seek jobs at which they have the same productivity as the current job holders. Yet for our purposes, this definition is too narrow, since insiders, entrants, and outsiders may have different productivities.

To make this idea more precise, it is useful to distinguish between labor turnover costs that are "production-related" and those that are "rent-related." The former are costs that are expended primarily to enhance worker productivity; the latter are not intrinsically related to productivity and may be the outcome of rent-creating activities. Most hiring and training costs ($C_E(L_E)$) tend to be production-related and many firing costs ($C_I(m - L_I)$) appear to be rent-related. In the unemployment equilibrium pictured in figure 3.2, there may be outsiders who are willing to work for a wage that would make them more profitable than the insiders, if only they faced identical remuneration for identical labor services. Outsiders and insiders would face identical choice sets in this sense if the outsiders were willing to work for less than the insider wage by an amount equal to the insider-outsider productivity differential plus the production-related turnover costs. However, the outsiders and insiders do not face identical choice sets in this sense due to the rent-related turnover costs. Even if the insider-outsider wage differential exceeds the insider-outsider productivity

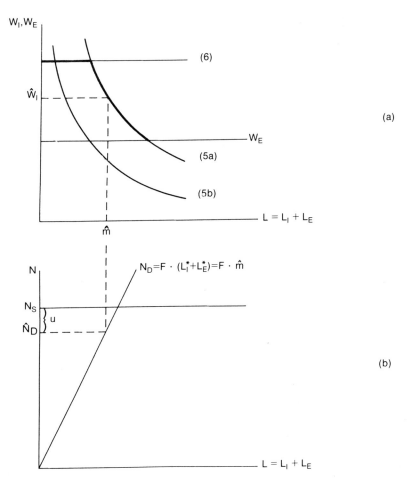

Figure 3.2
Unemployment in the insider-outsider theory.

differential plus the production-related turnover costs, the firms may nevertheless be unwilling to replace their insiders by outsiders. This will happen whenever the insider-outsider wage differential falls short of total (production-related *plus* rent-related) turnover costs.

Here, the outsiders are involuntarily unemployed in the sense that they face less favorable employment opportunities than the insiders. On account of the rent-related labor turnover costs, the outsiders face *discrimination* in the labor market.

As shown, the outsider and the firm may be unable to find a wage that induces both the outsider to work and the firm to employ him, given the insiders' activities, which, in effect, discriminate against outsiders. But, even though time-contracts thus may give rise to involuntary unemployment, is it not possible for the firm or the outsiders to make side-payments *to the insiders*, in order to give them an incentive to abstain from these activities? For example, such side-payments may take the form of profit-sharing or wage bonuses per entrant hired. But even though such arrangements may benefit the insiders, they may be unwilling to accept them because the insiders may fear that the admittance of low wage workers into the firm will give the employer an incentive to fire the insiders in the future. Besides, profit-sharing may be difficult for the insiders to monitor and may impose more risk on the insiders than they may be willing to accept at the new insider wage (see chapter 5). In this manner, risk-bearing, non-enforceability of contracts that are not subgame perfect, and difficulties in observing or verifying variables such as profits may be effective obstacles to eliminating involuntary unemployment through underbidding by way of side-payments to the insiders.

A central implication of the insider-outsider theory is that labor turnover costs are responsible for unemployment. However, in analyzing this issue, the one-period setting of our model is unduly restrictive. In a multiperiod context, a rise in labor turnover costs leads not only to a rise in the insider wage but also to a fall in the reservation wage. Thus, if the entrant wage is equal to the reservation wage, the firm faces countervailing wage movements: a rising insider wage and a falling entrant wage. Thus there may be no increase in the firm's present value of wage payments over a worker's remaining lifetime. Here the rise in turnover costs may not lead to a fall in employment (and a rise in unemployment).

In chapter 1, however, we discussed various plausible reasons why a rise in the insider wage may be associated with a rise in the present value of the firm's wage payments. First, suppose that the worker's discount rate exceeds the firm's rate and that the entrant wage is equal to the reservation wage.

Then a rise in the insider wage will lead to a sufficiently small decline in the entrant wage (derived from the worker's discount rate) so that there is a rise in the firm's present value of wage payments (computed by the firm's discount rate). Second, the entrant wage may not fall in tandem with the reservation wage. Insiders may prevent the entrant wage from falling in order to discourage underbidding or new hiring; alternatively, credit restrictions or minimum wage laws may provide floors for the entrant wage. In either event, a rise in the insider wage may then lead to reduced employment and increased unemployment.

3.4 Concluding Remarks

The efficiency-wage and insider-outsider theories of involuntary unemployment are built on quite different foundations. The former explain unemployment through firms' imperfect information about the productivities and about costs of their employees, the latter do so through insiders' market power, which is used to exploit labor turnover costs in the process of wage formation—and to some extent the turnover costs themselves can be manipulated by the insiders. In the efficiency wage theories, union activity is generally implied to be unimportant in determining the level of unemployment; in the insider-outsider theory, it may augment unemployment by amplifying labor turnover costs. In the efficiency wage theory, the "involuntariness" of unemployment is traceable to a genuine information cost for firms. In the insider-outsider theory, the "involuntariness" is mirrored in the more limited employment opportunity set of outsiders relative to insiders—a limitation that may be accentuated by social norms and legislation. In particular, the harassment version of the insider-outsider theory may be useful in explaining why outsiders may feel inhibited from underbidding, and the hiring/firing cost version may provide an underpinning for the notion that "job security legislation" may be at least partially responsible for unemployment. When comparing the realism of the two theories, the vital issue that remains is whether firms' imperfect information or workers' market power is more important in providing microeconomic foundations for the existence and persistence of involuntary unemployment in market economies.

Note

1. We are deeply indebted to Ben Lockwood, to whom the basic idea underlying this simple formulation is due.

4

Wage Setting, Unemployment, and Insider-Outsider Relations

Overview

The previous chapter compared and contrasted the salient ideas underlying the efficiency wage theory and the insider-outsider theory. In this chapter, we focus our attention exclusively on the insider-outsider theory and briefly investigate its conceptual underpinnings. It has been noted that the insiders derive their market power from labor turnover costs and that they may also engage in rent-creating activities that are designed to augment these costs. We now take a closer look at what these costs and rent-creating activities are, and how they may give rise to involuntary unemployment.

This chapter explores three distinct sources of unemployment related to labor turnover costs. One comprises government policy interventions, particularly legislation creating hiring and firing costs. A second may be identified as rent-creating activities of the insiders, making it costly for the firm to replace insiders by outsiders. A third source of unemployment is basically technological, regarding the relation between the rate of labor turnover and labor productivity (independently of insiders' rent-creating activities).

We examine each of these sources in turn. With regard to hiring and firing, it can be shown that the amount by which insiders can drive their wage above the outsiders' reservation wage depends on the magnitude of these costs.

In the previous chapter we focused on hiring, training, and firing costs, and divided these into "production-related" and "rent-related" costs. It can be shown that, under individualistic bargaining, the amount by which the insiders can drive their wage above that of the outsiders' reservation wage depends on the sum of the marginal hiring, training, and firing costs. Whenever this wage differential exceeds the insider-outsider productivity differential minus the production-related turnover costs, there is unemployment, which we have argued may be characterized as "involuntary" in a well-defined sense.

As we have seen, another set of labor turnover costs emerge when insiders protect themselves against attempts of outsiders to "steal" their jobs by threatening not to cooperate with these outsiders in the production process and to have unpleasant personal relations with them (i.e., to harass them). It can be shown that when insiders bargain individualistically with their firms, the insider-outsider wage differential depends on the marginal product differential between insiders and entrants (arising from insiders' cooperation activities) and the reservation wage differential (arising from insiders' harassment activities). As above, involuntary unemployment occurs whenever the insider-outsider wage differential exceeds the insider-outsider ability differential.

In the previous chapter, we discussed how a firm's labor turnover costs may be generated by workers' effort responses to their job security. The insiders are able to exploit this cost by raising their wage above the level at which outsiders would be willing to work, without giving the firms an incentive to replace them if the resulting productivity loss exceeds the insider-outsider wage differential.

Although the above explanations of involuntary unemployment are based on individualistic insider activities, the insider-outsider theory is also capable of rationalizing a variety of union activities. Given that labor turnover costs generate economic rent that is shared between firms and their insiders, unions may boost the wages of their members by augmenting the turnover costs and thereby increasing the amount of rent to be shared. In addition, they may help their members capture a larger share of this rent. In particular, unions can (a) provide leverage for the rent-creating activities of individual insiders, (b) give insiders new tools of rent creation (such as strike and work-to-rule threats), and (c) raise insiders' bargaining power. The first two activities are rent-augmenting; the third is share-augmenting.

The basic themes of this chapter are developed further in the rest of the book:

- *The most straightforward type of labor turnover costs—the costs of hiring, training, and firing—has already been considered in chapter 3.*
- *Chapter 5 examines the role of cooperation and harassment activities in the determination of wages, employment, and unemployment.*
- *Chapter 6 analyzes the effort effect of labor turnover.*
- *Chapters 7 and 8 rationalize union activities on the basis of hiring, training, and firing costs.*

As noted in chapter 2, a good conceptual test of theories of persistent involuntary unemployment in free-market economies is to ask whether it can explain why unemployment cannot be eliminated through underbidding. In particular: (a) Why are involuntarily unemployed workers unwilling or unable to gain jobs by underbidding their employed comrades? (b) Why are laid-off workers unwilling or unable to retain their jobs by underbidding? The lower wage bids may be initiated by the firms, the workers, or both in conjunction; "underbidding" is said to take place when the relevant parties accept such bids.

One obvious explanation could be "social norms," according to which underbidding is not an acceptable form of social behavior: "Thou shalt not steal the job of thy comrades by underbidding them" and "Thou shalt not permit job theft from underbidding" are widely accepted social precepts. These imply that existing wages become "fair wages," independent of current demand and supply pressures in the labor market—much as the so-called "wage norms" operate in studies of George Perry (1980), Arthur Okun (1981), and Daniel Mitchell (1985).

However, for an economist, it is natural to try to explore the rationale for such norms when attempting to answer the two questions above. Nowadays the preponderant answer to these questions is contained in the efficiency-wage theories. This chapter suggests a logically independent theory: the "insider-outsider" approach. In the efficiency-wage theories, all labor market power rests with the firms, who make the wage and employment decisions under asymmetric information. It is not in the firm's interest to accept the underbidding of involuntarily unemployed workers, because firms use wages as a screening device for productivity. In this case, the unemployment may be understood in terms of a conflict of interest between the firms and the unemployed workers.

By contrast, the insider-outsider approach places some labor market power into the hands of the employees. The crucial assumption is that it is costly to exchange a firm's current, full-fledged employees (the insiders) for unemployed workers (the outsiders), and that the rent associated with this turnover cost can be tapped by the insiders in the process of wage negotiation. Thus wages may be set so that involuntary unemployment results, but the outsiders are nevertheless unable to improve their position through underbidding, because the insiders make underbidding expensive for the firms to accept and disagreeable for the outsiders to pursue. Accordingly, involuntary unemployment arises out of a conflict of interest between the insiders and the outsiders. It should be observed that, unlike the efficiency-wage theories, the insider-outsider approach does not assume a direct effect of wages on productivity.

In what follows, we explore the insider-outsider approach by examining how persistent involuntary unemployment can arise under three separate types of cost from insider-outsider turnover: (i) the costs of hiring and firing (see chapter 3 and Robert Solow, 1985); (ii) the costs that arise when insiders are prepared to withdraw cooperation from entrants (and thereby reduce the entrants' productivity) or to damage entrants' personal relations with them (and thereby raise the entrants' disutility of work; see chapter 5); and (iii) the costs implicit in the adverse effect of labor turnover on work effort (see chapter 6). We then take a brief look at the implications of the insider-outsider approach for the theory of labor unions.

4.1 Hiring, Training, and Firing Costs

These are perhaps the most conspicuous turnover costs (for example, the expense of implementing mandatory hiring and firing procedures, engaging in litigation, making severance payments), and they take time to incur. These turnover costs have been examined in the previous chapter. With reference to these costs, let "insiders" be workers on whom all the hiring and training costs have been expended and whose dismissal would trigger the full range of firing costs, whereas "entrants" are associated only with hiring costs.

For the moment, suppose that the insiders are not unionized, so that we can assume the insider wage to be the outcome of an "individualistic" bargaining process between each insider and his firm whereby the insider takes the wages and employment opportunities of all other workers as given. We require that this bargaining process satisfy two general properties: (i) each insider captures some (or all) of the rent inherent in the hiring and firing costs and (ii) the greater this rent, the greater the insider wage.

Let W_I and W_E be the wages of insiders and entrants (respectively), let R be the outsiders' reservation wage, and let H be the marginal hiring and training costs, and F be the marginal firing costs. Then, under the conditions above, it can be shown that the insider wage will exceed the entrant wage by some positive amount that is not greater than the marginal firing costs:

$$W_E < W_I \leqslant (W_E + F). \tag{1a}$$

Here $W_I > W_E$ since insiders have some bargaining power, and $W_I \leqslant (W_E + F)$ since an insider wage that exceeds this upper bound would induce the firm to replace its marginal insider by an entrant. In the same vein, the entrant wage will exceed the outsiders' reservation wage by no more than the marginal hiring costs:

$$R \leqslant W_E \leqslant (R + H). \tag{1b}$$

Observe that W_E will exceed R if entrants have some bargaining power on account of the hiring costs, but that W_E will not exceed $(R + H)$ since the firm would otherwise have no incentive to employ the entrant.

Now consider an economy in which all wages are determined in this way and, at these wages, aggregate labor demand falls short of aggregate labor supply. To examine whether the resulting unemployment is involuntary, we distinguish between "production-related" and "rent-related" turnover costs. (For a discussion of these terms, see the previous chapter.) Suppose that each insider provides A efficiency units of labor whereas each entrant provides 1 efficiency unit of labor, where $A > 1$. For simplicity, we assume that all the hiring and training costs are production-related and all the firing costs are rent-related. Then the outsiders are involuntarily unemployed whenever

$$(R + H) < (W_I/A). \tag{2a}$$

The unemployment is involuntary in the sense that the outsiders are arbitrarily exposed to a more restricted opportunity set than the insiders.

Moreover, this unemployment will persist whenever the outsiders' reservation costs plus the marginal hiring and firing costs exceed the insider wage, normalized for skill differences:

$$R + H + F > (W_I/A). \tag{2b}$$

For, in that event, the firms have no incentive to replace insiders by outsiders.

4.2 Cooperation and Harassment

Another potentially important reason why insiders may have a stronger bargaining position than outsiders is that the insiders often have considerable latitude in choosing whether to be cooperative with entrants in the process of production or whether to have, or not to have, good personal relations with them. Thus, insiders are able to affect *both* entrants' productivity via work cooperation *and* their disutility of work via unfriendly attitudes, which we simply call "harassment." Firms generally find it impossible to monitor such cooperation and harassment activity perfectly, and the wage contracts cannot be made contingent on them. (Output-related wage contracts may not obviate this difficulty, because in many cases firms and/or insiders could find them incentive incompatible, too risky, or too costly to monitor, as shown in chapter 5.) Under these circumstances, insiders can protect themselves from underbidding by being prepared to withdraw cooperation from the underbidders or to damage their personal relations with them. In other words, the possibilities of pursuing cooperation and harassment generate economic rent that insiders can exploit in wage determination.

To begin with, let us examine the effects of cooperative activities alone. Suppose that wages are determined by the same individualistic bargaining process as above and that insiders can engage in cooperative activities while entrants cannot. Under these circumstances, entrants receive the reservation wage (and thus are not better off than the outsiders):

$$W_E = R. \tag{3a}$$

Suppose that each insider provides a_I efficiency units (given the level of cooperation among insiders) and that each entrant provides a_E efficiency units of labor (given the level of cooperation between insiders and entrants). Let $0 \leqslant a_I, a_E \leqslant 1$. It can be shown that the insider wage, generated by the bargaining process, will exceed the reservation wage by some positive factor that is not greater than the differential in the efficiency units of labor provided by the insiders and entrants:

$$R < W_I \leqslant R \cdot (a_I/a_E). \tag{3b}$$

Assuming for simplicity that cooperative activity has no direct utility cost to the insiders, it is in the insiders' interests to make this disparity as large as possible. They do this by cooperating with one another but refusing to cooperate with entrants. In other words, $a_E = 1$ and $a = A$, so that condition (3b) becomes

$$R < W_I \leqslant R \cdot A. \tag{3c}$$

In an economy that runs along these lines, persistent involuntary unemployment may exist in the following sense. The inherent ability difference between an insider (on the one hand) and an entrant or outsider (on the other) stems exclusively from their different individual abilities to provide cooperation to their colleagues. The corresponding ability-related marginal product differential may be evaluated as the amount by which their marginal products would differ under identical external condition of employment, viz., identical cooperation from their colleagues. Now observe that the bargaining process above may yield an insider wage that exceeds the reservation wage by more than the ability-related marginal product differential, so that the outsiders are involuntarily unemployed. Nevertheless, the firms may have no incentive to replace the insiders. The reason is that the insiders and outsiders do *not* face identical external conditions of employment: The insiders receive cooperation whereas the outsiders (through no fault of their own) do not. Thus, the firms do not find it worthwhile to hire outsiders, and consequently the unemployment persists.

By the same token, laid-off workers may be unable to retain their jobs by offering to work for lower wages. Specifically, suppose that there is a business downturn and that firms respond by laying off a number of employees. It can then be shown that it is in the best interest of the remaining employees to withdraw cooperation from the laid-off workers and thereby prevent underbidding.

Harassment activities can achieve a similar purpose. We observe that employees are free to decide how friendly or unfriendly they should be to fellow workers—activities whereby they can affect each other's disutility of work, but about which firms usually cannot obtain complete, verifiable, and objective information. Insiders can keep unemployed and laid-off workers from underbidding by creating the credible expectation that underbidders will be harassed. As a result, outsiders have a higher reservation wage than the insiders.

In the absence of any turnover costs except those generated through harassment activities, it can be shown that the insider wage will be greater than the insiders' reservation wage but will not exceed the entrants' reservation wage:

$$R_I < W_I \leqslant R_E. \tag{4}$$

If the outsiders were able to avoid harassment, they would be willing and able to do the insiders' work for less than the insiders' wage. Yet they do not have this option. Their choice set, even allowing for their abilities, is less favorable than that of the insiders. This is the sense in which the unemployment may be regarded as involuntary.

4.3 Effort and Labor Turnover

A third significant reason why firms might not comprehensively replace their high-wage insiders with low-wage outsiders is that the implied labor turnover would have an adverse effect on the morale of all their employees and consequently work effort and productivity would fall. As in some versions of the efficiency wage theories, we assume that firms have incomplete information on work effort and thus wages cannot be made dependent on it. Insiders know this and raise their wage above the level at which outsiders would be willing to work, but firms do not replace them since the associated productivity loss would dominate the reduction in labor cost.

To drive this point home in a simple way, suppose that future productivity is stochastically related to current work effort (due to lags in production or monitoring). Thus, firms cannot use current wages to reward workers for their current effort; at best, they can reward the stochastic output response to past effort. They can also use the turnover rate to stimulate effort by specifying a cutoff productivity, below which an employee is dismissed.

Let the firm's remuneration package consist of a wage and the cutoff productivity. The firm can raise the labor turnover rate by raising its cutoff productivity. This reduces the expected future reward that each employee receives for current effort. It can be shown that the effort response depends on a substitution effect and an income effect (see chapter 6). By the former, effort falls: The employee works less hard since he is more likely to be fired and thus less likely to be compensated for his effort. The income effect raises effort: The employee works harder in order to avoid the possibility of being fired.

In this context, turnover has an adverse effect on effort if the substitution effect dominates the income effect. Then the firm bears an effort-related cost of labor turnover. In particular, let the firm's production function now be $Q = f(e \cdot L_I + e \cdot L_E)$, where the effort level (e) depends inversely on the turnover rate (t): $e = e(t)$, e', $e'' < 0$. Given the insider wage (W_I) and the entrant wage (W_E), it is easy to show that the firm will set its labor turnover rate so that the effort cost of turnover is equal to the insider-entrant wage differential:

$$e' = W_I - W_e. \tag{5}$$

Consequently, the greater the insider wage, the greater the firm's turnover rate, and the smaller the firm's demand for insiders. The insiders are aware of this relationship and negotiate their wage in this context. Then, given that the insiders capture some of the economic rent associated with the effort-related turnover cost, there may be involuntary unemployment in the following sense: Insiders and outsiders have the same abilities and differ only in terms of their competitive positions. If the outsiders could gain employment without affecting employees' effort incentives, they could perform the same job as the insiders—and do it for less than the insider wage. But since that option is closed to them, they may be considered involuntarily unemployed.

4.4 Union Activity

Thus far our explanation of involuntary unemployment has not only avoided the presumption of government regulations, but also has made no reference to the activity of labor unions. However, the insider-outsider approach does suggest how unions may accentuate involuntary unemployment. It also provides several rationales for union activity and indicates how each can contribute to involuntary unemployment.

Assuming that unions are more responsive to the interests of their employed members than to those of the unemployed ones, there are many ways in which a union can help raise the wages of its insiders without reducing their chances of continued employment: (a) it may amplify the costs of hiring and firing (for example, severance pay, hiring and firing procedures); (b) it could increase the effectiveness and variety of cooperation and harassment activities; (c) it can augment insiders' bargaining power and thereby enable them to capture a greater share of the available rent from their jobs; (d) it can provide insiders with new rent-seeking tools—threats of strike and work-to-rule are the most prominent examples. (See chapters 7 and 8.) In this manner, the insider-outsider approach offers an explanation of how unions get their clout, and why employers choose to negotiate with unions rather than turn to nonunionized workers.

In short, the insider-outsider contributions described above may be seen as an attempt to rationalize simultaneously the existence of wage norms, involuntary unemployment,[1] and the economic role of labor unions.

Note

1. As noted in the previous chapter, our rationale for involuntary unemployment becomes more complex in an intertemporal setting, where we make the additional assumption that the insider wage is positively related to the present value of the firm's wage payments.

5   Cooperation, Harassment, and Involuntary Unemployment

Overview

The previous chapter discussed several different types of labor turnover costs that may give insiders power in the determination of wages, and hence help them influence employment and unemployment. We now examine one of these costs in depth, namely, that associated with insiders' cooperation and harassment activities.

This kind of analysis not only provides a microeconomic rationale for a macroeconomic equilibrium characterized by involuntary unemployment; it also gives an economic explanation for various observed behavior patterns among workers. In particular, it is often observed that

(a) people who work in close association over long periods of time tend to cooperate more, and have more supportive personal relations with one another than with newcomers,

(b) people who are not employed tend to observe the social norm that jobs should not be "stolen" from incumbent workers by underbidding their wages, and

(c) employers tend to discourage "job theft" by refusing to hire "predatory newcomers" (i.e., workers who attempt to gain jobs through underbidding).

We suggest that workers and firms often have economic motives for behaving in these ways. Insiders may be more cooperative and friendly to one another than to underbidding entrants in order to prevent the insider wage from being eroded: By creating more favorable conditions of work for themselves than for newcomers, they make it difficult for outsiders to gain employment through underbidding. Moreover, firms may be unwilling to hire outsiders at less than the prevailing wage because, given the insiders' unwillingness to cooperate with underbidders, it is not profitable for the firms to accept underbidding.

In short, the interdependence of employees who work in conjunction with one another is the centerpiece of this chapter. The traditional way of capturing worker interdependence in the theory of the firm is to assume that the cross-partial derivatives of the production function with respect to different labor types are not equal to zero. In that approach, however, the degree of productivity interdependence among workers is exogenously given. Our analysis departs from that approach by recognizing that (i) insiders may be able and willing to affect this productivity interdependence, (ii) workers' utilities of work are also interdependent, and (iii) the insiders may also be able and willing to influence this utility interdependence.

We define "cooperation activities" as ones whereby workers support one another in the process of production and thereby raise each other's productivities. "Harassment activities" refer to workers' activities that are designed to make each other's jobs more unpleasant and thereby raise each other's disutility of work. We assume that insiders are more effective cooperators and harassers than are entrants. Furthermore, firms are assumed to be unable to monitor these activities directly, and thus wages cannot be set contingent on them.

Our analysis shows how insiders' cooperation and harassment activities may give rise to involuntary unemployment. The insiders in our model are not malicious. They get no satisfaction from harassing or refusing to cooperate with entrants. Rather, their cooperation and harassment activities serve to improve their wages and protect their jobs. As result, the outsiders become victims of discrimination, in that they face a more limited choice set than the insiders. Even if they are prepared to work for a wage that is less than the insider wage by an amount sufficient to compensate the firm for their lack of cooperation skills, they may still be unable to find employment. This chapter provides a definition of involuntary unemployment as the outcome of such discrimination and investigates the conditions under which such unemployment exists in the macroeconomic equilibrium.

The last part of the chapter deals with the implications of insiders' activities for labor turnover within firms and wage-employment movements in response to cyclical macroeconomic shocks. We also explore the degree to which the involuntary unemployment above can be mitigated through the creation of new firms and through output-related wage contracts.

In order to understand how free-market economies may suffer from protracted spells of involuntary unemployment, it is important to explain why underbidding is not a preponderant feature of labor markets. In this context, we take "underbidding" to mean an agreement between a worker and a firm that a particular job be performed at less than the prevailing wage. (Whether the low-wage offer is made by the worker, the firm, or both is immaterial in this regard.) If underbidding occurred whenever unemployed workers were willing to work for less than the prevailing wages (normalized for any productivity differences), then involuntary unemployment would either disappear or be accompanied by the empirically unobserved phenomenon of persistent wage deflation.

In the absence of government intervention, underbidding failures can be rationalized by showing (a) why firms have no incentive to agree on low-wage bids in the presence of involuntary unemployment or (b) why workers lack this incentive. The recent theoretical literature on unemployment has pursued both of these routes. The efficiency wage theories (for example, George Akerlof, 1982; Jeremy Bulow and Lawrence Summers, 1986; Jim Malcomson, 1981; Carl Shapiro and Joseph Stiglitz, 1984; Andrew Weiss, 1980) have focused on route (a), and much of the labor union literature that has a bearing on unemployment and layoffs (for example, Ian MacDonald and Robert Solow, 1981; Andrew Oswald, 1982) takes route (b).

This chapter attempts to provide a rationale for what many people regard as a well-established social norm, namely, that workers should not "steal" jobs from their fellow workers by agreeing to work for lower wages, and that employers should not permit such "job theft."

Our analysis pursues the two routes above in the following way. Route (a): Firms may refuse to replace incumbent employees with workers who wish to underbid because they realistically expect that, if they did so, the remaining incumbents would withdraw cooperation from the underbidders in the process of production. Route (b): Unemployed workers may not agree to underbid because they realistically expect that, if they thereby succeeded in replacing some incumbents, their personal relations with the remaining incumbents would be unpleasant (i.e., they would be "harassed" by the incumbents).

In the standard literature on the theory of labor markets, harassment has received little attention, while the theory of teams (for example, Armen Alchian and H. Demsetz, 1972; Jacob Marshak and Roy Radner, 1972) recognizes employees' productivities to be interdependent. However, the crucial, distinctive feature of our analysis is that *cooperation and harassment activities do not occur automatically; rather, they lie within the control of the employees, especially the incumbents.*

In describing the causes and consequences of incumbents' cooperation and harassment activities, we adopt an "insider-outsider" approach to the labor market. The basic idea underlying this general approach is that there are labor turnover costs that generate economic rent that incumbent workers ("insiders") manipulate and exploit in the process of wage determination. In this chapter, the insiders are assumed to create a special, potentially important, variety of labor turnover cost by withdrawing cooperation from and by harassing the entrants who attempt to underbid. As a result, the insiders are able to raise their wages above the market-clearing level without inducing underbidding.

At these wages, the unemployed workers ("outsiders") would prefer to trade places with the insiders (i.e., they would prefer to be employed for insider wages under insider conditions of work rather than to be unemployed), but they do not have this option. They are victims of *discrimination*, because whenever they gain employment through underbidding, they receive less cooperation and more harassment than the insiders do. In fact, the outsiders may be willing to work for sufficiently less than the insider wages so as to compensate the firms for their more limited cooperation skills, but they may nevertheless be unable to find jobs. Given that the outsiders find themselves with lower productivity and higher disutility of work than the insiders, there may exist no wage that *both* induces firms to hire outsiders *and* induces outsiders to work. This is the sense in which involuntary unemployment can arise in our analysis.

Section 5.1 deals with the microeconomic behavior of workers and firms in our model. Section 5.2 describes the equilibrium of a single firm and its employees. In section 5.3, we incorporate this equilibrium in an aggregate analysis of the labor market and examine how involuntary unemployment can occur in this context. Section 5.4 deals with potential objections to our analysis. Finally, section 5.5 contains concluding remarks.

5.1 The Behavior of Economic Agents

5.1.1 The Underlying Setup

Though our explanation of involuntary unemployment rests on two distinct, logically independent arguments (one of which focuses on cooperation, the other on harassment), for brevity, the formal model in sections 5.2 and 5.3 deals with these arguments simultaneously.

The cooperation and harassment activities, which the insiders use to protect themselves against underbidding, may be defined as follows. "Cooperation" refers to all those activities in which workers help one another in the process of production and thereby raise their productivity. "Harassment" stands for all those activities whereby workers make one another's jobs more disagreeable (primarily by damaging their personal relations) and thereby raise their disutility of work.

In practice, those workers who have spent a long time at their jobs are often more capable of cooperation and harassment than their newly arrived counterparts. We capture this observation roughly by supposing that when workers first enter their firms, they are unable to cooperate with or harass other workers, but after a fixed period of time—call it the "initiation period"—they all gain identical access to these abilities.

Within this context, we identify three homogeneous groups of workers: (i) *insiders*, the "experienced" employees who are able to engage in the full range of cooperation and harassment activities; (ii) *entrants*, the "inexperienced" employees who have no access to these activities; and (iii) *outsiders*, the unemployed workers.[1]

In this section, we build a simple model that captures the role of insiders' cooperation and harassment activities in the formulation of wage and employment decisions within a firm. Our model is based on the following salient structural assumptions:

1. *Wage Decisions.* Each employee's wage is negotiated for one period at a time, where (for simplicity) the length of the period is assumed equal to the initiation period.[2]

2. *Outsiders Are Perfect Competitors for Jobs.* Thus, when an outsider is hired (and thereby turns into an entrant), the person's entrant wage is equal to his reservation wage (for the duration of the initiation period).

3. *Insiders Have Some Market Power.* Each insider sets his wage "individualistically" (taking the strategies of all other agents as given).[3]

4. *Monitoring.* An insider's wage cannot be made contingent on his cooperation and harassment activities, since the firm is unable to monitor these activities directly. (All that the firm can observe is its output and the number of insiders and entrants it employs.)

5. *Employment Decisions.* These are made unilaterally by the firms.

6. *Sequence of Decisions.* In the first stage of the decision-making process, the insider wage and the cooperation and harassment levels are set, taking into account how these decisions affect employment. The entrant wage is determined as well. In the second stage, the firms make the employment decisions, taking the insider and entrant wages, as well as the cooperation and harassment levels, as given.

5.1.2 The Firm

Consider a firm that has two variable factors of production: insiders (L_I) and entrants (L_E). Let a_I represent the level of cooperation among insiders (measured as the actual number of insiders divided into the number that would be required to produce the same output in the absence of cooperation among insiders), and let a_E stand for the level of cooperation between insiders and entrants (measured as the actual number of entrants divided into the number that would be required to produce the same output in the absence of cooperation from insiders). We shall call a_I and a_E the "labor endowments" of the insiders and entrants, respectively. The firm is assumed to know the levels of these endowments but it cannot observe the cooperation activities of individual workers. We write the firm's production function as $Q = f(a_I \cdot L_I + a_E \cdot L_E)$, $f' > 0$, $f'' < 0$, where Q is the level of output.

Let W be the insider wage and R_E be the entrant wage (which is equal to the entrants' reservation wage). All insiders are identical and receive the same wage, and similarly for entrants. The firm can observe W and R_E, but it cannot observe the harassment activities that are reflected in the level of R_E.

Within the two-stage, decision-making process specified in section 5.1.1 (with wages, cooperation, and harassment decisions made in the first stage and employment decisions made in the second), the firm's problem is to maximize its profit with respect to L_I and L_E, taking the insider and entrant wages, the overall cooperation, and harassment levels, as well as the production function f, as given. To present our analysis in the simplest possible way, we assume that the firm has a one-period time horizon.[4]

Let m be the firm's "incumbent work force," that is, the stock of insiders carried forward from the past. Since we assume that cooperation and harassment skills are firm-specific and that entrants acquire them only after they go through the initiation period, it is clear that $L_I \leqslant m$.

Thus, the firm's profit-maximization problem is

Maximize $\quad \pi = f(a_I \cdot L_I + a_E \cdot L_E) - W \cdot L_I - R_E \cdot L_E$

subject to $\quad L_I \leqslant m, \quad L_I, L_E \leqslant 0.$ (1)

Let $\lambda = a_I \cdot L_I + a_E \cdot L_E$ be the firm's effective work force (i.e., its work force in efficiency units of labor). Then the first-order conditions may be expressed as follows:

$$\frac{\partial \pi}{\partial L_I} = a_I \cdot f'(\lambda) - W \geqslant 0,$$

$$\frac{\partial \pi}{\partial L_I} \cdot (m - L_I) = 0;$$ (2a)

$$\frac{\partial \pi}{\partial L_E} = a_E \cdot f'(\lambda) - R_E \leqslant 0,$$

$$\frac{\partial \pi}{\partial L_E} \cdot L_E = 0;$$

(2b)

there we ignore the nonnegativity constraint on L_I and we assume that the firm is able to hire all the entrants it demands at the wage R_E.[5]

5.1.3 The Workers

Insider i has the following decision variables:

1. The level of his harassing activity directed at entrants: h_E^i (implicitly assuming that the insider harasses all entrants in equal measure). We assume that the insider does not harass other insiders.[6]

2. The levels of his cooperative activities directed at other insiders and entrants: a_I^i and a_E^i, respectively, defined analogously to a_I and a_E above. (We assume implicitly that he cooperates with all the other insiders in equal measure, and similarly for all the entrants.)

3. The insider i's wage: W^i.

The insider makes these decisions "individualistically"; that is, he takes the optimal cooperation, harassment, wage setting, and employment strategies of all other agents as given. Let us examine the role of each of these decision variables in the context of the insider's decision-making problem.

Since we are primarily concerned with the effect of insiders' cooperation and harassment activities on their wages and employment, it is natural to make the simplifying assumption that the insider i's cooperation and harassment activities do not affect his own utility directly, but only indirectly via the wage he is able to achieve.[7] In other words, the insider is assumed to regard the activities h_E^i, a_E^i, and a_I^i as neither desirable nor undesirable per se, and therefore (as shown below) he uses them only to support his wage claims.

We specify insider i's utility function quite simply as $\Omega^i = C^i - l^i$, where C_i is his consumption and l^i is his labor (in units of time). Labor is taken to be a discrete activity, with $l = 1$ for an employed worker and $l = 0$ for an unemployed one. We assume that each worker consumes his entire income in each period. For insider i, this means that $C^i = W^i$.

The insider's reservation wage, R_I^i, is defined as that wage (W^i) that makes him indifferent between employment (yielding utility $W^i - 1$) and unemployment (yielding utility 0):

$$R_I^i = R_I = 1 \qquad \text{for all } i. \tag{3a}$$

Let entrant j's utility be $\Omega^j = C^j - l^j - H_E$, where H_E stands for his disutility from being harassed by the insiders.[8] Naturally, we assume that

$$(\partial H_E / \partial h_E^i) > 0 \qquad \text{for any insider } i. \tag{3b}$$

Thus the entrant's reservation wage is

$$R_E^j = R_E = 1 + H_E \qquad \text{for all } j. \tag{3c}$$

We assume that each insider's harassing activity (h_E^i) is bounded from above and below, so that each entrant's disutility from being harassed (H_E) is also bounded as

$$0 \leqslant H_E \leqslant H, \tag{3d}$$

where H is a nonnegative constant (described in note 17).

We now turn to the insider i's cooperation activities and specify how they affect the productivities of the other insiders and the entrants. We wish to ensure, quite plausibly, that an insider is able to raise the marginal products of workers by cooperating with them. For this purpose, we make the following two assumptions:

$$\partial a_I / \partial a_I^i, \qquad \partial a_E / \partial a_E^i > 0, \tag{4a}$$

and

$$0 < \eta_I, \eta_E < 1, \tag{4b}$$

where $\eta_I = -(f''/f') \cdot a_I \cdot L_I$ and $\eta_E = -(f''/f') \cdot a_E \cdot L_E$ are the elasticities of the marginal product of labor with respect to the insider and entrant work forces. Thus, when an insider increases his cooperative activity with other insiders and entrants, the marginal products of the insider and entrant work forces rise:

$$\frac{\partial(a_I \cdot f')}{\partial a_I^i} = \frac{\partial a_I}{\partial a_I^i} \cdot \frac{1}{f'} \cdot (1 + \eta) > 0,$$

$$\frac{\partial(a_E \cdot f')}{\partial a_E^i} = \frac{\partial a_E}{\partial a_E^i} \cdot \frac{1}{f'} \cdot (1 + \eta) > 0.$$

Assumption (4a) means that the jobs within the firm are sufficiently interdependent so that an individual insider's cooperation with other insiders or entrants has a significant, positive effect on their labor endowments. This assumption is unnecessary to our analysis whenever insiders can influence a_I and a_E through coordinated (rather than individualistic) activity. Indeed this suggests that, in large plants with little job interdependence, insiders may have a special incentive to form a union. An insider-outsider explanation for the emergence of unions is to be found here.

We let each insider's cooperating activities (a_I^i and a_E^i) be bounded from above and below, so that the labor endowments of insiders and entrants (a_I and a_E) are bounded as follows:

$$1 \leqslant a_I, a_E \leqslant A, \tag{4c}$$

where A is a constant greater than unity.[9]

Finally, we turn to the insider's influence over his wage W^i. To reach our qualitative conclusions, we only need to assume that (a) each insider's wage captures at least some of the economic rent generated through his cooperation and harassment activities and (b) the greater this rent, the higher his wage. These properties hold in a variety of well-known bargaining games (for example, Shaked and Sutton, 1984) and are in accord with common-sense ideas on wage-setting processes. However, to make our exposition as simple as possible, we consider only the extreme case in which each insider sets his own wage unilaterally and individualistically (as noted in section 5.1). This means that each insider takes the wages and employment of all other insiders as given. Consequently, if he wishes to retain his job, he must set his wage so that the firm has an incentive to employ him in addition to all the other insiders it is employing. In other words, each insider regards himself as the marginal worker in the firm's employment decisions.

The insider i faces two wage-setting options: (i) he may set his wage at some level V^i, which is sufficiently low to ensure his continued employment, or (ii) he may achieve his reservation wage R_I^i by choosing not to be employed. Clearly, the insider will choose the first option only if the maximum achievable wage V^i, denoted by V_{max}^i, is at least as great as the reservation wage; otherwise, the second option is preferable:

$$W^i = \max[R_I, V_{max}^i]. \tag{5a}$$

V_{max}^i may be inferred from the firm's employment behavior as described by the first-order conditions (2a) and (2b). If entrants are not employed, then only (2a) is relevant for determining the maximum achievable wage: $W \leqslant a_I \cdot f'(\lambda)$ and thus V_{max}^i is the maximum of $[a_I \cdot f'(\lambda)]$ with respect to a_I^i and a_E^i. On the other hand, if entrants are employed (in addition to insiders), then both (2a) and (2b) are relevant and the first parts of (2a) and (2b) hold as equalities:

$$f'(\lambda) = f'(a_I \cdot m + a_E \cdot L_E)$$

$$= V^i/a_I = R_E/a_E,$$

and thus V^i_{max} is the maximum of $[(a_I/a_E) \cdot R_E]$ with respect to a_I^i, a_E^i, and h_E^i.
In short, V^i_{max} may be expressed as follows:

$$V^i_{max} = \max_{a_I^i, a_E^i, h_E^i} [\min\{a_I \cdot f'(a_I \cdot L_I), (a_I/a_E) \cdot R_E\}]. \tag{5b}$$

Substituting (5b) into (5a), and recalling that $R_I = 1$ and $R_E = 1 + H_E$, we obtain insider i's wage:

$$W^i = \max_{a_I^i, a_E^i, h_E^i} [1, \min\{a_I \cdot f'(a_I \cdot L_I), (a_I/a_E) \cdot (1 + H_E)\}]. \tag{5c}$$

5.2 The Microeconomic Equilibrium: The Firm and Its Employees

We now show how the equilibrium levels of wages, employment, and cooperation and harassment activities are determined through the interaction of a firm and its employees. Our concept of equilibrium (for the two-stage, decision-making process described above) may be specified as follows:

DEFINITION *In the Nash equilibrium of the firm and its employees, (a) each insider i maximizes his utility with respect to his decision variables W^i, a_I^i, a_E^i, and h_E^i, taking the strategies of the firm and the other employees as given, and (b) the firm maximizes its profit with respect to its decision variables L_I and L_E, taking the strategies of its employees as given.*

Let us now turn to the characteristics of this equilibrium.

5.2.1 Cooperation

Under equilibrium conditions, each insider cooperates fully with other insiders, but does not cooperate with entrants.

Intuitively, the reason is that (a) by cooperating with the other insiders, the insider raises the marginal product of the firm's incumbent work force and is thereby able to achieve a higher wage, and (b) by refusing to cooperate with entrants, the insider reduces the marginal product of the entrant work force, and consequently reduces the number of entrants hired, thereby raising the marginal product of the incumbent work force and achieving a higher wage.

This can be shown formally by deriving the cooperation activities a_I^i and a_E^i, which permit the insider i to earn his maximum achievable wage V_{max}^i. By the V_{max}^i equation (5b), the insider's optimal (equilibrium) levels of cooperation are $(a_I^i)^* = \max(a_I^i)$ and $(a_E^i)^* = \min(a_E^i)$, so that

$$a_I^* = A \quad \text{and} \quad a_E^* = 1. \tag{6a}$$

5.2.2 Harassment

Under equilibrium conditions, each insider harasses maximally all workers who enter the firm.

Intuitively, we see that by doing so, the insider maximizes the entrants' reservation wage and thereby discourages them from entering the firm, so that a minimal number of entrants are hired. Thus, the marginal product of the incumbent work force is maximized, so that the insider achieves the highest possible wage.

Formally, the V_{max}^i equation (5b) implies that the insider's equilibrium level of harassment (which permits him to earn his maximum achievable wage) is $(h_E^i)^* = \max(h_E^i)$, so that

$$H_E^* = H \tag{6b}$$

[recalling that, by (3d), H is the upper bound of H_E].

5.2.3 Wage Determination

Substituting the optimal cooperation levels (6a) and the optimal harassment level (6b) into the W^i equation (5c), we obtain the following wage equation:

$$(W^i)^* = W^*$$

$$= \max[1, \min\{A \cdot f'(A \cdot L_I), A \cdot (1 + H)\}] \quad \text{for all } i. \tag{7}$$

This equation has a straightforward interpretation. If the insider's reservation wage ($R_I = 1$) falls short of his maximum wage achievable through employment, $(\min\{A \cdot f'(A \cdot L_I), A \cdot (1 + H)\})$, then the insider sets his wage with two independent considerations in mind: W^i must be sufficiently low so that (a) the insider does not become unprofitable to the firm, that is,

$$W^i \leqslant A \cdot f'(A \cdot L_1) \tag{8a}$$

(for otherwise he would be dismissed), and (b) the insider remains at least as profitable as the marginal entrant, that is,

$$W^i \leqslant A \cdot (1 + H) \tag{8b}$$

(for otherwise he would be replaced by the entrant). We call (8a) the "absolute profitability constraint" (APC) and (8b) the "relative profitability constraint" (RPC) on the insider wage.

5.2.4 Employment Determination

Whether the insider wage is given by the reservation wage, the APC or the RPC depends on the size of the firm's incumbent work force m. Recall that the firm faces diminishing returns to labor (i.e., $f'' < 0$), and thus the larger the incumbent work force, the lower the incumbent's marginal product. There are three possible scenarios:

i. *A "large" incumbent work force*: Here the incumbent work force is so large that its marginal product is less than the insiders' reservation wage (R_1). In particular, $m > \bar{m}$, where $\bar{m}$ is the "maximum sustainable incumbent work force" (i.e., the largest possible number of incumbents that the firm may have an incentive to employ) and $\bar{m}$ is given by [10]

$$A \cdot f'(A \cdot \bar{m}) = 1. \tag{9}$$

When the incumbent work force is greater than its maximum sustainable level ($m > \bar{m}$), it is clear that the firm finds it worthwhile to reduce employment. What remains to be examined is how large the new work force will be and whether some insiders will be replaced by entrants.

To this end, note that in this scenario *the insider wage will be set equal to the reservation wage*:

$$W^* = R_1 = 1 \qquad \text{for } m > \bar{m}. \tag{10a}$$

The reason is that if W were set beneath this level, then some insiders would have an incentive to quit; whereas if W were above this level, then some insiders would be dismissed even though they prefer employment to unemployment and these insiders would consequently have an incentive to opt for a lower wage.

Given that the insider wage is at its minimum level $W = 1$, then [by (2a) and (9)] *the firm employs the maximum sustainable incumbent work force*:

$$L_I^* = \bar{m} \qquad \text{for } m > \bar{m}. \tag{10b}$$

Since the insiders' marginal product is equal to their reservation wage $(A \cdot f'(A \cdot L_I) = 1)$, the marginal product of an entrant (hired in addition to the insiders) must be less than his reservation wage $(f'(A \cdot L_I^*) < 1 + H)$. Thus, *the firm hires no entrants*:[11,12]

$$L_E^* = 0, \qquad \text{for } m > \bar{m}. \tag{10c}$$

ii. *An "intermediate" incumbent work force*: Here the incumbent work force is (a) small enough so that its marginal product exceeds the insiders' reservation wage but (b) large enough so that the marginal product of entrants (hired in addition to incumbents) falls short of the entrants' reservation wage. In particular, $\underline{m} \leqslant m \leqslant \bar{m}$, where $\underline{m}$ is the "minimum sustainable incumbent work force" (i.e., the smallest possible number of incumbents that the firm could employ without having an incentive to hire entrants). $\underline{m}$ is given by[13]

$$f'(A \cdot \underline{m}) = 1 + H. \tag{11}$$

Under these circumstances, *the firm hires no entrants*:

$$L_E^* = 0 \qquad \text{for } \underline{m} \leqslant m \leqslant \bar{m}, \tag{12a}$$

since [by (11)] the marginal product of an entrant is less than the entrant's reservation wage $(f'(A \cdot m) < 1 + H = R_E^*)$.

Consequently, in setting his wage, each insider is constrained not by the need to remain at least as profitable as the entrants (since entrants are never profitable in this scenario), but only by the need to keep his absolute profitability from falling below zero. In other words, the binding constraint on the insider wage [given by the wage equation (7)] is the APC [constraint (8a)], whereas the RPC [constraint (8b)] is redundant.[14] This means that *each insider sets his wage equal to the marginal product of the incumbent work force*:

$$W^* = A \cdot f'(A \cdot m) \qquad \text{for } \underline{m} \leqslant m \leqslant \bar{m}. \tag{12b}$$

At this wage, *the firm retains all its incumbents*:[15]

$$L_I^* = m \qquad \text{for } \underline{m} \leqslant m \leqslant \bar{m}. \tag{12c}$$

iii. *A "small" incumbent work force*: Here the incumbent work force is sufficiently small so that the marginal products of both the incumbents and some entrants (hired in addition to the incumbents) exceed their respective reservation wages. In particular, $m \leqslant \underline{m}$.

Under this scenario, the insiders cannot completely exclude the outsiders from getting jobs (regardless of their cooperation and harassment activities). Thus, each insider must set his wage with a view to his profitability vis-à-vis the entrants; that is, the binding constraint on the insider wage is the RPC [constraint (8b)].[16] By the wage equation (7), this means that *the insider wage is a markup (by the factor A) over the entrants' equilibrium reservation wage* $(R_E^* = 1 + H)$:

$$W^* = A \cdot (1 + H) \qquad \text{for } m \leqslant \underline{m}. \tag{13a}$$

At this wage, the marginal incumbent is just as profitable as the first entrant (hired in addition to the incumbent work force): $(\partial\pi/\partial L_I^*) = Af'(A \cdot m) - W^* = (\partial\pi/\partial L_E) = f'(A \cdot m) - (1 + H)$. Since the incumbent work force is "small," the first entrant generates positive profit; thus, the marginal incumbent does so, too. Consequently, *the firm retains all its incumbents*:

$$L_I^* = m \qquad \text{for } m \leqslant \underline{m}, \tag{13b}$$

provided (as shown below) that the firm lacks the incentive to replace all its incumbents by entrants.

Moreover, *entrants are hired until their marginal product is brought into equality with their reservation wage*: $A \cdot L_I^* + L_E^* = A \cdot \underline{m}$ [by (11)] and thus

$$L_E^* = A \cdot (\underline{m} - m). \tag{13c}$$

The firm has no incentive to replace *all* its insiders by entrants. If the firm were to pursue this replacement strategy, it is reasonable to assume that the entrants would still be harassed and thus their wage would still be $R_E^* = (1 + H)$: The mere fact that the insiders have been fired does not preclude their harassing the workers who have ousted them. The only effect replacement has on profit is that the wage falls (since the entrants are cheaper than the insiders) and labor productivity falls by the same amount (since the entrants cannot cooperate with one another).[17]

5.2.5 The Microeconomic Equilibrium

Our results above are summarized in the following proposition:

PROPOSITION 1 *For the Nash equilibrium, the insiders' cooperation and harassment activity levels are* $a_I^* = A$, $a_E^* = 1$, *and* $h_E^* = H$, *whenever* $L_E^* > 0$. *Let the firm's incumbent work force* (m) *be exogenously given. Then the equilibrium wage and employment levels may be characterized as follows:*

(I)   If $m > \bar{m}$,   then $W^* = 1$,

$L_I^* = \bar{m}$, $L_E^* = 0$.

Thus, if the incumbent work force (m) is "large," then the insiders receive their reservation wage ($W^* = 1$) and, in response, the firm employs the maximum sustainable incumbent work force ($\bar{m}$) and does not hire any entrants.

(II)   If $\underline{m} \leqslant m \leqslant \bar{m}$,   then $W^* = A \cdot f'(A \cdot m)$,

$L_I^* = m$, $L_E^* = 0$.

Thus, if the incumbent work force is "intermediate," then the insiders are paid the marginal product of the incumbent work force ($W^* = A \cdot f'(A \cdot m)$) and the firm retains all its incumbents and hires no entrants.

(III)   If $m < \underline{m}$,   then $W^* = A \cdot (1 + H)$,

$R_E^* = 1 + H$, $L_I^* = m$, $L_E^* = A \cdot (\underline{m} - m)$.

In other words, if the incumbent work force is "small," then the insider wage is a markup over the reservation wage (with the size of the markup depending on the insider-entrant cooperation differential A) and the firm retains all its incumbents and hires some entrants. The entrants receive the reservation wage, which is raised by the insiders' harassment activity.

Proposition 1 is illustrated in figure 5.1. The figure contains two demand curves: an *insider demand curve*, along which the insiders' marginal product is equal to the insider wage, assuming that only insiders are employed—$A \cdot f'(A \cdot L_I) = 0$—and an *entrant demand curve*, along which the entrants' marginal product is equal to the entrant wage (R_E), assuming that only entrants are employed—$f'(L_E) = R_E$. [Thus $f'(A \cdot L_I + L_E) = R_E$ is the demand curve for entrants hired in addition to a given insider work force L_I.]

Observe that the insider demand curve lies above the entrant demand curve (by a factor of A), because the insiders cooperate with one another but are not prepared to cooperate with entrants. The point at which the $R_I^* = 1$ line crosses the insider demand curve yields [by (9)] the maximum sustainable incumbent work force ($A \cdot \bar{m}$, in efficiency units). Similarly, the intersection of the $R_E^* = 1 + H$ line and the entrant demand curve yields [by (11)] the minimum sustainable incumbent work force ($A \cdot \underline{m}$, in efficiency units).

The RPC is denoted by the uppermost horizontal line in the figure. The APC coincides with the insider demand curve (since the APC is the locus

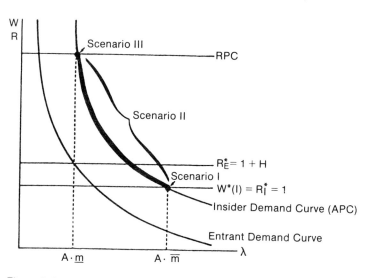

Figure 5.1
The macroeconomic equilibrium: RPC, $W^*(\text{III}) = A \cdot R_E^* = A(1 + H)$; insider demand
curve, $A \cdot f'(\lambda) = W^*$; entrant demand curve, $f'(\lambda) = R_E$.

of wage-employment points at which the absolute profitability of the
marginal insider is zero).

In figure 5.1, scenario II is depicted by the thick segment along the
insider demand curve. In other words, there is a continuum of equilibrium
points, each corresponding to a different incumbent work force:

$[W^*(\text{II}), \lambda^*(\text{II})]$

$$= [A \cdot f'(A \cdot L_I^*(\text{II})), (A \cdot L_I^*(\text{II}) + L_E^*(\text{II}))] = [A \cdot f'(A \cdot m), A \cdot m]. \quad (14\text{a})$$

Here the insiders prevent all entry into the firm through their cooperation
and harassment activities and set their wage so as to exploit all their
marginal rent ($W^*(\text{II}) = A \cdot f'(A \cdot m)$) and retain their jobs.

Scenario I is pictured by the lowest point on the thick line segment:

$[W^*(\text{I}), \lambda^*(\text{I})]$

$$= [R_I^*, (A \cdot L_I^*(\text{I}) + L_E^*(\text{I}))] = [1, A \cdot \overline{m}]. \quad (14\text{b})$$

Here the incumbent work force is sufficiently large so that the insider wage
is reduced to the reservation wage, and, in response, the firm employs only
the maximum sustainable incumbent work force.

Finally, scenario III is illustrated by the highest point on the thick line segment:

$[W^*(\text{III}), \lambda^*(\text{III})]$

$\quad = [A \cdot (1 + H), (A \cdot L_I^*(\text{III}) + L_E^*(\text{III}))]$

$\quad = [A \cdot (1 + H), A \cdot \underline{m}].$ (14c)

Here the incumbent work force is sufficiently small for some entrants to be profitable at their reservation wage. Thus, the insider wage is set so that the marginal incumbent is just as profitable as the marginal entrant ($W^*(\text{III}) = A \cdot (1 + H)$). In response, the firm retains all its incumbents and hires entrants until their marginal product (given by the entrant demand curve in the figure) is equal to their reservation wage (given by the line $R_E^* = 1 + H$ in the figure). Thus the firm's total work force, in efficiency units, is equal to what it would be if the minimum sustainable incumbent work force were employed ($\lambda^*(\text{III}) = A \cdot \underline{m}$).

Figure 5.1 shows quite simply what the insiders' cooperation and harassment activities are meant to achieve. By cooperating with other insiders, each insider raises the insider demand curve (in the figure) and is thereby able to achieve a higher wage than would otherwise have been possible. This is true for one of two reasons: (i) when entrants are not profitable (in scenario II), so that the insider wage is equal to the marginal product of the incumbent work force ($W^*(\text{II}) = A \cdot f'(A \cdot m)$), cooperation among insiders raises this marginal product; and (ii) when entrants are profitable (in scenario III), so that the insider wage is a markup over the entrant wage ($W^*(\text{III}) = A \cdot (1 + H)$), cooperation among insiders raises the firm's cost of replacing an insider by an entrant and thereby increases the markup between the insider wage (W) and the entrant wage (R_E).

When the insider withdraws cooperation from potential entrants, he lowers the potential entrant demand curve (in the figure) and, once again, raises the cost of replacing insiders by entrants.

Finally, when the insider increases his harassment of potential entrants, he raises the entrants' reservation wage, which is the basis on which the insider wage is marked up.

Observe that the insiders' threats to withdraw cooperation and to harass entrants are credible. Given that the firm has already hired a fixed amount, L_E, of entrants, it remains in the insiders' interest to fulfill their threats. For in withdrawing cooperation, each insider causes a reduction in a_E and thereby also reduces the firm's effective work force ($\lambda = a_I^* \cdot L_I^* + a_E \cdot L_E$); as a result, he is able to raise his marginal product and his wage [i.e., for given L_E, $(\partial W_E^i / \partial a_E^i) = a_I \cdot f'' \cdot (\partial a_E / \partial a_E^i) < 0$ for any insider i]. Further-

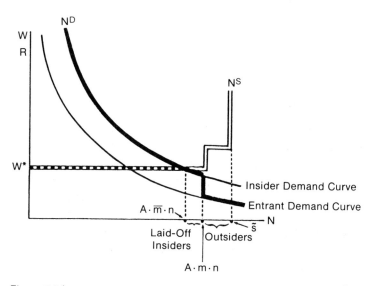

Figure 5.2A
Scenario I: N^D, aggregate labor demand curve (solid line); N^S, aggregate labor supply curve (doubled line); W_*, wage-setting curve (dotted line).

more, each insider still has an incentive to fulfill his harassment threat because, in doing so, he raises the entrants' reservation wage and is thereby able to achieve a higher wage for himself.

5.3 The Aggregate Labor Market: Involuntary Unemployment

We now shift the focus of our attention from the microeconomic equilibrium within a firm to unemployment in the labor market. Consider an economy that contains a fixed number n of identical firms and a fixed number s of workers. The wage and employment decisions are made in a decentralized fashion within each firm, along the lines indicated in the previous section.

Aggregate labor market activity may be described in terms of three building blocks:

i. *The aggregate labor demand curve*, denoted by N^D (the thick downward-sloping curves) in figures 5.2A–5.2C. (These figures picture the labor market under scenarios I–III, respectively.) When aggregate labor demand (N^D, in efficiency units) is less than or equal to the aggregate incumbent work force ($A \cdot m \cdot n$, also in efficiency units), employment decisions are

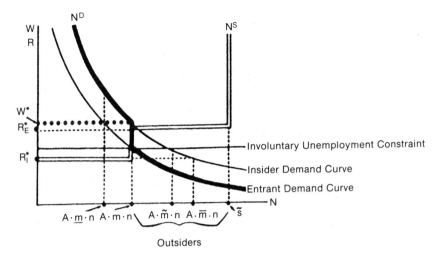

Figure 5.2B
Scenario II: Key given in figure 5.2A.

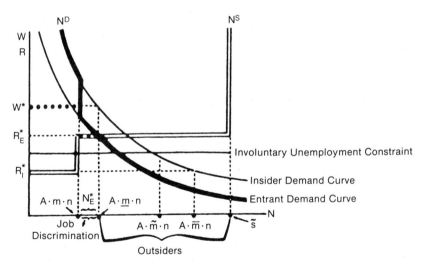

Figure 5.2C
Scenario III: Key given in figure 5.2A.

made along the aggregate insider demand curve:

$$N^D = n \cdot g(W^*/A) \qquad \text{for } 0 \leqslant N^D \leqslant A \cdot m \cdot n \tag{15a}$$

[by equation (2a), with $a_I = A$], where $g = (f')^{-1}$. Yet when aggregate labor demand exceeds the aggregate incumbent work force, employment decisions are given by the aggregate entrant demand curve:

$$N^D = n \cdot g(R_E^*) \qquad \text{for } N^D > A \cdot m \cdot n \tag{15b}$$

[by equation (2b), when $a_E = 1$].

ii. *The aggregate labor supply curve*, denoted by N^S (the doubled line step functions) in figures 5.2A–5.2C:

$$W = R_I^* \qquad \text{for } 0 \leqslant N^S \leqslant A \cdot m, \tag{16a}$$

$$W = R_E^* \qquad \text{for } A \cdot m < N^S \leqslant \tilde{s}, \tag{16b}$$

where N^S is measured in terms of efficiency units of labor and $\tilde{s}$ is the total labor force in efficiency units ($\tilde{s} = A \cdot m + (s - m)$).

iii. The *wage-setting curve*, denoted by W^* (the dotted horizontal lines) in figures 5.2A–5.2C. When the aggregate incumbent work force is "large" (figure 5.2A), insiders receive their reservation wage:

$$W^* = 1 \qquad \text{for } N^D > A \cdot \bar{m} \cdot n. \tag{17a}$$

When this work force is "intermediate" (figure 5.2B), workers receive their marginal product:

$$W^* = A \cdot f'(A \cdot m) \qquad \text{for } A \cdot \underline{m} \cdot n \leqslant N^D \leqslant A \cdot \bar{m} \cdot n. \tag{17b}$$

When it is "small" (figure 5.2C), workers receive a markup over the entrant wage (which is equal to the entrants' reservation wage):

$$W^* = A \cdot R_E^* = A \cdot (1 + H) \qquad \text{for } 0 \leqslant N^D < A \cdot \underline{m} \cdot n. \tag{17c}$$

Figures 5.2A–5.2C are drawn so that the labor force $\tilde{s}$ exceeds the demand for labor at the equilibrium insider wage W^*; thus, some workers remain unemployed. The question to which we now turn is whether this unemployment is *involuntary*.

Clearly, it is not involuntary in scenario I, figure 5.2A. Here the wage-setting curve (W^*) passes through the intersection of the aggregate labor demand curve (N^D) and supply curve (N^S). Employment (in efficiency units) curve (N^S) is $A \cdot \bar{m} \cdot n$, leaving ($\tilde{s} - A \cdot \bar{m} \cdot n$) workers unemployed—voluntarily so, since the incumbents who lose their jobs [($m - \bar{m}$) in number] prefer to be unemployed than to work for their marginal product $(W^* = R_I^* > A \cdot f(A \cdot m))$ and the outsiders $[(s - m)$ in number] would be unwilling to work at the prevailing wage even if they were not harassed $(R_E^* > R_I^* = W_I^*)$.

In scenarios II and III, the nature of unemployment is a more complex matter. The reason is that insiders and outsiders in our labor market have different employment opportunities. The difference is twofold:

a. They do not face "identical conditions of employment" (ICE), that is, job attributes lying outside the workers' control. Insiders are able to work under full cooperation and without harassment from the other insiders, whereas outsiders do not have this option.

b. Even under ICE, insiders, and outsiders are not equally productive. Even if insiders and outsiders received equal cooperation from their colleagues, the outsiders would still be less productive since they (unlike the insiders) are unable to engage in cooperative activities with others.

These differences suggest that, in order for unemployment to be involuntary, it is not sufficient for workers to be unsuccessful in finding jobs at less than the prevailing wage. Differences in ability should be included in our conception of involuntary unemployment, but differences in conditions of employment (lying beyond the workers' control) should be excluded.

Let the prevailing "efficiency wage" be defined as the prevailing wage normalized for differences in productivity. Then, we propose the following definition of involuntary unemployment:

DEFINITION *A worker is involuntarily unemployed over a particular period of time if he does not have a job during that period, even though he would wish to work at an efficiency wage that is less than the efficiency wage of a current employee, provided that he had the opportunity to be employed under identical conditions of employment (ICE) as that employee.*

This definition is easily extended to a multiperiod context.[18] The definition is meant to capture the idea that outsiders are out of work because they have a smaller choice set—in terms of wages received per efficiency unit of labor—than the insiders. In our model, an insider's efficiency wage is (W/a_I). Under ICE, an outsider's efficiency wage is (R_E^{ICE}/a_E^{ICE}). If outsiders are involuntarily unemployed, then their choice set is smaller than that of the insiders in the sense that

$$(R_E^{ICE}/a_E^{ICE}) < (W/a_I). \tag{18a}$$

Defining $x \equiv (a_E^{ICE}/a_1)$ as the ratio of an entrant and insider's labor endowments under identical conditions of work,[19] our condition for involuntary unemployment becomes

$$W > x \cdot R_E^{ICE} = x \cdot R_I^* = x. \tag{18b}$$

This means that, under identical conditions of employment, an outsider would be cheaper (in terms of efficiency wages) than an insider. (An outsider's labor costs, normalized for productivity differences is $x \cdot R_E^{ICE}$, whereas an insider's labor cost is W.) The reason why the firms in our analysis nevertheless do not replace insiders by outsiders is that these workers do *not* in fact face identical conditions of employment. Under *actual* conditions of employment (in which insiders receive cooperation and no harassment, whereas potential entrants receive harassment and no co-operation), an outsider is more expensive (in terms of efficiency wages) than an entrant. There is no underbidding because insiders rob their firms of the incentive to employ outsiders.

Our definition of involuntary employment sheds light on the nature of unemployment in scenarios II and III, as shown in figures 5.2B and 5.2C, respectively. Observe that, in both figures, the wage-setting curve (shown by the dotted horizontal line W^*) crosses the N^D curve to the left of the intersection of the N^D and N^s curves. This implies that the outsiders $(\tilde{s} - A \cdot m \cdot n)$ are willing to work for less than the prevailing insider wage (W^*), but are unable to do so. In order for this unemployment to be involuntary, we require that condition (18b) be satisfied, so that the insider wage lies above the "involuntary unemployment constraint," $W^* = x$, in figures 5.2B and 5.2C.[20]

The wage $W = x$ corresponds to a particular size $(\tilde{m})$ of the firm's incumbent work force:

$$x \equiv A \cdot f'(A \cdot \tilde{m}). \tag{19}$$

Thus, we see that the outsiders $(s - A \cdot m \cdot n)$ are involuntarily unemployed only if the aggregate incumbent work force is less than $n \cdot \tilde{m}$. It is easy to show that

$$\underline{m} < \tilde{m} < \bar{m}.^{21} \tag{20}$$

This means that when the aggregate incumbent work force is "small" (scenario I), all the unemployment is involuntary. However, when the aggregate incumbent work force is "intermediate" (scenario II), the unemployment is involuntary when $m < \tilde{m}$ and voluntary when $m \geqslant \tilde{m}$. (As figure 5.2B is drawn, it is involuntary.)

The workers who enter the firm in scenario III face a similar form of discrimination as the outsiders, in that they have a smaller choice set (in wage/efficiency-labor space) than the insiders. In particular, if the entrants and insiders faced identical conditions of employment, then each entrant's compensation per efficiency unit of labor would be less than that of each insider $(R_E^{ICE}/a_E^{ICE}) < (W/a_I)$. Hence, in figure 5.2C the distance $(A \cdot n \cdot (\bar{m} - m))$ may be called "job discrimination."

Our conclusions concerning the existence of involuntary unemployment are summarized in the following proposition:

PROPOSITION 2 *Consider a labor market described by the aggregate labor demand curve* (15a) *and* (15b), *the aggregate labor supply curve* (16a) *and* (16b), *and the wage-setting curve* (17a)–(17c). *Let aggregate incumbent work force, $m \cdot n$, be historically given (where n is the number of firms and m is the size of each firm's incumbent work force). If this work force happens to fall short of a particular critical level, $\tilde{m} \cdot n$ [by (19)], then there is involuntary unemployment.*

Although our model deals with the simultaneous performance of co-operation and harassment activities, our explanation of involuntary unemployment may rest on each of these activities alone. If insiders engage in cooperation but no harassment activities, then the equilibrium within the firm is given by proposition 1 with $H = 0$ and involuntary unemployment arises under the conditions in proposition 2. When harassment but no cooperation activities are performed, we must not only set $A = 1$ in proposition 1, but we must also assume that the firm faces some costs of replacing insiders by outsiders. The reason is that, in the absence of such costs, the firm would always find it worthwhile to fire all its harassing insiders and hire entrants who (by assumption) are incapable of harassing.[22]

5.4 Some Potential Objections

We now turn to some potential objections to our explanation of wages, employment, and unemployment.

5.4.1 Labor Turnover

If incumbent workers are able to restrict labor turnover of their firms, why do firms often have large labor turnover rates in practice? Is our analysis inapplicable whenever a firm's work force has large simultaneous inflows and outflows?

When our model is extended to include quits and retirements of employees, it is able to account for simultaneous inflows and outflows. In particular, suppose that $r \cdot m$ randomly chosen[23] incumbents in each firm quit or retire at the end of each time period (where $0 < r < 1$). If the incumbent work force initially exceeds its minimum sustainable level ($m > \underline{m}$), then the separations cause this work force to shrink. As it does so, the insider wage (W) and the marginal product of the insiders and potential entrants rise. However, once the incumbent work force falls beneath $\underline{m}$, the marginal product of potential entrants is so high that the insiders are no longer able to prevent all outsiders from being hired. Consequently, work force inflows and outflows occur simultaneously. In the stationary equilibrium, they are of equal magnitude. It can be shown[24] that these flows are $r \cdot L_I^* = L_E^* = (r \cdot A \cdot n \cdot \underline{m})/(r + A)$, and the associated level of unemployment is $u = s - L_I^* - L_E^* = s - (1 + r) \cdot (A \cdot n \cdot \underline{m})/(r + A)$.

Another reason why insiders' discriminatory activities do not preclude labor turnover in the real world is the following. Suppose that a firm employs "teams" of heterogeneous workers who are complementary to one another in the production process. In this context, insiders have no incentive to prevent the replacement of workers who have quit or retired. On the contrary, since all members of a team are complementary, it is in the insiders' interest to cooperate with and avoid harassing new entrants who fill vacancies on the team. In this light, it becomes clear that our analysis, in the case of heterogeneous labor, applies not to labor turnover within teams, but rather to turnover of teams (namely, the replacement of a team of insiders by a team of entrants).

5.4.2 Creation of Firms

Does our explanation of involuntary unemployment hinge on an assumption that the number of firms in the economy is fixed? Would free entry of firms lead to the elimination of this unemployment?

Our analysis suggests that when insider market power is widespread, entry of new firms (which have no insiders) may be a potentially important route to reducing unemployment. However, it is worth noting that, in practice, the creation of firms is often a lengthy process. Thus, even if free entry would eventually permit full employment to be achieved, the involuntary unemployment may nevertheless last a long time.

Moreover, the existence of involuntary unemployment does not necessarily generate an incentive to create new firms. The mere fact that insiders keep outsiders from being hired by the existing firms does not mean that new firms would find it profitable to hire these outsiders. Observe that new firms, in our analysis, are at a disadvantage vis-à-vis the existing firms, since new firms can employ only entrants (who are unable to cooperate with one another), whereas existing firms also employ insiders (who do cooperate with one another). There are of course many other reasons why new firms may be unprofitable even when existing firms are not—for example, setup costs, capital market imperfections, scarcity of entrepreneurial skills, and reduction of product prices due to entry of firms. Hence, the involuntary unemployment of section 5.3 may persist even after all profitable opportunities for entry of firms have been exhausted.

5.4.3 Output-Related Wage Contracts

Does our explanation of involuntary unemployment hinge on our assumption that time-rate wages are the only form of labor remuneration? Could output-related wage contracts be used to bribe the insiders not to discriminate against entrants, thereby making the employed and unemployed workers as well as the firms better off and eliminating the unemployment?

Although Pareto-superior alternatives to time-rate wages may exist under some circumstances, they may not be available in others. In fact, they are never available for unemployment generated through differential harassment activities. The reason is that the firm is unable to infer the performance of these activities from the variables it can observe—namely, its total output, its employment of insiders and entrants, and its wages[25]—and thus it has no opportunity to reward insiders for forgoing harassment of entrants.

The matter is not quite so simple for cooperation activities. Although the firm cannot observe these activities directly, it is able to observe its total output. Thus, it may reward its insiders for cooperating with entrants by sharing the proceeds of its output with these insiders . This could take the form of profit or revenue sharing.

Yet there are a variety of obstacles to designing and implementing such output-related wage contracts. Consider the following three significant ones, which are analyzed formally in Lindbeck and Snower (1985a):

Monitoring-Cost Difficulty. Since profit and revenue-sharing schemes are generally costly for workers to monitor,[26] managers may have an incentive to use their superior position in composing profit or revenue figures to their own advantage. In response, the employees may have an incentive to implement monitoring procedures (and possibly also to engage in litigation). The gains from profit or revenue sharing may not fully compensate the firm and its employees for these monitoring costs.

Risk-Aversion Difficulty. Profit and revenue-sharing schemes inevitably involve the imposition of risk on employees. If these employees are risk averse, then they thereby suffer a utility loss. The firm may be unable to compensate them for this loss without robbing itself of the incentive to implement such schemes.

Market-Power Difficulty. When an insider decides to cooperate with entrants, he loses something and gains something: (i) he loses market power vis-à-vis the entrants and thus his time-rate wage sinks toward the reservation wage; and (ii) he gains some of the profit or revenue that accrues as a result of his cooperation with the entrants. In order for the output-related wage contract to induce insider-outsider cooperation, the second effect must outweight the first. However, that will happen only if the firm relinquishes at least a certain amount of its gross profit. Yet if the firm does so, it may find that its net profit is lower than in the non-cooperative equilibrium, and then it has no incentive to implement the contract.

These difficulties, and perhaps others, help explain why output-related wage contracts do not play a particularly prominent role in today's labor markets. However, there is no reason to believe that the difficulties are necessarily insuperable; indeed, the model of differential cooperation activities surely suggests that there is a real-world case to be made for seeking alternatives to time-rate contracts. Be that as it may, time-rate wages are in fact the predominant form of labor remuneration, and our analysis indicates how involuntary unemployment may arise when they are used.

5.4.4 Economic Recovery

Given that insiders can prevent outsiders from getting jobs, does our analysis imply that they can prevent employment from recovering after a recession? In particular, suppose that there has been an upswing in business conditions, shifting the insider and entrant demand curves in figure 5.1 to the right. Does our analysis lead to the counterfactual implication that insiders invariably take advantage of such an upswing by raising their wages so that employment remains unchanged?

To see why this potential objection does not hold, let us consider how our macroeconomy responds to an upswing in each of the three scenarios.

(Lindbeck and Snower, 1985a, contains a formal analysis of the repercussions of business variations.) To begin with, note that the minimum and maximum sustainable incumbent work forces ($\underline{m}$ and $\bar{m}$, respectively) rise in an upswing, so that the dividing lines between the three scenarios in figure 5.1 shift to the right. If the incumbent work force is "large" (before and after the upswing), then the insider wage remains at $W^*(I) = R_I^* = 1$ and more insiders are retained on account of the upswing. If the incumbent work force is "intermediate" (before and after the upswing), the insiders raise their wage ($W^*(II)$) by the full amount of the upward shift of the insider demand curve (without thereby encouraging entry of new employees), and as a result, employment remains unchanged. Finally, if the incumbent work force is "small" (before and after the upswing), the insiders are unable to raise their wage, for otherwise they would induce the firm to replace them by entrants. Consequently, the insider wage remains at $W^*(III) = A \cdot (1 + H)$ and the firm hires more entrants on account of the upswing.

In short, under scenarios I and III, insiders do *not* prevent employment from rising in an upswing, but they do have this effect under scenario II. In this connection, it is important to mention that if insider wages are assumed to be the outcome of a bargaining process that splits the marginal rent between the insiders and their employers, then an upswing will lead to a rise in employment even under scenario II.

The degree to which an upswing leads to higher wages versus higher employment may depend on the size of this upswing. Consider, for example, a labor market suffering from unemployment and stuck in scenario II. If the upswing is "small," so that the labor market remains in this scenario, then employment will continue to stagnate while insider wages rise. Yet if the upswing is "large" so that the labor market moves into scenario III, then insider wages rise to a particular markup over entrants' reservation wages and employment expands (the larger the upswing, the greater the expansion). Here we observe that a large business stimulus reduces the level of unemployment whereas a small stimulus is unable to do so.

As another example of how the magnitude of the upswing matters to the wage-employment response, consider a labor market in scenario I. Here a "small" upswing (which maintains the existence of scenario I) keeps wages stable and induces firms to fire fewer incumbents than they would have done in the absence of the upswing. Yet if the upswing is large enough to put the labor market into scenario II, then all incumbents are retained and wages rise.

5.5 Concluding Remarks

This chapter has outlined how insiders' cooperation and harassment activities may give rise to unemployment. The central idea is that firms find it costly to substitute outsiders for insiders, and that insiders manage to capture at least some of the associated economic rent in the process of wage determination. Consequently, insiders raise their wages above the level at which outsiders would be willing to work, but firms nevertheless lack the incentive to replace insiders by outsiders or to add outsiders to their work forces.

In general, the insider-outsider turnover cost can come in many guises—for example, hiring, training, and firing costs (Lindbeck and Snower, 1984a), morale effects of labor turnover (Lindbeck and Snower, 1984b)—and this chapter explores another one: the insiders' ability and incentive to cooperate with and harass some workers but not others. This ability enables them to create rent and thereby drive up their wages.

In this context involuntary unemployment can arise in the sense that outsiders are unable to find work even though they would be just as profitable to the firm as the insiders, provided that they faced identical conditions of employment. It is the insiders' cooperation and harassment activities that ensure that these conditions are not the same for insiders and outsiders.

Our analysis has a variety of empirical implications. On the whole, these do not square with those of the natural-rate hypothesis, since employment within our framework is not uniquely determined by preferences, endowments, and production technologies. Rather, our analysis suggests that the size of the incumbent work force may be an important determinant of employment, since insiders may have market power over wages whereas outsiders do not. As we have seen (in section 5.2.5), past employment (by virtue of its influence on the current incumbent work force) may affect current employment. In particular, over an "intermediate" range of incumbent employment levels ($\underline{m} \leqslant m \leqslant \bar{m}$), there is inertia in employment; but this inertia disappears at "low" incumbent employment levels ($m < \underline{m}$) and at "high" ones ($m > \bar{m}$).

Our model also includes the size of the incumbent work force as an argument in the insider wage equation. In particular, over an "intermediate" range of incumbent employment levels, the insider wage is determined in the traditional way, namely, from the relevant marginal productivity condition associated with an estimated labor demand curve (for insiders); yet at "high" and "low" incumbent employment levels, the insider wage is given by the reservation wage (proxied, for example, by unemployment pay, Social Security benefits, etc.) and a markup over the reservation wage, respectively. The reservation wage itself depends on the size of the incumbent work force in our model (since insiders have an incentive to harass other workers only when the incumbent work force is sufficiently small).

Of course, when conducting empirical studies, it is important to take heed of the production technologies under consideration. To the extent that these differ from the diminishing returns to labor assumed in our model, our predictions (regarding the effect of the incumbent work force on employment and wage formation) must be altered accordingly.

Furthermore, our analysis suggests that business upswings will tend to generate fewer jobs in countries with large insider power (due, for example, to unions' ability to exploit cooperation and harassment opportunities) than in countries where insiders are weak. Moreover (as shown in section 5.4.4) whether a business upswing leads primarily to higher wages or higher employment may depend on the magnitude of this upswing relative to the size of the incumbent work force.

Our model also has implications for cyclical variations in labor market activity. As shown in Lindbeck and Snower (1985a), the movement of wages and employment in an upswing and a downswing may not be symmetric. In particular, a downswing may be characterized by stable insider wages and a contraction of the incumbent work force through retirements and layoffs, while an upswing (as in section 5.4.4) may take the form of rising insider wages and only modest (if any) increases in employment.

In these and other respects, our insider-outsider approach yields an interrelated set of predictions about labor market activity.

Notes

1. We assume all jobs to provide opportunities for cooperation and harassment. If this assumption were to be relaxed, the "outsiders" would also include employees in jobs without such opportunities.

2. In other words, there are no "long-term" wage contracts (extending over the employees' lifetimes). If such contracts were possible and if employees lacked market power on entering the firms, then involuntary unemployment could not exist.

3. The assumption of unilateral wage setting by insiders is made only for expositional simplicity, as noted in section 5.2.2.

4. With regard to our analytical conclusions, this turns out not to be a restrictive assumption. Naturally, if the firm has a multiperiod time horizon, it faces an inherently intertemporal problem, since the entrants hired in one period become insiders in the next. Lindbeck and Snower (1985a) extend our model to a two-period, overlapping-generations setting.

5. Since $L_I \leqslant m$, the marginal incumbent may generate positive profit, as shown by the inequality in (2a). Since $L_E \geqslant 0$, the marginal potential entrant may generate negative profit, as shown by the inequality in (2b). Finally, we assume that $A \cdot f'(0) > 1$, where A is the upper bound on a_I, as given in (4c), so that it is always profitable to the firm to employ some insiders: $L_I^* > 0$.

6. This assumption could be derived from more basic postulates. For example, we could assume that each insider finds it disagreeable to harass the other insiders and then show that, in the Nash equilibrium (described below), no insider is able to achieve a higher wage by harassing other insiders. Thus, each insider chooses not to harass the other insiders.

7. Allowing the insider's cooperation and harassment activities to affect his utility directly has self-evident implications for our results. In practice, of course, this direct utility effect might be positive or negative. For example, an insider can generally be expected to derive disutility from harassing workers who do not threaten his welfare, but he may well gain utility from harassing workers who engage in underbidding (e.g., "scabs") and thereby threaten his position. The same may be said of an insider's attitudes to cooperation. For example, cooperation among insiders may provide utility in the form of companionship, but this is most unlikely to be the case between insiders and workers who underbid them.

8. Recall that the entrants, unlike the insiders, are unable to perform harassment activities. Furthermore, note that H_E is the same for every entrant (since we have assumed that each insider harasses all entrants in equal measure).

9. The assumption that A is a constant is merely an expositional simplification. Our analysis could be easily be extended to cover the possibility that A is an increasing function of L_I (i.e., the more insiders there are, the greater the potential for cooperative activity). In that case, we would require that the marginal product of insiders (in the Nash equilibrium described below) diminishes as more insiders are hired:

$$\partial(a \cdot f')/\partial L_I = A \cdot f'' + A' \cdot f' < 0.$$

(This implies that the demand curve for insider labor is downward sloping.)

10. *Proof*   If the firm is not constrained by $L_I \leqslant m$ in its maximization problem (1), then [by the first-order condition (2a)] its demand for insiders (L_I^*) rises with a_i and falls with W. By (3a) and (4c), $\max(a_I) = A$ and $\min(W) = R_I = 1$. Substituting these values into the insider demand function (2a), as equality, yields (9).

11. The firm has no incentive to replace some (but not all) of its insiders by entrants, since the profit contribution from replacing one insider by one entrant is

$\Phi = (\partial\pi/\partial L_E) - (\partial\pi/\partial L_I)$

$\quad = (W - R_E) - (A - 1)\cdot f'(\lambda) < 0,$

by (2a) and (2b), and

$(d\Phi/dL_E)|_{dL_E = -dL_I} = (A - 1)^2 \cdot f'' < 0.$

Clearly this applies to all three scenarios.

12. The firm has no incentive to replace all of its insides by entrants for the following reason. In the equilibrium for scenario I, the firms's profit is $\pi^*(I) = f[A\cdot g(1/A)] - g(1/A)$, where $g = (f')^{-1}$. If the firm replaced all its insiders by entrants, its profits would be $\hat{\pi} = f[g(1 + H)] - (1 + H)\cdot g(1 + H)$. (Here the entrants are harassed by the insiders whom they ousted, e.g., through picket lines, social ostracism, and perhaps even violence by the displaced insiders.) To compare $\pi^*(I)$ and $\hat{\pi}$, consider the expression $\pi(x) = f[g(x)] - x\cdot g(x)$, where x is an arbitrary number. It can be shown that $\pi'(x) < 0$. Furthermore, $(1 + H) > 1 > 1/A$. Thus, $\pi^*(I) > f[g(1/A)] - (1/A)\cdot g(1/A) > \hat{\pi}$.

13. *Proof* If $m = \underline{m}$, then $L_E^* = 0$, provided that $a_E = 1$ and $R_E = 1 + H$. [The reason is that, by (2b), $(\partial\pi/\partial L_E) = f'(A\cdot \underline{m}) - (1 + H) = 0.$] If $m < \underline{m}$, then $L_E^* > 0$ for any feasible a_E and R_E. [The reason is that $(\partial\pi/\partial L_E) = a_E\cdot f'(A\cdot \underline{m}) - R_E > 0$ for any feasible a_E and R_E.]

14. Formally, this may be shown as follows. Since $m \geqslant \underline{m}$ then [by (11)] $f'(A\cdot m) \leqslant 1 + H$. Since $m \leqslant \bar{m}$, then [by (9)] $A\cdot f'(A\cdot m) \geqslant 1$. Therefore, $1 \leqslant A\cdot f'(A\cdot m) \leqslant A\cdot(1 + H)$. By the wage equation (7), we obtain (12b).

15. The firm has no incentive to replace all of its insiders by entrants, for the following reason. As in note 12, we consider the expression $\pi(x) = f[g(x)] - x\cdot g(x)$, for any arbitrary x, and we recall that $\pi'(x) < 0$. If the firm pursues the replacement strategy, its profit is $\hat{\pi} = \pi(x)$ for $x = (1 + H)$. In the equilibrium for scenario II, its profit is $\pi^*(II) = f(A\cdot m) - A\cdot f'(A\cdot m)\cdot m$. In this case, $\pi^*(II) = \pi(x)$ for $g(x) = A\cdot m$ and $x = (W/A)$, since $(W/A) = f'(A\cdot m)$. Furthermore, observe that $(W/A) \leqslant (1 + H)$ in scenario II. Consequently [by $\pi'(x) < 0$], $\pi^*(II) \geqslant \hat{\pi}$.

16. Formally, it follows from $m < \underline{m}$ that $f'(A\cdot m) > 1 + H$. Thus, $A\cdot f'(A\cdot m) > A\cdot(1 + H) > 1$. By the wage equation (7), we obtain (13a).

17. To make this point formally, recall that if the replacement strategy is pursued, then profit is $\hat{\pi} = f[g(1 + H)] - (1 + H)\cdot g(1 + H)$. Under scenario III, the firm's profit is $\pi^*(III) = f[g(1 + H)] - A\cdot(1 + H)\cdot m - (1 + H)\cdot A\cdot(\underline{m} - m) = f[g(1 + H)] - (1 + H)\cdot g(1 + H)$, which is equal to the profit under the replacement strategy. If the insiders do not capture the entire rent from their cooperation and harassment activities, or if the firm bears any further labor turnover costs, then $\pi^*(III)$ will exceed $\hat{\pi}$.

18. For our analysis, the relevant period is the single period over which the firm and the workers optimize their objectives. In a multiperiod context, our definition may be restated in terms of present values: A worker is involuntarily unemployed

if he unsuccessfully seeks work (under ICE) for a discounted stream of efficiency wages that is less than the corresponding discounted stream of a current employee, over the same set of time periods. In other words, an outsider is involuntarily unemployed if he has less favorable opportunities than a current employee to earn a present value of wage income for a given stream of productive services. Under our simplifying assumption that outsiders turn into insiders after a single period of work (the initiation period), our intertemporal definition of involuntary unemployment reduces to the condition that the outsider has less favorable opportunities than a current employee *during the initiation period*. Observe that our definition involves a comparison of the wage-labor service opportunities of an outsider and a current employee over a *unique set* of time periods. It is *not* concerned with a comparison of those opportunities over an outsider's future working lifetime with those over an insider's past, present, and future working lifetime. We believe that the notions of unemployment commonly adopted by the news media, politicians, and compilers of unemployment statistics are more readily captured by the former comparison than the latter. For a discussion of the relation between the magnitude of labor turnover costs and the level of unemployment in a multiperiod context, see pp. 8 and 73.

19. The ratio of the insiders and entrants' marginal products under identical conditions of employment is $[(a_I \cdot f'(\lambda))/(a_E^{ICE} \cdot f'(\lambda))] = a_I/a_E^{ICE}$.

20. Clearly, $1 < x < A$, because the insider is able to engage in cooperative activity whereas the entrant is not. [If insiders and entrants had equal cooperative abilities, then $x = 1$; when insiders cooperate fully with one another but not at all with potential entrants, then $(a_E/a_I) = A$.]

21. *Proof* $\tilde{m} < \bar{m}$, since $x > 1$ (by note 20) and given the definition of $\tilde{m}$ (in (19)) and $\bar{m}$ [in (9)]. Furthermore, $\tilde{m} > \underline{m}$, since $x < A$ (by note 20) and given the definitions of $\tilde{m}$ and $\underline{m}$ [in (11)].

22. Formally, by the definition of H^c given in note 17, if $A = 1$, then $H^c = 0$ and thus $H = 0$. This implies that the insiders would be unable to erect entry barriers against the outsiders, and thus there could be no involuntary unemployment.

23. The assumption of random choice is made only for expository simplicity, guaranteeing that all workers have the same reservation wage. Had we assumed that workers retire after reaching a particular age, then (a) the reservation wage would rise with age; (b) the firm would hire the youngest entrants available; and (c) it is the reservation wage of these entrants that would be relevant to insider wage determination.

24. Suppose that the incumbent work force is $\hat{m}$ ($< \underline{m}$) when it first falls short of m. In that period of time, the firm hires $L_E^* = A \cdot (m - \hat{m})$. Then, in the next period, the incumbent work force becomes $(1 - r) \cdot \hat{m} + A \cdot (m - \hat{m})$. In general, $m_t = (1 - r) \cdot m_{t-1} + A \cdot (m - m_{t-1})$. Assuming that $r + A < 1$, the incumbent work force rises monotonically to its stationary level $(A \cdot n \cdot \underline{m})/(r + A)$.

25. We assume that firms do not know what the outsiders' reservation wages would be in the absence of harassment (for example, they do not know whether

these reservation wages are the same as those of the insiders). Thus they cannot infer the presence of harassment by observing the entrant wages (in the event that scenario III obtains).

26. For instance, managers often have considerable latitude in their choice of profit and revenue accounting practices (for example, how to price intermediate goods and inventories, how to evaluate the firm's debt in real terms, and how to treat depreciation and obsolescence).

6

Job Security, Work Incentives, and Unemployment

Overview

Whereas the previous chapter showed how insiders' cooperation and harassment activities can generate labor turnover costs that may be responsible for involuntary unemployment, we now turn to a quite different source of labor turnover costs: the effect of job security on effort. When firms affect their employees' job security by changing the "labor turnover rate"—by which we mean the rate at which insiders are replaced by outsiders—they can affect work effort. If effort falls in response to a reduction in job security, then the cost of labor turnover is given by the associated effort forgone.

This chapter has a double purpose: (i) It shows how the effect of job security on effort may provide another explanation of why involuntarily unemployed workers may be unable to find jobs through underbidding, and (ii) it examines the relation between job security and productivity.

Regarding the first purpose, we argue that if employers were to replace their high-wage insiders by comparatively low-wage outsiders, this could have a significant, adverse effect on the morale and effort input of the workforce. Employers have an incentive to resist underbidding whenever the effort-related loss in productivity more than outweighs the associated saving of labor cost.

We assume that the firms cannot directly observe the work effort of each individual employee, and thus wages cannot be paid in proportion to the effort expended. Nevertheless, by observing their produced output, firms may be able to infer what the average relation between microeconomic job security and effort must be. In that case, they can use job security as an incentive mechanism.

We provide a particularly simple model of the relation between effort and job security. Suppose that firms can observe the output of each employee and that this output is stochastically related to the employee's past effort. Furthermore, suppose that firms offer the following termination contract: If the employee's output exceeds a specified output target, then the employee is retained; otherwise he is fired. When an employee expends more effort on the job, he raises his chances of being retained and thereby raises his expected future remuneration. In this sense, the workers' expected remuneration may be viewed as a reward for past effort.

When a firm raises the rate at which it replaces insiders by outsiders, it reduces this effort reward. The resulting change in effort may be described by a substitution effect (i.e., the greater the reward, the greater the effort input) and an income effect (i.e., the greater the reward, the greater the worker's expected income—ceteris paribus—and the more leisure and less effort the worker can afford to enjoy). If the substitution effect dominates the income effect, then the firm faces an effort-related cost of labor turnover.

The insiders take this cost into account in the process of wage setting. To fix ideas, we assume that the wage is set unilaterally by a union that comprises all the firm's insiders. The union sets the insider wage above the minimum level at which outsiders would be prepared to work, but most union members nevertheless escape dismissal. The effort-related cost of turnover plays a dual role in this model: It explains both why the union has market power and why the firm lacks the incentive to replace all its insiders by outsiders.

In this context, it is clear that our assumption of firm-specific insider unions is merely illustrative. Our qualitative conclusions still hold when insiders are organized informally, or when they bargain individualistically with their firms, or when only a fraction of the firm's workforce is unionized.

As in the previous chapter, involuntary unemployment can arise in this setting, in the sense that the outsiders have a smaller choice set than the insiders. In contrast to the previous chapter, however, the choice set must now be described in terms of the insider wage received in return for a particular amount of effort expended. The outsiders face a wage-effort trade-off that is inferior to that of the insiders, because when outsiders replace insiders, the firm's labor turnover rate rises and, as result, work effort may fall. The outsiders do not have the opportunity to offer the same amount of effort as the insiders in return for the same wage, because firms cannot monitor effort directly and the outsiders would have no incentive to expend the requisite amount of effort once the turnover rate has declined.

Turning now to the second purpose of this chapter, our analysis can also shed light on the relation between job security and productivity. Let us distinguish between "microeconomic" and "macroeconomic" job security. Microeconomic job security is related to the rate at which a firm fires its employees (possibly replacing them by new entrants). It may be measured by an employee's probability of being retained by his firm. By contrast, macroeconomic job security is measured by the probability of finding a new job.

In the presence of any labor turnover costs (including the effort-related costs to be analyzed in this chapter), the labor market ceases to be an "auction market," in which all workers of equal productivity have an equal chance of finding a job in any given period of time. Rather, an insider's retention probability exceeds an outsider's employment probability. In other words, the link between micro- and macroeconomic job security is broken in the presence of labor turnover costs. The former depends on microeconomic conditions within the firm; the latter depends on macroeconomic conditions across firms.

Our analysis shows that a rise in macroeconomic job security unambiguously reduces work effort. The more likely a worker is to find a new job, the smaller the penalty associated with losing his current job on account of insufficient effort. Consequently, the less effort the worker will expend. On the other hand, as we have seen, a rise in microeconomic job security may encourage or discourage work effort, depending on whether the substitution effect of remuneration on effort dominates the income effect or vice versa.

The distinction between micro- and macroeconomic job security is useful in assessing the debate concerning the relation between job security and productivity. This debate has become particularly heated in the past decade, fueled by job security legislation, the recent productivity slowdown, and the rise in average unemployment levels in mature capitalist economies.

Some people of "conservative" persuasion tend to argue that job security stifles productivity since it reduces the incentive to work hard. This is said to be a major deficiency of the welfare state and is also reputed to extend to centrally planned economies, where employment guarantees frequently coexist with low productivity. In this spirit, some observers have called unemployment a "worker discipline device." The opposing view in this debate is represented by those who argue that job security promotes productivity because it encourages workers to establish reputations for hard work in order to keep their jobs and earn promotions.

Our analysis suggests that the contenders in the controversy above may be talking at cross purposes. The former view deals with macroeconomic job security and with what may in fact be regarded as the "income effect" of microeconomic job security. The latter is concerned with what we have called the "substitution effect" of microeconomic job security. Thus it is not surprising that the contenders reach different conclusions.

There is no intrinsic one-to-one relation between macro- and microsecurity. Government macroeconomic policies that affect the demand for labor have a more immediate effect on the former than on the latter. An individual firm's hiring and firing decisions have an obvious bearing on the microsecurity of its employees, but they generally have no effect on macrosecurity. In this way, the distinction *between macro- and microeconomic job security may help the assessment of how policies that affect job security may influence productivity.*

6.1 Introduction

In this chapter we examine how firms may influence job security in order to provide work incentives. We explore what this behavior of firms implies for productivity and unemployment.

Firms may influence job security through their firing and hiring decisions. The greater the rate at which a firm replaces its incumbent works by newly hired workers (which we call the "turnover rate"), the lower is its employees' probability of retaining their jobs, i.e., the lower is the "microeconomic job security" of the employees. (We define the turnover rate solely in terms of the firm's and hiring decisions since we do not consider voluntary quits in this chapter.)

We assume that firms have imperfect information about their employees' effort and thus they are unable to make wages contingent on effort. If, however, the employees' effort is related to their microeconomic job security, then firms may indirectly be able to influence effort—and hence productivity—through changes in the turnover rate.

To model the relation between the turnover rate and effort, we assume that a worker's output lags behind his effort input, and thus workers who are retained receive remuneration that is related to their past effort. In this context, a fall in the turnover rate has a substitution effect and an income effect on effort. By the substitution effect, effort rises: An employee who is more likely to receive a reward for his current efforts will work harder. The income effect pulls in the opposite direction: The reduced risk of loosing his job raises the worker's expected income and enables him to afford working less hard. If the substitution effect dominates the income effect, a rise in microeconomic job security (generated by a fall in the turnover rate) stimulates effort and thereby productivity; if the income effect dominates, productivity is reduced.

Such changes in microeconomic job security must not be confused with changes in what we call "macroeconomic job security," which is measured by a worker's probability of finding a job in the economy after dismissal from his current position. We show that a rise in macroeconomic job security unambiguously reduces work effort. Our analysis of the comparitive roles of macro- and microeconomic job security sheds some light on the ongoing controversy about whether job security helps or hinders productivity.

The firm's use of the turnover rate as an incentive device for productivity provides a new rationale for involuntary unemployment. When the substitution effect of labor turnover on effort dominates the income effect, then a rise in the turnover rate is costly to the firm since it reduces work effort. The insiders, of course, are aware of this effort cost of turnover. Indeed, this cost gives the insiders market power by way of the possibility of making threats. The insiders are assumed to exercise this market power in the process of wage negotiation. Thus, the insiders are able to drive their wage above the market-clearing level without necessarily facing dismissal.

Under these circumstances, the outsiders are unable to find jobs, even though they are willing to work for less than the insider wage and are identical to the insiders in terms of potential job performance (i.e., if an outsider had the same opportunity to fill a job slot as an insider, he would be equally productive). In this sense, the unemployment is involuntary.

Our concept of involuntary unemployment captures the notion that the outsiders have no jobs because they face a smaller choice set than the insiders. Each insider has the opportunity of receiving the insider wage in return for expending a particular effort level. The outsiders do not have this opportunity, since they can only replace the insiders if the firm's turnover rate were raised, and this, in turn, would reduce the worker's effort and hence be costly to the firm.

Our analysis hence explains the absence of underbidding when there is involuntary unemployment—an explanation that is commonplace in business circles, but that has been neglected by main-stream economic theory: Employers may not accept indiscriminate underbidding by outsiders, because the increased turnover that would be necessary to take advantage of such underbidding would reduce labor productivity by more than the firm's wage bill.

There is a vague similarity between the rationale for involuntary unemployment in this chapter and that offered by some variants of the efficiency wage theory, viz., the moral hazard models [in these models work effort is variable—e.g., Calvo and Wellisz, 1978, Malcolmson, 1981; Shapiro and Stiglitz, 1984] and the quit models [see, e.g., Calvo, 1979; Stiglitz, 1974]. In both the present model and these efficiency wage models, firms have imperfect information about their employees' effort and firms seek to influence their labor turnover rates. Beyond that, however, the similarity ends. In the efficiency wage models, firms use *the wage* as a screening device for productivity and employees have no market power, whereas in our model firms use *the turnover rate* to influence productivity, which gives incumbent workers ("insiders") market power in the wage setting.

The salient difference between these models becomes obvious when we compare the sequence of decisions within them. In the efficiency wage models, the firm first makes the wage and employment decisions (taking the wage effect on effort into account), and the workers then make the effort decision and/or decide whether to quit their current jobs (taking the wage as given). Involuntary unemployment can arise when the profit-maximizing wage levels of all firms in the economy exceed the market-clearing level.

In our model, by contrast, we have the following sequence of decisions. In the first stage, the insiders (possibly through negotiation with their firm) set the insider wage (taking all subsequent decisions into account); in the second stage, the firm makes the employment decisions and, in so doing, sets the turnover rate (accepting the wages as given and taking into account the effect of turnover on effort); and in the third stage, the employees (insiders and entrants) make the effort decision (accepting all previous decisions as given). Involuntary unemployment can arise when the wages set by the insiders are above the market-clearing wage level.

The chapter is organized as follows. Section 6.2 deals with the firm's use of labor turnover as a screening device for effort. On this basis, section 6.3 deals with workers' effort decision (and, in particular, with the effect on turnover of effort). Section 6.4 describes the firm's turnover decision (taking the effort decision into account). Section 6.5 deals with the exercise of insider power in wage determination (taking the effort and turnover decisions into account) and shows how involuntary unemployment can arise in this context. Section 6.6 discusses what our analysis has to say about the influence of job security on worker productivity. Finally, section 6.7 contains our concluding remarks.

6.2 Firms' Monitoring of Effort

Our point of departure is that the firm is unable to monitor the work effort of an employee accurately and instantaneously. However, we assume that firms are able to observe the output of each employee. The relation between the employee's effort and the associated output is taken to be lagged and stochastic.

Let the production function relating effort (e) and output (q) for a particular worker take the following simple form:

$$q_{+1} = e \cdot [\gamma], \tag{1}$$

where q_{+1} is next period's output and γ—which we call the "productivity factor"—is a random variable with mean unity and constant variance. We assume that $0 \leqslant \gamma \leqslant \gamma^{max}$, where γ^{max} is a finite, positive constant (since it is certainly not reasonable to suppose that a worker can produce infinite output with finite effort). Let the productivity factors of different workers be identically and independently distributed, so that our analysis can proceed in terms of a representative worker.

To fix ideas, we assume that the employer is unable to observe the effort input e, but can observe output q (with a one-period lag) and knows the distribution (but not the realized value) of γ. Given this information structure, the employer makes the hiring and firing decisions in such a way as to provide an effort incentive: He chooses a 'production target" Q, and a worker whose output q falls short of it is fired; otherwise he is retained.

The density of the productivity factor, $G[\gamma]$, and the corresponding density of q (for a given level of effort), $H(q)$, are pictured in figures 6.1a and 6.1b. The retention probability—which is our measure of "microeconomic job security"—is given by the figures' shaded areas, which denotes the probability that the productivity factor exceeds the target $\bar{\gamma}$, and equivalently, the probability that the workers output, q_1, exceeds the production target Q:

$$\sigma = \int_Q^{max(q)} H(q)\, dq = \int_{\bar{\gamma}}^{\gamma^{max}} e_{-1} \cdot G(\gamma)\, d\gamma, \tag{2}$$

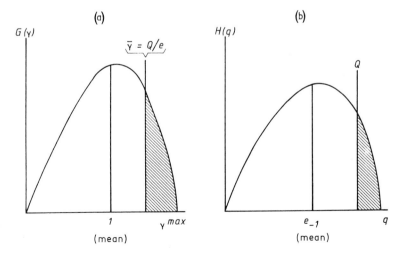

Figure 6.1
The worker's retention probability.

where $\bar{\gamma} = Q/e_{-1}$ is the "target productivity factor," viz., the productivity factor that corresponds to the output target Q. Observe that $\max[q]$ is finite, since e and $\gamma^{\max}$ are finite. Thus, the level of the output target that is just sufficient to ensure that *all* current insiders are replaced by entrants, which we call $Q^{\max}$, is finite as well.

For nondegenerate densities, where $G[\gamma] > 0$ for $0 < \gamma < \gamma^{\max}$, we find that the worker's rentention probability depends positively on the worker's level of effort and negatively on the output target:

$$\sigma = \sigma(e_{-1}, Q). \qquad\qquad (3)$$
$${\scriptstyle(+)\ (-)}$$

6.3 The Effort Decision

For simplicity (but without substantial loss of generality), we assume that each worker has a working lifetime of two periods. Let each worker's per period separable utility function be $U = U(Y, e)$, where Y is income and $U_Y > 0$, $U_e < 0$, U_{YY}, $U_{ee} < 0$, and $U_{Ye} = 0$. For an insider (i.e., a worker who was employed in the previous time period and whose output in that period exceeded the firm's production target Q), $Y = W$ (the insider wage); for an entrant, $Y = R$ (the entrant wage); and for an outsider, $Y = 0$, We assume that workers are unable to insure themselves against dismissal (for the standard moral-hazard reasons).

An employee expends effort over his working lifetime so as to maximize the present value of his expected utility (taking wages and employment opportunities as given). The utility of an entrant (in his first period of work) is

$$U_1 = U(R, e_1),$$

where the subscript identifies the time period of the working lifetime.

The entrant's effort decision e_1 is made with a view to his income in the following time period. This income cannot be perfectly foreseen. If the worker is retained (and thereupon becomes an insider), his income will be W. If he is fired, he faces a probability $[\rho]$ of being employed as an entrant at another firm, receiving R. With probability $[1 - \rho]$ he remains unemployed and receives nothing. Thus, the insider's expected utility (in his second period of work) is

$$U_2 = \int_{\bar{\gamma}^e}^{\gamma^{\max}} U(W, e_2) \cdot G(\gamma)\, d\gamma + (1 - \sigma) \cdot \{\rho \cdot U[R, \eta_2]$$

$$+ (1 - \rho) \cdot U[0, 0], \qquad\qquad (4)$$

where $\bar{\gamma}^e$ is the expected target productivity factor (viz., the $\bar{\gamma}$ expected by the insider), and e_2 is his effort in the second period when he is retained and $[\eta_2]$ is his effort when he has been fired and rehired.

The insider's effort decision in the second period, e_2, does not play a crucial role in generating our qualitative conclusions. Unlike the first-period effort decision, e_2 cannot be directly influenced by the firm's output target, since the insider leaves the firm at the end of the second period regardless of the level of the output target. Since we have assumed that $U_{\gamma e} = 0$, the first-period effort decision does not depend on the second-period effort decision. Thus, let us set e_2 at some arbitrary given level, which may, for example, be equal to e_1 (since insiders may wish to preserve their reputation among friends as conscientious individuals) or to the minimal effort level, $\min(e_2)$ (since they receive no material rewards for efforts in the second period).

Which e_2 we choose makes no difference to our analysis of the relation between job security and productivity, and our explanation of how involuntary unemployment can arise, though it may affect the magnitude of such unemployment. For unemployment is involuntary whenever outsiders are unable to find jobs even though they are prepared to work for less than the prevailing "efficiency wage," viz., the nominal insider wage normalized for the insider-entrant effort differential. The lower is the ratio (e_2/e_1), ceteris paribus, the smaller is the normalized "efficiency wage" $W \cdot (e_2/e_1)$, thus the easier it is for the outsiders to underbid the insiders and the more such underbidding will take place (Note that e_2/e_1 is the ratio of insiders to entrant effort.)

The present value of an entrant's expected utility is

$$U_1 + (1/(1 + r)) \cdot U_2,$$

where r is the discount rate. Maximizing this present value with respect to e_1, we obtain the following first-order condition:

$$U_e + \frac{\partial \bar{\gamma}^e}{\partial e} \cdot \frac{\partial}{\partial \gamma} \left\{ \left(\int_{\bar{\gamma}^e}^{\gamma^{max}} U[w, e_2] \cdot G(\gamma) \, d\gamma \right. \right.$$

$$- \frac{\partial \sigma}{\partial e} \cdot \{ \rho \cdot U[R, \eta_2] + (1 - \rho) \cdot U[0, 0] \} = 0. \tag{5}$$

In order words, the marginal disutility of effort (the first term) is set equal to the marginal utility of the expected insider income due to the effort-induced increase in the retention probability (the second term) and due to the reduced risk of receiving entrant income (the third term).

In this context, the effort effect of labor turnover may be analyzed by examining the influence of a rise in the expected output target Q^e on the effort level e_1. Letting $[\phi]$ be the left-hand expression of (5), this effort may be expressed as follows:

$$\frac{\partial e_1}{\partial Q^e} = -\frac{\partial \phi / \partial Q^e}{\partial \phi / \partial e_1},$$ (6)

where $[\partial \phi / \partial e_1]$ is assumed to be negative, so that the second-order condition for utility maximization is satisfied. Thus, the sign of the effort effect of turnover $(\partial e_1 / \partial Q^e]$ coincides with the sign of $[\partial \phi / \partial Q^e]$:

$$\frac{\partial \phi}{\partial Q^e} = \frac{\partial^2 \bar{\gamma}^e}{\partial e \, \partial Q} \cdot \frac{\partial}{\partial \gamma} \left\{ \left\{ \int_{\bar{\gamma}^e}^{\gamma^{max}} U[W, e_1] \cdot G(\gamma) \, d\gamma \right. \right.$$

$$- \frac{\partial^2}{\partial e \, \partial Q} \cdot \left\{ \rho \cdot U[R, \eta_2] + (1 - \rho) \cdot U[0, 0] \right.$$

$$- \frac{\partial \bar{\gamma}^e}{\partial e} \cdot \frac{\partial \bar{\gamma}^e}{\partial Q} \cdot \frac{\partial^2}{\partial \gamma^2} \left\{ \int_{\bar{\gamma}^e}^{\gamma^{max}} U[W, e_2] \cdot G(\gamma) \, d\gamma \right\}.$$ (7)

The first two right-hand terms of equation (7) may be identified as the *substitution effect* of the effort reward on effort; the third term may be termed the *income effect*:

Term 1: A rise in Q^e reduces $(\partial \bar{\gamma} / \partial e)$ [since $(\partial^2 \bar{\gamma} / \partial e \, \partial Q) = -(1/e)^2 < 0$]. In other words, a rise in Q^e gives the worker greater leverage in raising his retention chances through effort (i.e., reducing γ through e). In this respect, the effort reward increases; hence term 1 is positive.

Term 2: A rise in Q^e, as shown, raises the worker's leverage on his retention chances through effort and thereby reduces his risk of receiving income of an entrant or of becoming an outsider. Hence, term 2 is of opposite sign to term 1, and of smaller absolute value, since the income of an insider exceeds that of an entrant or outsider.

Term 3: As noted, a rise in Q^e increases $\bar{\gamma}^e$ and thereby reduces the expected value of the effort reward. If $U_{YY} < 0$ over the relevant range, then the associated utility loss becomes progressively greater and—obversely—the utility loss to be avoided through a given rise in effort becomes progressively greater as well.

In sum, a rise in the expected output target Q^e has counterveiling effects on work effort. These effects correspond to the commonplace idea that workers who face greater chances of dismissal (*ceteris paribus*) may work less hard if they find that their effort is less likely to be rewarded (the first two terms), or they may work harder for fear of losing their current labor income (the first term).

Employers find the process of labor turnover costly when turnover has an adverse influence on effort, i.e., when the sum of all the effects in equation (7) is negative, so that

$$e = e(Q^e).$$
$$(-)$$

(8)

6.4 The Turnover Decision

Having examined how employees make their effort decisions (taking wages and employment opportunities as given), we now turn to firms' employment decisions (taking wages as given, and considering how the employment decisions influence effort).

To make our unemployment analysis free of systematic expectational errors, we assume that each worker has rational expectations, so that the perceived and actual probabilities of job retention are equal. We assume that there is an effort cost of labor turnover, i.e., $e' < 0$ in equation (8), and that $e'' < 0$. Thus the firm has an incentive to equalize the job retention probabilities of its employees, so that each employee faces the same probability of keeping his job, rather than granting some workers more job security than others.

Let $L_{I,t}$ be the number of insiders retained and $L_{E,t}$ be the number of entrants hired by the firm in time period t. Then the expected output of the firm in that period is $e \cdot (L_{I,t} + L_{E,t})$. Then the expected profit in period t is $X_t = e \cdot (L_{I,t} + L_{E,t}) - W \cdot L_{I,t} - R \cdot L_{E,t}$. We assume that the firm is a profit maximizer with an infinite time horizon, and the present value of expected profit is

$$PV = \sum_{t=1}^{\infty} \left(\frac{1}{1-r}\right)^t \cdot X_t,$$

(9)

where the discount rate r is the same as that of the workers.

Since our analysis centers on the implications of replacing insiders by outsiders, rather than on those of expanding or contracting the firm's workforce as a whole, it is convenient to assume that the size of the firm's workforce is fixed. To this end, suppose that the firm has an exogenously given factor—call it "capital"—and that the relation between this factor endowment (K) and the number of workers is characterized by fixed coefficients:

$$L_{I,t} + L_{E,t} = v \cdot K = \underline{L} \tag{10}$$

(where v and $\underline{L}$ are positive constants).

We focus our attention on static equilibrium conditions, in which the effort of employees and the employment of insiders and entrants (and, by implication, the job retention probability $[\sigma]$) remains constant through time.

We define the firm's current labor turnover rate T as $T = 1 - \sigma$, where $\sigma = L_I/\underline{L}$ is the retention probability. Then the current profit of the firm may be expressed as follows (suppressing the time subscripts whenever we need to refer only to the current and previous periods of time):

$$X = e \cdot \underline{L} - W \cdot L_I - R \cdot (\underline{L} - L_I)$$
$$= [e + (W - R) \cdot T] \cdot \underline{L} - W \cdot \underline{L} \tag{11}$$

by equation (10).

As shown in the previous section, the current turnover rate (when correctly anticipated by the workers) affects the effort of entrants in the previous time period; it has no other effort effects. (This major simplification follows from our two-period, overlapping generations setup. If workers could remain employed for more than two periods, then the current turnover rate would affect the effort of all vintages of past employees who had a chance of remaining with their firm in the current period.)

The firm's control variable is its output target Q, whereby its hiring and firing decisions are made. A rise in the current output target has two effects on the firm's present value (PV): (i) it reduces the expected effort level of the employees in the previous time period [in accordance with equation (8)] and (ii) it reduces the firm's labor cost per employee by the insider-entrant wage differential. Thus,

$$\underset{Q}{\mathrm{argmax}}(PV) = \underset{Q}{\mathrm{argmax}}(Z), \quad \text{where } Z = (1 + r) \cdot e_{-1} + (W - R) \cdot T. \tag{12}$$

(dZ/dQ) may be interpreted as the firm's marginal gain from raising the output target.

In order to provide a simple and clear derivation of the equilibrium level of the output target, we specify the following convenient functional forms for the effort function [relating the effort level to the expected output target, equation (8)] and the retention function [relating the retention rate to the effort level and the output target, equation (3)]. The effort function [equation (8)] is

$$e_{-1} = -(b/2) \cdot (Q^e)^2, \tag{8'}$$

where the coefficient b measures the impact of the turnover rate on effort. When the substitution effect of turnover on effort exceeds the income effect, the coefficient is positive; when the income effect dominates, the coefficient is negative. (For simplicity, but without substantial loss of generality, we ignore the effect of the wages on effort.) The retention function [equation (3)] is

$$\sigma = 1 - a_1 \cdot Q + a_2 \cdot e_{-1}, \tag{3'}$$

where a_1 and a_2 are positive constants. Thus the turnover function is

$$T = a_1 \cdot Q - a_2 \cdot e_{-1}. \tag{13}$$

Substituting the effort and turnover function into the firm's objective Z, we find how the firm's profit depends on the actual and expected levels of the output target:

$$Z = (W - R) \cdot [a_1 \cdot Q + \frac{a_2 \cdot b}{2} \cdot (Q^e)^2] - (1 + r) \cdot \frac{b}{2} \cdot (Q^e)^2. \tag{14}$$

This summary of the gains and losses associated with the actual and expected targets is illustrated in figure 6.2. Here, a rise in the actual target (in the top left box) has a direct, positive effect on the turnover rate (in the top right box). If the rise in the actual target leads to a rise in the expected target (in the bottom left box), then effort is reduced (in the bottom right box). The fall in effort, in turn, means that more workers fail to meet the given output target, and therefore the turnover rate rises.

Observe how these terms depend on the actual and anticipated output targets. If the actual output target (Q) is raised while the anticipated target (Q^e) remains constant, then the firm achieves a labor cost saving without

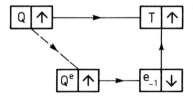

Figure 6.2
The profitability effects of a rise in the output target.

any effort loss. On the other hand, if the anticipated target rises while the actual target remains constant, the firm experiences an effort loss as well as a labor cost saving, since a rise in the anticipated target reduces effort, which raises the turnover rate. We concentrate on the nontrivial decision-making problem of the firm in which $(1 + r) > a_2 \cdot (W - R)$, so that the effort loss exceeds the labor cost saving (from a rise in the anticipated target).

In short, an increase in the actual output target (*ceteris paribus*) makes the firm better off, whereas a rise in the anticipated output target (*certeris paribus*) makes the firm worse off. Moreover, the anticipated and actual targets are related to one another, since we assume that workers' expectations are rational, in the sense that each worker's expectation of the output target is the best possible forecast (conditional on the worker's information set) of the firm's actual target.

The firm then faces a time consistency problem. In the current period, it has the incentive to raise the actual output target to its maximum level, so that all current insiders are replaced by entrants. In this way it achieves a maximum labor cost saving. However, with regard to the next period, when the successful current entrants will have turned into insiders, the firm has the incentive to announce that no insiders will be replaced. If this announcement is believed—so that the anticipated output target is at its minimum level—the firm thereby induces the current entrants to expend maximum effort on the job.

However, once the next period arrives, it is again in the firm's interests to set the actual target at its maximum level while trying to drive the anticipated target to its minimum level. In other words, the firm has an incentive to renege on its previous announcement. We assume that the firm cannot enter into a binding contract to implement its announced target, and thus the announcement will in fact be disregarded. Since the employees have rational expectations, they cannot be systematically deceived; i.e., they will not repeatedly believe an announcement that is repeatedly disregarded. In short, the announcement cannot remain "credible."

The firm has a choice. It can implement a target that maintains its credibility or one that disappoints its employees' expectations and thereby destroys its credibility. From the set of noncredible targets, the one that maximizes the present value of the firm's profit we call the "optimal noncredible target."

When the firm destroys its credibility by raising its actual target above the level necessary to maintain credibility, it gains something and loses something. Its gain is a current reduction in labor cost as it replaces more high-wage insiders by low-wage entrants. It's loss is a future reduction in work effort, as employees' expectations eventually adjust to the new, higher actual target.

To establish the conditions under which the firm gains and loses credibility, we specify the employees' expectations formation mechanism. We assume that expectations about the current output target are formulated at the beginning of the current time period (when the employees make their effort decision). At that time, each employee has accurately observed his previous period's output, and remembers accurately the firm's actual output target and his expected output target in the previous period. In other words, his current information set is

$$I = (q_{-1}, Q_{-1}, Q^e_{-1}).$$

Note that the firm's current output target is not in this information set, since the employees can infer this target only once their current output has been produced (at the end of the current period).

In this context, we consider the following expectations formation mechanism, which will be shown to be rational:

$$Q^e_t = Q_{t-1}. \tag{15}$$

In others words, each employee expects the output target of period $t - 1$ to be implemented in period t. At the initial (current) period of time ($t = 1$) the expected target is given at some arbitrary level (viz., the actual target level at time $t = 0$):

$$Q^e = \underline{Q}^e. \tag{16}$$

By the expectations formation mechanism (15), a credible trajectory is one in which the actual targets through time are equal to the initial expected target: $(Q_{t=0}, Q_{t=0}, \ldots)$. The present value from implementing a credible target is

$$\underline{PV} = \left(1 + \frac{1}{r}\right) \cdot \{(W - R) \cdot a_1\} \cdot \underline{Q}^e$$

$$- \left(1 + \frac{1}{r}\right) \cdot \frac{b}{2} \cdot [(1 + r) - (W - R) \cdot a_2] \cdot (\underline{Q}^e)^2. \tag{17}$$

To derive the optimal noncredible target, we begin by considering an arbitrary sequence of output targets $(Q^o_{t=1}, Q^o_{t=2}, \ldots)$ that are not necessarily credible. The present value from implementing this sequence of targets is

$$\text{PV}^\circ = \left(\frac{1}{1+r}\right) \cdot \{(W-R)\cdot a_1 \cdot Q^\circ_{t=1} - \frac{b}{2}\cdot[(1+r)-(W-R)\cdot a_2]\cdot (Q^*)^2\}$$

$$+ \sum_{t=2}^{\infty} \left(\frac{1}{1+r}\right)^t \cdot \{(W-R)\cdot a_1 \cdot Q^\circ_t$$

$$- (Q^\circ_{t-1})^2 \cdot \frac{b}{2}\cdot[(1+r)-(W-R)\cdot a_2]. \tag{18}$$

Maximizing this present value with respect to each target, we obtain

$$\frac{\partial \text{PV}^\circ}{\partial Q^\circ_t} = \left(\frac{1}{1+r}\right)^t \cdot (W-R)\cdot a_1 - \left(\frac{1}{1+r}\right)^{t+1} \cdot Q^\circ_t \cdot \frac{b}{2}$$

$$\cdot[(1+r)-(W-R)\cdot a_2] = 0, \tag{19a}$$

which implies that

$$(W-R)\cdot[a_1 + \frac{b\cdot a_2}{2\cdot(1+r)}\cdot Q^\circ_t] = \frac{b}{2}\cdot Q^\circ_t. \tag{19b}$$

The left-hand expression in equation (19b) is the "marginal gain" from an increase in the target level Q°_t (viz., a rise in the target raises the turnover rate, which reduces the firm's labor cost); the right-hand expression is the "marginal loss" (viz., a rise in the target reduces effort). These terms are illustrated in figure 6.3.

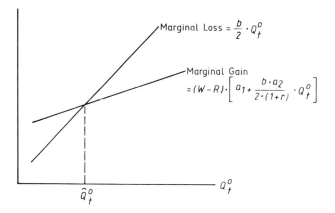

Figure 6.3
The marginal gain and loss from the production target.

Solving equation (19b) yields the optimal noncredible target (which lies at the intersection of the marginal gain and marginal loss curves in figure 6.3),

$$\hat{Q}_t^o = \hat{Q}^o = \frac{(1+r)\cdot(W-R)\cdot a_1}{b\cdot[(1+r)-(W-R)\cdot a_2]},\tag{20}$$

provided (as we in fact assume) that $Q^o \leqslant Q^{max}$. (Otherwise $Q^o = Q^{max}$.)

Note that the optimal noncredible target is stationary through time and does not depend on the initial expected target $Q^e = Q^*$, since this initial expected target is taken as given in the present value maximization. By implication, the trajectory of optimal noncredible targets is time consistent: The trajectory $(Q_2^o, Q_3^o, \ldots)$ that maximizes the present value from time $t = 1$ onward, given the initial expectation $Q_0^e = \underline{Q}^e$, is identical to the trajectory $(Q_2^o, Q_3^o, \ldots)$ that maximizes the present value from time $t = 2$ onward given the first-period expectation that $Q_1^e = Q_1^o$.

The marginal benefit (MB) from implementing the optimal noncredible target is

$$MB = PV^o - \underline{PV}.\tag{21}$$

To evaluate this marginal benefit, let us define the constant $\alpha = Q^e/Q^o$. Then, by equations (17) and (18), it is easy to show that $MB > 0$ whenever

$$\underline{Q}^o < \frac{2\cdot(1+r)\cdot\{(W-R)\cdot a_1\}\cdot(1-\alpha)}{b\cdot[(1+r)-(W-R)\cdot a_2]\cdot(1-\alpha^2)}.$$

By equation (20), this inequality reduces to the simple expression

$$(\alpha - 1)^2 > 0.\tag{22}$$

Thus when $Q_{r=0}^e = Q^o$, the marginal benefit is zero; otherwise it is unambiguously positive. Thus the firm will implement the optimal noncredible target.

The qualitative properties of the optimal noncredible target may be summarized as follows:

a. The stronger the effect of the target on effort, the lower the target. (A rise in the coefficient b raises the marginal loss curve by more than the marginal gain curve in figure 6.3.)

b. The stronger the effect of the target on the turnover rate, the greater the target. (A rise in the coefficient a_1 raises the marginal gain curve and leaves the marginal loss curve unchanged.)

c. The stronger the impact of effort on the turnover rate, the greater the target. (A rise in the coefficient a_2 raises the marginal gain curve and leaves the marginal loss curve unchanged.)

d. The greater the discount rate, the lower the target. (A rise in r raises the marginal loss curve and leaves the marginal gain curve unchanged.)

e. The greater the insider wage, the greater the target. (A rise in W raises the marginal gain curve and leaves the marginal loss curve unchanged.)

6.5 Wage Determination and Involuntary Unemployment

As noted in the introduction, we assume that entrants receive their reservation wage (R), whereas the insider wage (W) is controled by the insiders themselves. (Our basic conclusions would not be affected if we assumed that the insider wage was the outcome of a negotiation process, such as a Nash bargain between the firm and the insiders, in which the insiders have some market power.) We here define the reservation wage to be the wage offered during the initiation period that makes an entrant indifferent between accepting employment and remaining unemployed. Let the insider wage be set unilaterally by a union that comprises all the insiders in a firm. We assume (for simplicity) that this union seeks to maximize the current wage income of those employees of the firm who are insiders at the beginning of the period and the union does not take the welfare of other workers (entrants and outsiders) into account. The union is assumed to take the reservation wage as given when the insider wage is set. (This means that each union covers a sufficiently small proportion of the economy-wide insider workforce so that changes in the insider wage paid by one firm have no appreciable effect on the reservation wage.)

In the conventional theories of union behavior, the union exerts influence on the wage (in that it either sets the wage unilaterally or engages in wage bargaining with the firm), but we are not told where this influence comes from. In particular, the conventional theories do not explain why firms do not break the union's power by replacing all their unionized employees by nonunionized, unemployed workers whenever the union demands a wage above the reservation wage. By contrast, in our model the source of union power may be identified as the effort effect of labor turnover. When the union is aware that turnover is costly to the firm (when turnover is inversely related to effort), the union is able to raise the insider wage above the reservation wage without necessarily bringing about the dismissal of the union members.

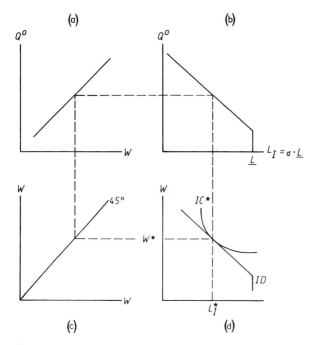

Figure 6.4
Wage determination.

The union's objective is

$$\text{Maximize } V = W \cdot L_I = W \cdot [\sigma] \cdot \underline{L}. \tag{23}$$

The union faces a trade-off, since a rise in the insider wage W is associated with a fall in the retention ratio $[\sigma]$. The reason is that a rise in W raises the firm's output target [by equation (20)] and this, in turn, reduces the retention ratio (both directly and indirectly via the fall in effort). The positive relation between W and Q^o and the inverse relation between Q^o and $[\sigma] \cdot \underline{L} = L_I$ are illustrated in figures 6.4a and 6.4b, respectively. These two relations imply an inverse relation between the insider wage and the firm's demand for insiders, as shown by the ID curve in figure 6.4d. (Note that wages are here determined in the same way as in the standard monopoly union model, except that the union here cares only about the insiders.)

The union's aim is to set the insider wage so as to achieve its most preferred point on the insider demand curve (ID). The highest attainable indifference curve is denoted by IC* in figure 6.4d, and the most preferred point is given by (L_I^*, W^*).

The first-order condition for an interior optimum in the union's problem (23) is

$$\frac{dV}{dW} = \sigma \cdot \underline{L} + W \cdot \sigma_w \cdot \underline{L} = 0,$$

which implies that

$$(\sigma_w / \sigma) \cdot W = -1. \tag{24}$$

In other words, the elasticity of the retention ratio with respect to the insider wage must be equal to -1.

Given the effort function (13), the optimal noncredible target (20), and the retention function (3′), the above elasticity may be expressed as follows:

$$\frac{\sigma_w}{\sigma} \cdot W = -\frac{(1 + r)^2 \cdot a_1 \cdot [a_2 \cdot Q + (a_1 / b)] \cdot W}{1 - a_1 \cdot Q + a_2 \cdot e_{-1}}, \tag{25}$$

where Q is the firm's output target. Consequently [by equation (24)], the union will set the insider wage at the following level:

$$W^* = \frac{[1 - a_1 \cdot Q - (a_2 \cdot b/2) \cdot Q^2]}{a_1 \cdot (1 + r)^2 \cdot [a_2 \cdot Q + (a_1 / b)]}, \tag{26}$$

where W^* is the wage which maximizes the union's preference function.

Figure 6.5 illustrates the aggregate demand and supply curves of our labor market. We assume that there are a fixed number (n) of firms and (s) of workers in the economy. All firms are identical; so are all unions, all

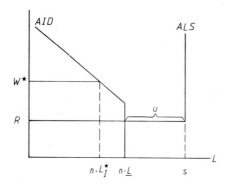

Figure 6.5
Involuntary unemployment.

insiders, all entrants, and all outsiders. The aggregate labor supply curve is denoted by ALS and the aggregate insider demand curves is given by AID.

The figure shows how involuntary unemployment can arise in our model. At the equilibrium wage W^*, $n \cdot L_i^*$ insiders are employed and $(n \cdot \underline{L} - n \cdot L^*)$ entrants are employed as well. The remaining u workers are unemployed. If insiders and entrants provide an equal amount of effort on these jobs, this unemployment may be termed involuntary, in the sense that the outsiders have a more limited choice set than the insiders. The insiders and outsiders have identical job characteristics, since they are equally productive under identical conditions of work. Nevertheless, the insiders receive a higher wage in the current period than that offered to outsiders. (See also the discussion on pp. 8 and 73.)

The firms do not find it worthwhile to replace all their insiders by outsiders because these workers do not face the same opportunities. Insiders are able to continue working without thereby reducing the effort expended by the firms' employees. By contrast, when outsiders take over the insiders' jobs, they raise the turnover rate and consequently lower employees' effort.

It is important to observe how our explanation of involuntary unemployment depends on the impact of labor turnover on effort. Suppose that the economy is initially in an equilibrium where labor turnover is inversely related to effort (i.e., the substitution effect of the turnover rate on effort exceeds the income effect) and there is involuntary unemployment. Thereupon, suppose that there is an exogenous change in workers' preferences so that the substitution effect falls relative to the income effect and thus the impact of labor turnover on effort becomes weaker (viz., a rise in the turnover rate elicits a smaller fall in effort than heretofore).

This change may be portrayed by a fall in the coefficient b [of the effort function (13)]. The repercussions of this change are portrayed in figure 6.6. For any given insider wage W, the firm's output target (the optimal credible or the noncredible target) rises, as shown in equations (20) and (21) and in figure 6.6a. As result, the firm's insider demand curve (ID in figure 6.6d) falls. Consequently, the union reduces its wage [as shown in figure 6.6d and implied by equations (20) and (26)] and the demand for insiders falls. In short, the weaker the impact of labor turnover on effort, the more successful the outsiders are in underbidding the insiders and the lower level of involuntary unemployment.

As the coefficient b falls towards zero (at which point the substitution effect of turnover on effort is equal to the income effect), the firm's output target rises monotonically without bound [by equations (20) and (21)].

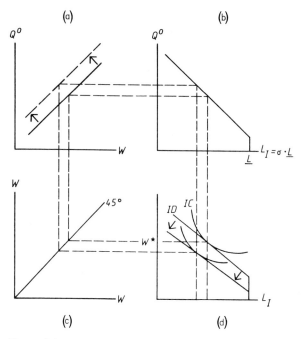

Figure 6.6
The effects of a change in the effort impact of turnover.

Recall that Q^{max} (the output target that is just sufficient to ensure that all the current insiders are replaced by entrants) is finite. Thus, there exists a positive level of b, $\underline{b}$ (so that the substitution effect still dominates the income effect) at which the firm's output target is Q^{max} and the outsiders are completely successful in underbidding the insiders. Under these circumstances, involuntary unemployment disappears.

Note that our explanation of involuntary unemployment does *not* require that $b > \underline{b}$ over the entire range of turnover rates. Rather, there is a stability argument to be made. As long as $b \leqslant \underline{b}$, firms replace all their high-wage insiders by low-wage outsiders. This process continues until either the existing involuntary unemployment has disappeared *or* the impact of turnover on effort turns sufficiently negative so that $b > \underline{b}$.

6.6 Job Security and Worker Productivity

Our analysis of the morale effect of labor turnover also sheds light on the controversy concerning the relation between job security and worker productivity. Some people have argued that many collective bargaining agreements and welfare state measures to promote job security have robbed workers of their motivation. Workers who are reasonably sure of remaining employed allegedly have no need to exert themselves at their current jobs. On the other side of the barricades are those who argue that job security enables workers to benefit from their work effort and thus provides a crucial effort incentive. (This is the case in our analysis when the substitution effect of labor turnover on effort dominates the income effect.) For example, Japan, which grants its workers a higher degree of job security than most other capitalist economies, is generally agreed to have comparatively high work morale. It is also often argued that the employees in firms with comparatively high job security (e.g., IBM) work comparatively hard to establish reputations.

In the light of our analysis, the above controversy blurs the distinction between two entirely separate aspects of job security, with separate implications for work effort. As noted in section 6.1, the first is microeconomic job security (measured by the worker's perceived probability of retaining his current job) and the second is macroeconomic job security (characterized by the worker's perceived probability of regaining employment once he has been fired).

There is no immutable relation between these probabilities. The former reflects the employment conditions in a particular firm—in particular, its labor turnover rate, its survival prospects, and the prospects of capital-labor substitution. The latter reflects the economy-wide employment conditions—in particular, the ratio of vacancies to job searchers, the availability of job information, and the accessibility of government employment creation schemes.

Furthermore, micro- and macroeconomic job security have different effects on work effort. With regard to microeconomic security, we have seen that $(\partial e/\partial \bar{Q})$ may in general be positive or negative; i.e., the substitution effect of the turnover rate on effort may be greater or smaller than the income effect. However, with regard to the macroeconomic security, $(\partial e/\partial \rho)$ [implied by equation (5)] can be shown to be unambiguously negative. In particular, a rise in ρ reduces the expected income differential between workers who are retained and those who are fired. In this way macroeconomic job security mitigates the gains from job effort. Consequently, the substitution effect is negative. Moreover, a rise in the re-employment probability raises each worker's total expected income and thereby induces him to consume more leisure on the job, i.e., provide less effort. Thus, the income effect is negative as well.

The upshot of these considerations is that light can be shed on the controversy between productivity and job security by distinguishing between micro- and macroeconomic job security. The effects of these two kinds of job security may go in opposite directions, and, in the context of this chapter, they actually do when there is involuntary unemployment. The contestants in the controversy may have been talking past one another by adopting different concepts of job security.

6.7 Concluding Remarks

This chapter has examined various guises of the relation between worker productivity and job security, and explores the possibility of involuntary unemployment emerging as result.

The qualitative conclusions of our analysis could also have been reached if the effort rewards took the form of promotions. Promotions—like the rewards in our analysis—are usually awarded for past job achievements, and workers' endeavors to establish reputations are aimed at reaping future rewards for current effort.

Within this framework, we have seen that when wages are such that workers prefer employment to unemployment and insiders receive more remuneration than outsiders, outsiders may nevertheless be unable to underbid the insiders. This can happen when labor turnover has an adverse effect on work effort. In that event, there is persistent involuntary unemployment.

7   Strike and Lockout
       Threats and Fiscal Policy

Overview

Since the insider-outsider theory focuses on the market power of insiders in the process of wage determination, it is easy to get the impression that our theory applies exclusively to labor unions, and that wherever labor unions are absent, our theory is inapplicable. To dispel this impression, chapters 3 and 5 have assumed that insiders bargain individualistically with their employers, and we have shown that the insiders can nevertheless gain market power if the labor turnover costs are of significant magnitude relative to the wage per pay period. (Chapter 6 assumed union wage setting, but our argument for the existence of involuntary unemployment did not depend on the existence of unions.)

However, it is undoubtedly true that the labor turnover costs associated with an insider are generally much larger when insiders perform their rent-creating activities in conjunction with one another than when they act individualistically. Insiders may collude through formal or informal organizations. The most common formal organization of this type is, of course, the labor union. Most unions do in fact appear to be dominated by insiders, rather than by entrants and outsiders. Consequently, we may expect unions to represent the interests of insiders more than those of outsiders.

As we have observed briefly in chapter 4, unions serve a fourfold purpose for insiders:

i. they are able to augment the rent-creation done by individual insiders,

ii. they characteristically have more bargaining power than any of their individual members,

iii. they may operate as an interest group in the political process and, as such, lobby for job security legislation, and

iv. they can provide rent-creating tools—such as strike and work-to-rule threats —that are generally not available to unorganized workers.

Each of these purposes is important in its own right, but the wage-employment consequences of the first three are much more transparent than those of the fourth. For this reason, we now focus our attention on the fourth purpose. In particular, this chapter deals with strike threats (as well as an important employer response: lockout threats), while the next chapter covers both strike and work-to-rule threats.

Our aim is to provide a rationale for strike threats based on the market power of insiders, which, in turn, is derived from the existence of hiring, training, and firing costs. (It is clear, however, that any other labor turnover costs could serve our purposes equally well.) We consider a firm-specific union that calls a strike when the firm rejects its wage proposal. Then the firm has a choice between bearing the costs of worker replacement (viz., firing the strikers and hiring and training new recruits instead) or the costs of keeping the strikers' positions vacant. We analyze the case in which the former costs exceed the latter, so that the firm prefers the strike option to the replacement option—which appears to be quite common in practice.

The union members may prefer the strike option as well. For when the union members are uncertain about whether the firm will accept or reject their wage proposal, the strike option may provide them with a higher expected present value of income than the replacement option. The reason is that the union members have a greater probability of returning to their previous positions after a strike than of finding new employment after they have been replaced by the firm (and thereby have lost their privileged status as insiders).

In our analysis, what gives unions their clout are the labor turnover costs. For, in the absence of these costs, the firm would find it profitable to replace all its strikers rather than to accept the strike and keep the strikers' positions vacant. The traditional union literature has largely ignored the questions of where union clout comes from. This literature has been concerned more with describing the effects of union power on wages and employment rather than the causes of this power.

Yet our endeavor to explain the causes of union power has unavoidable implications for the effects of union power as well. In our analysis—unlike the traditional union literature—wages are not merely determined by maximizing a union utility function subject to a labor demand function (in the "monopoly union model") or to an iso-profit function (in the "efficient bargain model"). Labor turnover costs play a crucial role as well. These costs not only help explain why unions have clout but also impose special constraints on union behavior. In particular, the union in our analysis faces what we call a "proposal acceptance constraint" (within which the firm has an incentive to accept the union's wage proposal, given the costs of striking) and a "credibility constraint" (within which the union's wage proposal is credible).

Beyond this, the chapter is also concerned with the role of lockout threats as firms' responses to strike threats. In practice, lockouts serve various purposes. For example, they enable the firm (i) to deplete the union's strike fund and thereby moderate the union's wage claims, (ii) to avoid paying the wages of nonstrikers (who may be unprofitable in the absence of the striking workers), and (iii) to gain information about the union's objectives and constraints.

This chapter focuses attention exclusively on the first rationale. Here, the effect of the lockout threat on union wages operates via the union's credibility constraint. As noted, the lockout reduces the union's strike fund payment. The lower this payment, the greater an insider's individual incentive to break the strike rather than to observe it. Thus, the lockout threat reduces the maximum wage that gives each insider an individual incentive to observe a strike once the union has called it.

In this analytical context, we find an as yet unexplored channel whereby fiscal policies may affect wages. Variations in unemployment benefits, payroll and income taxes, and public employment all have an impact on the credibility of strike threats. The resulting effect on wages is quite independent from the standard fiscal policy channels in the macro literature. Our analysis suggests that when marginal productivity considerations dominate wage determination, the fiscal policies affect wages in the conventional ways; but when credibility considerations dominate, the effects may run in the opposite direction.

7.1 Introduction

The existence of strikes and strike threats has long posed a problem for economic theory. Strikes reduce the total gain from productive activity to be shared among the firms and their employees. If there is, then, a common potential interest in avoiding strikes, why do strike threats occur in the first place? What makes strike threats credible and effective in wage bargaining? Furthermore, why do employers sometimes respond to strike threats by issuing lockout threats? All these questions have received little attention in the theoretical literature on labor markets.

This chapter suggests an explanation of strike and lockout threats in which labor turnover costs play a particularly important role. We consider an economy in which firms engage in wage bargaining with their unionized employees, and, in this context, we find that strike and lockout threats can be explained as rational behavior of the agents. We also find that these threats can make a significant difference to the effectiveness of fiscal policies.

Our chapter departs from the standard literature on the theory of labor unions, which has been dominated by two models of union behavior:

i. In the "monopoly model," the union sets the wage while the firms unilaterally make the employment decisions. Here, the union maximizes its utility function subject to its labor demand function.

ii. In the "efficient bargain model," the wage and employment decisions are made jointly by the union and the firms. In this case, the union may be viewed as maximizing its utility function subject to an isoprofit function.

These models are analyzed in Dixon (1987), MaCurdy and Pencavel (1982), McDonald and Solow (1981), Nickell (1982), Oswald (1985), and others. In Nickell and Andrews (1983), the union and the firms bargain over the wage, while firms make the employment decisions. Manning's model (1987) encompasses the monopoly model and the efficient bargain model.

This literature leaves a fundamental question unanswered: What gives unions their clout? In other words, what stops firms from ignoring the unions' demands and dealing with nonunionized workers instead?

This chapter suggests a particularly simple answer: Firms could, in principle, ignore the strike threats of their unionized employees by firing them, and, in doing so, the firms may incur substantial labor turnover costs. To avoid these costs, the firms may have to make wage concessions to the current employees.

Our rationale for strike threats rests on insider power derived from the existence of hiring, training, and firing costs. Let us begin by observing that a firm's production technology together with its costs of hiring, training, and firing determine an upper bound on the insider wage: if the insider wage exceeds this bound, then the firm finds it profitable to replace its insiders by entrants; below this bound, the firm lacks this incentive. Now suppose that the insiders have imperfect information about their firm's technologies and hiring-training-firing costs and consequently do not know precisely what this upper bound is. Furthermore, suppose—for the moment—that the insiders set their wage, and that the firm's only feasible responses are to retain or dismiss these insiders. Then the insiders face a straightforward trade-off—the higher their wage, the greater their probability of dismissal. The insiders will set their wage so as to maximize their utility subject to this trade-off. For example, if the insiders are risk-neutral and their utility is linearly related to their income, then they will set their wage so as to maximize their expected income.

Paradoxical as it may sound, the opportunity to strike may serve to make both the insiders *and* their firm better off. To see this, observe that, when workers go on strike, the employer need not fire them; rather, their positions could be kept vacant pending the outcome of the disagreement.

The cost to the firm of keeping the strikers' positions vacant is the profit forgone; the cost of replacing the strikers by new entrants is the cost of hiring, training, and firing plus the productivity differential between the strikers and the new entrants minus the associated wage differential. If the former cost is less than the latter, the firm will be better off under the strike threat than under the replacement threat.

Moreover, the insiders may be better off as well, since workers whose positions are kept vacant during a strike usually have a greater chance of working as insiders in the future than those who are fired. In particular, during a strike, the present value of insiders' income depends, among other things, on the probability of returning to their previous jobs. Under the replacement option, the present value of insiders' income depends, in part, on their probability of finding a new job and gaining insider status on that job. Since the insiders' probability of returning to their positions after the strike is generally greater than their probability of finding new insider positions, the present value of their incomes under the strike may well exceed that under the replacement option. In that event, the insiders will prefer the strike threat to the replacement threat.

In this chapter we assume that the strike threat is Pareto superior to the replacement threat in the above sense, and thus the insider wage will be set with reference to the costs that the strike incurs to the insiders and firm. Observe, however, that our rationale for strike threats ultimately rests on the costs of hiring, training, and firing. For, in the absence of these costs, the firm would find it worthwhile to replace all its strikers rather than keep their positions vacant. Needless to say, *any* labor turnover costs—not just the costs of hiring, training, and firing—could serve this purpose. Thus, our analysis of strike threats could just as well be based on the costs of cooperation and harassment differentials (described in chapter 5) or the effort cost of labor turnover (described in chapter 6).

Our strike explanation differs from the ones suggested in the literature, where strikes are regarded as

• an "information-gathering device" in situations where employees are not perfectly informed about each other's preferences or about market conditions (e.g., Bishop, 1964; Cross, 1965; Harsani, 1956; Hayes, 1984; Reder and Newman, 1980) or

• an "expectations-revising device" when union management seeks to convince its rank and file that its wage demands are unacceptably high to employers (e.g., Aschenfelter and Johnson, 1969; Farber, 1978).

Our answer to the question why unions have clout has important implications for the theory of union behavior. No longer can wage determination be explained merely in terms of the maximization of union utility
subject to a labor demand function or an isoprofit function. The amount of
damage that the union is potentially able to inflict on the firms (viz., the
profits forgone in the event of a strike)—which we call "union punch"—is
of critical significance as well.

We also show how the *credibility* of strike threats is an important,
independent influence on wage bargaining. A union that threatens to strike
must be able to induce its members to observe the strike once it has been
called.

Just as strike threats can give unions leverage in wage bargaining, so
lockout threats can perform an analogous function for the firms. The latter
threats are credible whenever the firms find it cheaper to lock strikers out
than to exchange them (for nonunionized workers) or retain them without
lockout (in anticipation that the conflict will be resolved).

It will be shown that once strike and lockout threats are taken into
account in the bargaining between unions and firms, the conventional fiscal
policy effects on wages need to be modified, in that a new channel of fiscal
policy influence arises. We indicate that these effects depend on whether
union punch or union credibility constitutes binding constraints on the
union's wage-setting problem, and we show that variations in fiscal policy
instruments (such as unemployment benefits, income taxes, and public
employment) affect union punch and credibility in quite different ways.

The chapter is organized as follows. Section 7.2 presents an overview of
agents' behavior in our model. Section 7.3 outlines our model of union
behavior. Section 7.4 is concerned with the formulation of the union's wage
proposal and strike threat as well as the firm's lockout threat. Section 7.5
examines the effectiveness of fiscal policies under strike threats and lockout
threats. Finally, section 7.6 contains our concluding remarks.

7.2 The Model of Agents' Behavior

The turnover costs generate economic rent, which may be seized by the
firms and their employees in the wage bargaining process. We assume that
the insiders manage to capture some of this rent, whereas the entrants
receive their reservation wage (R). Thus, the insider wage (W) is greater
than R.

Characteristically it takes time for entrants to achieve a sufficiently
strong position in their firms in order to generate labor turnover costs

should they be replaced. For simplicity, we suppose that entrants remain such for a finite span of time, which we call the "initiation period."

Next, we assume that wage contracts are implementable only for a limited time period; for simplicity, let it be equal to the initiation period. Thus, at the end of the initiation period, the bargaining position of the entrants is the same as that of the insiders. In fact, the entrants *become* insiders, receiving the new, higher insider wage.

Our model economy comprises a government and a fixed number of firms and workers. The firms produce a nondurable consumption good by means of labor and capital. They distribute their profits to the workers. The workers buy the consumption good and offer labor services. There are no entries or retirements from the labor force. The government employs workers to produce public services.

Employment and production decisions are made by the firms and the government. Workers decide how much to consume. The insider wage is determined through a bargaining process, described below. We shall analyze the agents' decisions under stationary Nash equilibrium conditions, in which the capital stock is constant and each private agent sets his decision variables under the assumption that all other agents have set their decision variables optimally with regard to their objectives and constraints.

The activities of the various agents may be described as follows:

7.2.1 The Government

The government has three policy instruments:

i. public employments (L_G),

ii. unemployment benefits (B per unemployed worker), and

iii. an income tax rate (τ).

Each instrument is parametrically fixed.[1]

For simplicity we assume that the government offers each of its employees the insider wage prevailing in the private sector.[2]

7.2.2 The Firms

The firm produces a homogeneous consumption good (Q) and has three factors of production at its disposal: insider labor (L_I), entrant labor (L_E), and capital (K). All firms in the economy are identical.

Since we are not concerned with factor substitution, let there be a fixed ratio of capital to total labour input, so that[3]

$$Q = \min[(L_I + L_E), K],\tag{1}$$

where the capital stock (K) is exogeneously given.

Let $C_E = C_E(L_E)$ be the firm's cost of acquiring entrants, where C_E', $C_E'' > 0$ for $L_E > 0$, $C_E(0) = 0$, $\lim_{L_E \to 0} C_E' = \tilde{c}_E$, and $\tilde{c}_E$ is a positive constant (i.e., C_E is finitely large for all positive L_E). Let $C_I = C_I(m - L_I)$ be the firm's cost of dismissing insiders, where m is the incumbent workforce (i.e., the number of insiders employed by the firm at the beginning of the current time period), C_I', $C_I'' > 0$ for $m > L_I$, $C_I(0) = 0$, $\lim_{L_I \to m} C_I' = \tilde{c}_I$, and $\tilde{c}_I$ is a positive constant (i.e., C_I is finitely large for all $0 \leqslant L_I < m$).

In making its production and employment decisions $(Q, L_I$ and $L_E)$, the firm faces a given insider wage (W), an entrant wage (R), and the capital stock (K). The firm maximizes the present value of its profit, which in each period is

$$\pi = Q - W \cdot L_I - R \cdot L_E - C_E(L_E) - C_I[m - L_I]\tag{2}$$

(where revenue and costs are all evaluated in terms of the consumption good).

7.2.3 The Workers

Each worker's utility is a function of consumption (C) and labor (l): $U = U(C, l)$, where $U_C > 0$ and $U_l < 0$. For simplicity, work is taken to be a discrete activity: Each employee provides one unit of labor $(l = 1)$; each outsider provides none $(l = 0)$. The worker consumes his entire income.

Every worker (whether employed or unemployed) receives the same exogenous, lump-sum profit income, $\sigma \cdot \pi$, where σ (<1) is the ratio of firms to employees. An outsider's disposable income is $(B + \sigma \cdot \pi) \cdot (1 - \tau)$; that of an insider is $(W + \sigma \cdot \pi) \cdot (1 - \tau)$; and that of an entrant is $(R + \sigma \cdot \pi) \cdot (1 - \tau)$.

For simplicity, let workers have a two-period time horizon and a zero rate of time discount. Then the entrants' reservation wage (R) (which, we assume, is the same as the wage that entrants are offered) may be defined as follows:

$$U[(R + \sigma \cdot \pi) \cdot (1 - \tau), 1] + U[(W + \sigma \cdot \pi) \cdot (1 - \tau), 1)]$$

$$= 2 \cdot U[(B + \sigma \cdot \pi) \cdot (1 - \tau), 0].\tag{3a}$$

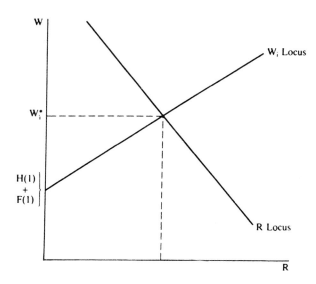

Figure 7.1
The equilibrium insider and reservation wages.

The trade-off between W and R [equation (3a)] is pictured by the R locus in figure 7.1.

7.2.4 Insider Wage Determination

Our analysis consistent with several alternative ways in which economic rent may be divided between a firm and its employees through insider wage determination. Quite generally, we only require that the wage bargain satisfy two properties:

i. insiders capture some of the economic rent generated by the labor turnover costs that would be incurred if they were replaced by entrants, and

ii. the greater this rent, the greater the insider wage.[4]

Yet this chapter is not concerned with the precise way in which wage bargaining schemes split rent between employers and employees, but rather with the rationale for strike and lockout threats as well as the associated fiscal policy implications. Thus, let us consider a particularly transparent special case of wage bargain: The wage demanded by the insiders is at its maximal level subject to the condition that no insider is fired.

If insiders were to bargain "individualistically" (i.e., each insider acts independently of all other insiders), then each insider would set his wage high enough so that his firm would be indifferent between retaining him and replacing him by an entrant. Hence the insider wage is

$$W_i = R + [H(1) + F(1)] \tag{3b}$$

(where the subscript i stands for "individualistic" bargaining). Under these circumstances, entrants have no opportunity to enter the workforce. Equation (3b) is pictured by the W_i locus in figure 7.1. Here, W_i^* and R^* are the equilibrium insider and reservation wages, respectively.

7.3 Labor Union Activity

Let a "union" simply be a collective of workers engaged in some well-defined economic activity. Since we have assumed that insiders have more market power than other workers, it is natural for us to restrict our attention to unions consisting only of insiders. We endeavor to explain the behavior of such unions in terms of their members' individualistic interests. (The underlying presumption is that a union that is not beneficial to its members is unlikely to persist).

We consider only one type of union activity: the strike. This is given one purpose, namely, to back up the union's wage demands. In other words, the strike is a *wage-preserving device*. (By contrast, the next chapter examines the strike as a *job-preserving device*). In particular, we suppose that the union, consisting of all the insiders of a firm, makes a wage proposal to that firm and it is the firm's rejection of this proposal that provokes the strike. The strike is "won" by the workers if the firm is induced to accept the proposal after all; it is "lost" if the proposal is irrevocably rejected, in which case the wage remains beneath the union's asking price.

We also consider a common countermove available to the firm: the lockout. We focus on one purpose for this activity: The lockout enables the firm to deplete the union's strike fund and thereby diminish the union's bargaining power and moderate its wage proposals.[5,6]

The union's strike threat may be defined in terms of the following implicit contract between the firm and its insiders:

If the firm accepts the union's wage proposal, then none of the employees will strike; yet if the proposal is rejected, then some (possibly all) of the employees will strike.

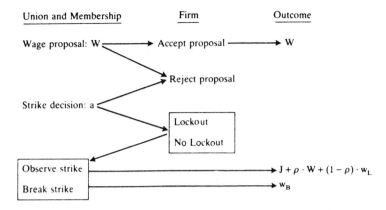

Figure 7.2
The sequence of decisions.

The steps in the bargaining process under this contract may be set out as follows (see figure 7.2). *First,* the union makes a wage proposal, *W*. *Second,* the firm decides whether to accept or reject this proposal. If it is accepted, *W* becomes the insider wage. *Third,* if the proposal is rejected, the union decides what proportion (*a*) of the firm's workforce is to be called out on strike.[7] *Fourth,* the firm decides whether or not to undertake a lockout in response to the strike. *Fifth,* each union member decides whether to observe or break the strike (given the lockout decision).

The strike and lockout decisions are inherently intertemporal. A strike is conducted with a view to achieving a particular wage in the future; a lockout is imposed in order to reduce the union's wage demands in the future. We can capture the essence of the problem in two time periods. Suppose that the firm and the union have a two-period time horizon and that both are risk-neutral. Let both parties expect a strike, once begun, to last for only one time period. For simplicity (but without loss of generality) we assume that both parties have a zero rate of time discount.

Let ρ be each party's subjective probability that the union will win the strike.[8] We assume that ρ is inversely related to the size of the union's wage proposal: $\rho = \rho(W)$, $\rho' < 0$.

If the strike is observed, the union member receives a strike-fund payment, J, in the first period. His remuneration in the second period depends on whether the strike is won or lost. With probability ρ, he expects to receive W; with probability $(1 - \rho)$, he expects to receive a lower wage— call it w_L (where L stands for a "lost" strike). Thus, the present value of his expected income is $J + [\rho \cdot W + (1 - \rho) \cdot w_L]$, as shown in figure 7.2.

On the other hand, if the strike is broken (i.e., the union members do not respond to the strike call), then the wage is also lower—call it w_B.

Since we are not concerned with specific mechanisms for dividing economic rent between employers and employees, we do not provide choice-theoretic foundations for the determination of w_L and w_B. There are, however, obvious upper and lower bounds on these wages. If union members lose or break their strike, they can be expected to give up some of their market power. Consequently, w_L and w_B must fall short of W. Furthermore, union members cannot receive a wage beneath W_i, for were they to face this possibility, they would have an incentive to leave their union and bargain individualistically. In sum, $W > w_L$, $w_B \geqslant W_i$. For simplicity, we make the simplifying assumption that $w_L = w_B = w = g(W, W_i)$, where $W_i \leqslant w < W$ and $g_1, g_2 \geqslant 0.$[9]

As in section 7.2, we let the union maximize the insider wage subject to the condition that no insiders are fired.[10] In the analysis below, we examine the Nash equilibrium of the bargaining process above (i.e., the firm's decisions are exogenously given to the union and vice versa).

We require that this equilibrium have the following properties:

a. The equilibrium strike threat is credible. This means that if the firm rejects the union's wage proposal, the union members have an incentive to observe (rather than break) the strike.

b. The equilibrium wage proposal is not rejected by the firm and hence does not provoke a strike.

The prerequisites of condition (a) are examined in the next section; those for (b) are given in the appendix. Whereas condition (a) is plausible and straightforward, condition (b) reflects the selective focus of chapter. We are here concerned only with strike and lockout threats; the actual conduct of strikes and lockouts is easy to examine within the framework of our analysis, but for the sake of brevity we do not do so. (Our perspective is analogous to that of oligopolistic entry deterrence, where entry into the industry is effectively eliminated—threats are made but need not be carried out).

Of course, the bargaining strategies of the firm and the union depend on their subjective probabilities of the strike outcome; yet since the strike is not provoked, these probabilities do not have objective counterparts. Both parties are assumed to have perfect information about the circumstances under which the threats take effect and both recognize whether the threats are credible.[11]

Having described the salient characteristics of the equilibrium state, we now turn to the way in which the union formulates its wage proposal.

7.4 The Wage Proposal and the Lockout Decision

The lockout decision described above is a discrete one: Either the firm locks out all its nonstriking union members or it does not.[12] *First* (in section 7.4.1) let us examine the union's wage proposal when the firm chooses the lockout option in response to the strike threat; *second* (in section 7.4.2) we see what happens to this wage proposal when the firm does not choose the lockout option; *third* (in section 7.4.3) we show how the firm makes its lockout decision.

7.4.1 Strike Threat with Lockout Threat

Suppose that whenever some insiders strike, the firm locks out the rest. Recall that the union's wage proposal (W) is such that the firm has no incentive to fire any insiders. Furthermore, we assume that the labor acquisition and dismissal functions [$H(L_E)$ and $F(m - L_I)$] are such that, in the solution to the firm's profit maximization problem, $L_I + L_E = K$, from equation (1). Thus, the union's wage proposal is set so that $L_I = K$, which is a positive constant, which we hereafter call $\bar{L}$ for short.

Thus, if the firm accepts the wage proposal, then the present value of its profits is

$$\pi^a = 2 \cdot [1 - W] \cdot \qquad \qquad (4)$$

(where the superscript a stands for "acceptance" of the wage proposal).[13]

On the other hand, if it rejects this proposal, then the union calls a strike, whereupon the firm locks out all the remaining insiders. In that case, the firm's first-period profit is zero. In the second period, the union either wins the strike (in which case the insider wage is W) or it loses it (in which case the insider wage is w). Hence the expected present value of the firm's profit when the union's wage proposal is rejected is

$$\pi^l = \rho \cdot [1 - W] \cdot \bar{L} + (1 - \rho) \cdot [1 - w] \cdot \bar{L} \qquad \qquad (5)$$

(where the superscript l stands for the case of "lockout").

We can now fully specify the union's wage proposal. The wage is set as high as possible, subject to three conditions: (i) no strike is provoked, (ii) the strike threat is credible, and (iii) no insiders are fired. Let the maximal wage satisfying the first condition (given the lockout threat) be called the *proposal acceptance wage*, W_{PA}^l. Let the maximal wage satisfying the second constraint be the *credible threat wage*, W_{CT}^l. The third constraint is simply a nonnegativity condition on profit and the maximal wage associated with it is the *zero-profit wage*, W_{ZP}^l.

Hence, the union's wage proposal must be

$$W^l = \min(W_{PA}^l, W_{CT}^l, W_{ZP}^l). \tag{6}$$

The zero-profit wage is not analytically interesting; so let us assume that it is never binding: $W_{ZP}^l \geqslant \min(W_{PA}^l, W_{CT}^l)$.

The proposal acceptance wage (W_{PA}^l) is sufficiently high so that the firm's profit from accepting this wage is the same as the profit from rejecting it: $\pi^a = \pi^l$. In other words,

$$[1 - W_{PA}^l] \cdot \overline{L} \cdot \{1 + (1 - \rho)\} = \{1 - w\} \cdot \overline{L} \cdot (1 - \rho).$$

Thus,

$$W_{PA}^l = 1 - [(1 - w) \cdot (1 - \rho)/(2 - \rho)]. \tag{7}$$

We call this the *proposal-acceptance constraint* in the event of a lockout.[14]

The credible-threat wage (W_{CT}^l) is such that, if the union's wage proposal is rejected, then each union member is just on the margin of indifference between observing and the breaking the strike. This is the case when the worker's ex post utility from striking (i.e., his utility once the proposed wage is rejected) is equal to his ex post utility from not striking.

Let X be the (exogenously given) proportion of the union's total strike fund made available to the union members in the current time period. Let J be the payment per worker from this available fund. Since both the strikers and the lockout victims are entitled to the payments, $J = (X/\overline{L})$.

Suppose that each worker observed the strike. Then, in the first period, each receives the strike fund payment (J) and profit income[15] $(\sigma \cdot \pi)$; in the second period, each receives W if the strike is won, or w if it is lost, in addition to profit income $(\sigma \cdot \pi)$. Thus, each worker's ex post utility from observing the strike is

$$U^s = U\{(J + \sigma \cdot \pi) \cdot (1 - \tau), 0\} + \rho \cdot U\{(W^l + \sigma \cdot \pi) \cdot (1 - \tau), 1\}$$

$$+ (1 - \rho) \cdot U\{(w + \sigma \cdot \pi) \cdot (1 - \tau), 1\}. \tag{8a}$$

Now suppose instead that each worker breaks the strike. Then they receive w in both periods. The associated ex post utility is

$$U^b = 2 \cdot U\{(w + \sigma \cdot \pi) \cdot (1 - \tau), 1\}. \tag{8b}$$

At the credible-threat wage (W_{CT}^l),

$$U^s - U^b = 0. \tag{9}$$

Let us call this the *credible-threat constraint*.

Equations (8a), (8b), and (9) indicate what makes the strike threat credible in our model. Supposing (quite plausibly) that $J \leqslant w$ (so that a worker's first-period income is less when he observes the strike than when he breaks it), then our model allows only one reason why a worker may find it worthwhile to observe a strike—namely, that his second-period income from doing so ($\rho \cdot W + (1 - \rho) \cdot w$) is sufficiently large relative to that from breaking the strike (w).

This rationale for observing the strike rests on our assumption that all union members are identical (having the same utility function and facing the same J, π, τ, σ, W^1, w, and ρ), so that the strike is either observed by all members or broken by all members. By implication, whenever the strike is broken, *all* members receive w in both periods.

In practice, however, union members are heterogeneous, and thus some may observe a strike while others break it. If the strikers win, the strike breakers may well receive the same wage as the strike observers. Then, unless the union is able to enforce the strike decision voted by its members, there is a "free rider" problem (since the strike breakers reap the benefits of the strike without paying the cost).

Nevertheless, there are practical circumstances in which this free rider problem does not occur. For example, in firms with few workers, each worker may realize that by breaking the strike, he reduces the chances of winning the strike and thereby reduces his expected income. In addition, workers may expect that, after the strike is won, those who observed the strike may harass the strike breakers (thereby raising each strike breaker's marginal disutility of work) or refuse to cooperate with them in the process of production (thereby reducing each strike breaker's productivity, perhaps in sufficient magnitude to induce the firm to lay off the strike breaker). (Lindbeck and Snower, 1985a, have analyzed how insiders use cooperation and harassment activities to prevent underbidding by outsiders; here we suggest that insiders may so so to prevent underbidding by strike breakers.)

Extending our model to include cooperation and harassment activities and to make ρ dependent on the number of strike breakers would complicate our analysis without shedding new light on the ways in which the union's wage proposal (W) and its strike fund payments (J) affect its strike threat credibility. Thus, we simply retain our assumption that strike breakers receive w in both periods and therefore do not become free riders.

For expositional purposes, it is convenient to think of credibility as a matter of degree and let $\Omega = U^s - U^b$ measure how credible the strike threat is (viz., the greater Ω, the "more credible" the threat). In these terms, it is clear that a rise in J makes the threat more credible, since the utility from observing the strike is increased while the utility from breaking it remains unchanged:

$$(\partial \Omega / \partial J) = U_C \cdot (1 - \tau) > 0 \qquad \text{[by equations (8a), (8b)].}$$

On the other hand, a rise in the wage proposal (W^l) has countervailing effects on credibility:

$$\frac{\partial \Omega}{\partial W^l} = U_C \cdot (1 - \tau) \cdot [\rho + (1 - \rho) \cdot g_1 - 2 \cdot g_1] + \rho' \cdot \Gamma,$$

where

$$\Gamma = U\{(W_{CT}^l + \sigma \cdot \pi) \cdot (1 - \tau), 1\} - U\{(w + \sigma \cdot \pi) \cdot (1 - \tau), 1\} > 0.$$

For a given probability of winning the strike (ρ), U^s rises when the strike is won [by the amount $\delta \cdot U_C \cdot (\Gamma - \tau)$] and when the strike is lost [by the amount $U_C \cdot (1 - \tau) \cdot g_1$]. U^n rises as well [by the amount $2 \cdot U_C \cdot (1 - \tau) \cdot g_1$]. Moreover, ρ falls and this reduces U^s (since the chance of receiving W falls relative to the chance of receiving w).[16]

Thus a rise in the wage proposal (W) makes the strike threat less credible [i.e., $(\partial \Omega / \partial W_{CT}^l) < 0$] when

$$g_1 > \frac{\rho' \cdot \Gamma}{U_C \cdot (1 - \tau) \cdot (1 + \rho)} + \frac{\rho}{(1 + \rho)},$$

and the threat becomes more credible when the inequality runs the other way.

In sum, there are two possible ways in which the wage can affect strike threat credibility.

a. The *credibility-reducing wage*: When the wage falls, workers have a greater inducement to observe the strike, on the grounds that they are more likely to win the strike. We call this the *bird-in-the-hand* case, because the reasoning is that "one bird in the hand is worth two in the bush."

b. The *credibility-enhancing wage*: When the wage rises, workers have a greater inducement to observe the strike, on the grounds that their wage income is higher when they win the strike. We call this the *pie-in-the-sky* case, because the workers are being induced to strike through the chance of "a pie in the sky."

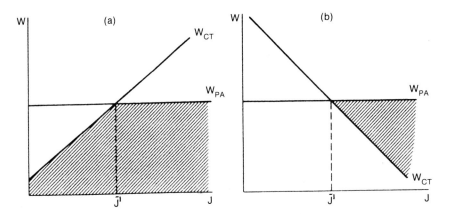

Figure 7.3
The wage proposal in the event of a lockout.

Figure 7.3a illustrates the "bird-in-the-hand" case. The credible-threat constraint [W_{CT} of equation (9)] is upward-sloping since W reduces credibility whereas J raises it:

$$(\partial W_{CT}^l / \partial J^l) = -(\partial \Omega / \partial J^l)/(\partial \Omega / \partial W_{CT}^l) > 0.$$

The proposal-acceptance constraint [W_{PA} of equation (7)] is pictured as well. (It is horizontal since J has no direct effect on the firm's profit.) The union's feasible region is given by the shaded area. The wage proposal that the union makes depends on what the existing level of J is. If $J^l < \tilde{J}^l$, then $W^l = W_{CT}^l$; and if $J^l > \tilde{J}^l$, then $W^l = W_{PA}^l$.

Figure 7.3b deals with the "pie-in-the-sky" case. Here the credible-threat constraint is downward sloping since W and J both raise credibility:

$$(\partial W_{CT}^l / \partial J) = -(\partial \Omega / \partial J^l)/(\partial \Omega / \partial W_{CT}^l) < 0.$$

(Once again, the feasible region is the shaded area.) If the union's strike fund is so small that $J^l < \tilde{J}^l$, then it is impossible to establish threat credibility (i.e., $\Omega < 0$). (In this case, union members are unable to gain economic rent from their strike threat.) If $J^l > \tilde{J}^l$ then $W^l = W_{PA}^l$. Note that the credible-threat constraint is never binding in the case.

(It is interesting to note that the relation between W_{CT}^l and J^l need not be monotonic, and thus, for a unique set of functional forms U and ρ, the wage may be credibility-reducing at some levels and credibility-enhancing at others.)

7.4.2 Strike Threat without Lockout Threat

Now suppose that the firm decides not to impose a lockout. In the event of a strike, the firm keeps all the remaining employees on the production line. As above, if the firm accepts the union's wage proposal (W), its profit is given by π^a of equation (4). Yet if it rejects this proposal, the union now calls $a \cdot \bar{L}$ of the firm's workforce out on strike. As a result, the firm's first-period profit is generated wholly by the remaining employees $((1 - a) \cdot \bar{L})$. These workers receive a wage w, which is lower than the one the firm rejected. In the second period, all employees receive W if the union wins the strike, or w if the union loses. Thus, the expected present value of the firm's profit, after rejection of the union's wage proposal, is

$$\pi^n = [1 - w] \cdot (1 - a) \cdot \bar{L} + \rho \cdot [1 - W] \cdot \bar{L}$$

$$+ (1 - \rho) \cdot [1 - w] \cdot \bar{L} \tag{10}$$

(where the superscript n stands for the case of "no lockout" threat).

Once again, the proposal-acceptance wage (W_{PA}^n) sets $\pi^a > \pi^n$. Consequently, the proposal-acceptance constraint in the absence of a lockout is

$$[1 - W_{PA}^n] \cdot \bar{L} \cdot \{1 + (1 - \rho)\} = [1 - w] \cdot \bar{L} \cdot \{1 - a + (1 - \rho)\}. \tag{11}$$

In contrast to the lockout case, the number of workers threatening to strike makes a difference to the proposal-acceptance wage. The greater $(a \cdot \bar{L})$, the smaller the firm's first-period profit in the event of a strike, and thus (if $g_1 = 0$, so that w is unaffected by W_{PA}^n) the higher W_{PA}^n (at which the firm is indifferent between accepting and rejecting the wage proposal). [Yet if $g_1 > 0$, then $(\partial W_{PA}^n / \partial(a \cdot \bar{L})) > 0$ only if the effect of W_{PA}^n on w is sufficiently small, viz., only if $g_1 < (1 - g)/(1 - W_{PA}^n)$.] Furthermore, the greater $(a \cdot \bar{L})$, the smaller the strike fund payment (J) [for recall that $J = (X/(a \cdot \bar{L})]$, where X—the overall strike fund available to union members in the current period—is exogenously given]. Thus, there is an inverse relation between W_{PA}^n and J^n as pictured in figure 7.4. Whereas J is fixed in the case of lockout at $J^l = (X/\bar{L})$, it is now endogenous to the union's decision making.

The credible-threat constraint remains the same as in the case of lockout [see equation (9)]. (Thus $W_{CT}^a = W_{CT}^l$.) Figure 7.4a depicts the "bird-in-the-hand" case and figure 7.4b is about the "pie-in-the-sky" case. (The latter figure is illustrative only, since the proposal-acceptance constraint need not be flatter than the credible-threat constraint.)

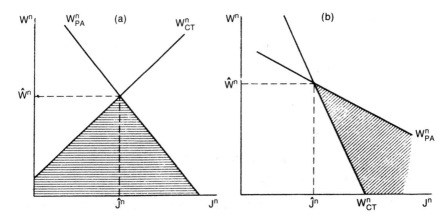

Figure 7.4
The wage proposal in the absence of a lockout.

The shaded areas in the figures are the union's feasible regions for the wage proposal. The union chooses the maximal attainable wage, lying at the intersection of the two constraints in figures 7.4a and 7.4b: $W^n = \hat{W}^n$.[17]

7.4.3 The Lockout Decision

Having examined the union's wage proposal in the presence and absence of the lockout threat, we now find the conditions under which this threat will and will not be used.

A firm that stages a lockout earns less profit in the current period than one that does not.[18] Consequently, the firm can be induced to lock out union members only if this provides a future profit advantage that outweighs the current profit loss. In our model, the only conceivable future advantage lies in the possibility that the lockout threat may enable the firm to achieve a lower insider wage than it could otherwise have done. There is only one way for this to work, namely,

a. the lockout threat reduces the strike fund payment, J, and

b. a reduction in J leads to a fall in the union's wage proposal,[19] W.

Condition (a) holds only if the credible-threat constraint is binding in wage determination. Condition (b) holds only if the wage proposal is credibility-reducing (and, by implication, W and J have opposite effects on Ω).

In sum,

PROPOSITION 1   *In the bargaining process above, the lockout threat is used only if*

a. *credible-threat constraint (9) is binding, i.e.,* $W = W_{CT} < W_{PA}$, *and*
b. *the union's wage proposal is credibility-reducing.*

In this light, it is convenient to examine the lockout decision under two different circumstances:

- a credibility-enhancing wage proposal and
- a credibility-reducing wage proposal.

When the wage proposal is credibility-enhancing, the strike threat will not provoke a lockout threat (by proposition 1b) and then the proposal is determined as shown in figure 7.4b. Here, $W^n = W^n_{PA} = W^n_{CT}$.

On the other hand, when the wage proposal is credibility-reducing, this proposal is made as shown in figure 7.5. Here the proposal-acceptance and credible-threat constraints in the presence and absence of lockout are superimposed on each other. Observe that if $a = 1$, then $W^l_{PA} = W^n_{PA}$.[20]

The figure pictures a well-known rationale for lockout in the real-world conduct of labor conflict: It is meant to reduce the union's ability to support

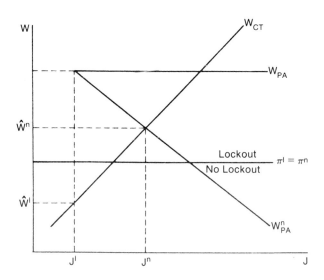

Figure 7.5
The lockout decision and the corresponding wage proposals (when these proposals are credibility-reducing).

their members during the conflict and consequently make it more desirable for these members to break the strike than to observe it. In order for the union to reestablish its strike-threat credibility (i.e., to convince the firm that a strike call would be heeded), the wage proposal is reduced.

The lock-out threat is used if $\pi^l > \pi^a$, which implies [by equations (4) and (5)] that

$$W^n > W^l \cdot \left(\frac{\rho}{2}\right) + \left(\frac{1-\rho}{2}\right) \cdot w + \frac{1}{2}. \tag{12}$$

This condition is contained in figure 7.5. When W^n lies above the $\pi^l = \pi^n$ line, the lockout threat is operative; otherwise it is not.[21]

In this way, our model of wage determination is closed: Having shown how the union formulates its wage proposal in the presence and absence of a lockout threat, we find in equation (12) the condition under which this lockout threat becomes operative.

7.5 The Effectiveness of Fiscal Policies

We now examine the implications of our analysis above for the influence of fiscal policies on wage determination. The fiscal policies take the form of changes in the policy instruments enumerated in section 7.2.1: public employment (L_G), unemployment benefits (B), and the income tax rate (τ).

With respect to public employment, it is instructive to make a distinction regarding the security of job tenure that it provides. At one extreme is "permanent" public employment, where the available government jobs remain in the hands of an identifiable, invariant group of workers (viz., permanent tenure). At the other extreme is "rotating" employment, where the government jobs rotate randomly among the outsiders, so that each applicant has an equal chance of receiving such a job (viz., limited tenure). The realism of both extremes is open to question. In practice, current increases in government employment raise the employment chances of some, but not all, workers who are currently unemployed.

We are concerned with how the fiscal policies above affect the labor market directly, but not indirectly via other markets, such as the product market. The reason for this emphasis is that we intend to compare the impact of fiscal policies in the presence and absence of strikes and lockouts, and these forms of work disruption have their proximate influence on the labor market.

The effect of the fiscal policies on wages will be examined under our three different bargaining scenarios:

i. individualistic bargaining,

ii. union bargaining under combined strike and lockout threats, and

iii. union bargaining under strike threat alone.

i. *Individualistic bargaining*: Increases in unemployment benefit (B), the income tax rate (τ), and rotating government employment (L_G) all raise the entrants' reservation wage (R) for any given level of W_i. (However, an increase in permanent government employment does not affect the employment probability of the currently unemployed workers and thus leaves R unchanged, for any given W_i.) In terms of figure 7.1, these policies shift the R locus upward.[22] The W_i locus remains unchanged (since the policies do not directly affect the labor turnover costs). Thus, the equilibrium insider and entrant wages (W_i^* and R^*, respectively) both rise.

PROPOSITION 2   *Under individualistic bargaining (as described above), an increase in unemployment benefits (B), the income tax rate (τ) or rotating government employment (L_G) raises the insider wage (W).*

Here, *marginal productivity considerations* dominate wage determination: Insider wages are bid up to the point at which insiders are just profitable as entrants.

ii. *Union bargaining under combined strike and lockout threats*: Under these circumstances, *strike credibility considerations* dominate wage determination. As we have seen, a lockout threat is not made in our economy unless it succeeds in reducing the union's strike threat credibility and thereby reduces the insider wage. Here marginal productivity considerations lose their influence over wage determination: Even if it were possible to raise the wage without inducing firms to replace insiders with entrants (*ceteris paribus*), unions nevertheless do not do so in order to preserve the credibility of their strike threat.

Now, it is interesting to observe that the fiscal policies above *reduce* this credibility. The reason is that, by raising the individualistic wage (i.e., the wage achievable under individualistic bargaining), these policies improve the expected remuneration the insiders would receive in the event of losing a strike. Thus, the utility from observing the strike falls relative to the utility from breaking it. Recalling that the lockout threat is used only when the wage is credibility-reducing, it is clear that the unions can regain their lost strike-threat credibility by reducing their wage demands. In order to regain strike threat credibility, the unions must reduce their wage demands.

Let us see how this works concretely in our model.

By proposition 1, when the strike and lockout threats occur together, the credible-threat constraint is binding (i.e., $W = W_{CT}$) but the proposal-acceptance constraint is redundant (i.e., $W < W_{PA}$). This means that union members are on the margin of indifference between observing and breaking a strike, but they do not face the prospect of dismissal.

From inspection of the credible-threat constraint (9), it is evident that the only way in which increases in B and rotating L_G can affect the union wage proposal (W) is via the individualistic wage (W_i). Recall that W_i may be positively related to w, the wage received after a strike is lost or broken. Note that strike breakers are more likely to receive w than strike observers.[23]

An increase in B or rotating L_G raises W_i, which, in turn, raises the utility from breaking a strike by more than the utility from observing it. In this manner, the fiscal policies rob the strike threat of credibility. Since the union members were initially on the margin of indifference between observing and breaking a strike, after the fiscal policies have been implemented, the strike threat is no longer credible. By proposition 1, under combined strike and lockout threats, the wage proposal is credibility-reducing. Thus, the only way for the union to restore its strike threat credibility is by reducing its wage proposal (W). Thus, the credible-threat constraint shifts downward. As shown, given the strike fund payment under lockout (J^l), the wage proposal (W) falls.

An increase in the income tax rate (τ) has the same, dampening effect on W via W_i. In addition, it has a direct, negative impact on strike threat credibility [see equation (9)], leading to a further fall in W.

PROPOSITION 3   *Under unionized bargaining with combined strike and lockout threats (as described above), an increase in unemployment benefits (B), the income tax rate (τ), or rotating government employment (L_G) reduces the insider wage.*

These are startling results. Here the effect of the above fiscal policies on wages is the opposite of that under individualistic bargaining. The reason is that whereas these policies raise the proposal-acceptance wage (which is relevant to individualistic bargaining), they reduce the credible-threat wage (which is relevant to unionized bargaining under combined strike and lockout threats). Of course, it is well to remember that this chain of causation is merely one channel whereby fiscal policies may influence wage determination. Other channels, e.g., those identified in neoclassical and Keynesian macro models, may be operative as well.

iii. *Union bargaining under strike threat alone*: Now *both marginal productivity and strike credibility considerations* become relevant to wage determination.

The reason for this may be found in the fact that the union's decision concerning the number of potential strikers now plays a role in the union's wage proposal.[24] If a strike occurs, a rise in the number of precommitted strikers reduces expected profits as well as the strike fund payment (*ceteris paribus*). The lower the expected profits (viz., the higher the cost of the strike to the firm), the greater the wage that the firm is willing to pay. The lower the strike fund payments, the less credible is the strike, and (if the wage proposal is credibility-reducing) the lower the wage that the union can credibly demand. Here the union faces a trade-off. It will set the number of potential strikers so that the wage gain from threatened profit reduction is exactly offset by the wage loss from credibility reduction. In other words, marginal productivity and strike credibility considerations are weighted off against each other.

Concretely, as we have seen in section 7.4, the strike threat can occur in the absence of a lockout threat when the wage proposal is either credibility-reducing (as in figure 7.4a) or credibility-enhancing (as in figure 7.4b). In either event, the equilibrium insider wage (W^n) is given by the intersection of the proposal-acceptance constraint and the credible-threat constraint.

The fiscal policies above stimulate the individualistic wage and thereby they (a) reduce strike credibility and (b) reduce expected profit (by raising the reservation wage). The first effect lowers the union's wage demand; the second stimulates it. The overall fiscal policy impact on wages depends on which of these effects is dominant.

In particular, increases in B, τ, and rotating L_G all raise the individualistic insider wage (W_i^*, as shown in section 7.3.1). Consequently, they shift the proposal-acceptance constraint upward [by equation (10)]. If the wage proposal is credibility-reducing, the credible-threat constraint shifts downward; yet if the proposal is credibility-enhancing, this constraint shifts upward. In either case, the effect on the equilibrium insider wage (W^n) is ambiguous.

PROPOSITION 4   *Under unionized bargaining with strike threat but no lockout threat (as described above), an increase in unemployment benefits (B), the income tax rate (τ), or rotating government employment (L_G) has an ambiguous effect on the insider wage.*

The result is in line with our observations concerning the way in which marginal productivity and credibility considerations influence the effectiveness of fiscal policies. The two considerations pull the insider wage in

Bargaining scenario	Binding conditions on wage determination	Effect of expansionary fiscal policies
Individualistic	Marginal productivity conditions	Rise in wages
Combined strike and lockout	Strike credibility conditions	Fall in wages
Strike threat alone	Marginal productivity and strike credibility conditions	Ambiguous change in wages

Figure 7.6
The effect of fiscal policies on wage determination.

opposite directions; and since they are both operative when the strike threat occurs alone, the movement of the insider wage is ambiguous.

The results of all the policy exercises above are summarized in figure 7.6.

7.6 Concluding Remarks

The main thrust of this chapter lies in its contribution to the theory of union behavior. As noted, the theory thus far has been dominated by models in which the union sets the wage so as to maximize its utility function subject to a labor-demand constraint or a minimum-profit constraint. This literature overlooks the fact that the union's influence over the wage depends on (a) its ability to "punish" firms that do not accede to its wage demands (i.e., "union punch") and (b) its ability to fulfill its threats under the appropriate conditions (i.e., "union credibility"). This chapter has focused on the influence of union punch and credibility on wage formation. In this context, a rationale for strikes and lockout threats has been developed. We have indicated that when the costs and hiring and firing generate economic rent that workers can exploit through their wage demands, strike threats and lockout threats may be explained as rent-seeking devices.

As shown, the partial-equilibrium effects of fiscal policies are quite different depending on whether there is individualistic bargaining, unionized bargaining in the presence of strike and lockout threats, or unionized bargaining in the presence of strike threat alone. The case of individualistic bargaining generates conventional results. The unconventional results under unionized bargaining all stem from a single source: the union's formulation of wage proposals so as to preserve strike threat credibility.

Since the mainstream literature on fiscal policy and wage formation (both the perfect competition and the union models of the labour market—e.g., Dixon, 1986; Layard and Nickell, 1986) do not take the issue of strike threat credibility into account, it is not surprising that they get different results from ours.

It is worth emphasizing that the policy exercises above are concerned only with the direct effects of fiscal policies on the labor market (and not with the indirect effects operating through other markets). The reason for this focus of attention is that in this way the role of strike threats and lockout threats in wage formation can be brought into sharp relief. In other words, the main purpose of our fiscal policy exercises is to highlight the operation of our union model, rather than to serve as a foundation for policy recommendations.

Another word of warning regarding the practical applications of our analysis is vital as well. We have dealt with economies in which wages are determined entirely through individualistic bargaining, or entirely through unionized bargaining under strike and lockout threats, or entirely through such bargaining under strike threats alone. However, real-world economies comprise many sectors in which bargaining proceeds in different ways. In some sectors the bargaining is individualistic; in others it is unionized. In some instances (in West European countries rather than in the United States) employers make regular use of lockout threats; in others they do not. The macroeconomic effectiveness of fiscal policies in economies with such sectoral differences lies beyond the scope of this chapter. Moreover, our analysis has considered only a limited set of reasons for the strike and lockout threats. As noted, strike threats may be more than wage-preserving devices and lockout threats may be aimed at more than depleting unions' strike funds. Yet these other functions also lie beyond the chapter's scope. In view of these caveats, our analysis should be seen as only a first step in explaining strikes and lockout threats and in exploring the effectiveness of fiscal policies when unions play an active role in wage determination.

Appendix

The following are sufficient conditions for the absence of strikes for the Nash equilibrium.

Whenever the union's wage proposal exceeds a critical value—call it W^*—the firm rejects it (and thereby provokes a strike), and whenever the proposal lies beneath W^*, the firm accepts it. Given that the strike threat is credible, rejection of the proposal implies that the insider receives an expected income of $Y = J +$

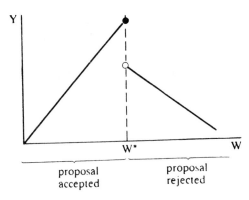

Figure 7A
The income-wage proposal relation.

$[\rho \cdot W + (1 - \rho) \cdot w]$. We assume that $\rho' < [1/(W - w)]$, so that $[\partial Y/\partial W] < 0$. In other words, whenever the firm rejects the wage proposal, the union has an incentive to reduce the proposed wage.

Let $Y^* = J + [\rho \cdot W^* + (1 - \rho) \cdot w]$. We assume that the levels of J, w, and ρ are such that $Y^* < W^*$. In other words, the maximum labor income under rejection of the wage proposal falls short of the maximum income under acceptance.

Under these circumstances, the union has an incentive to make a wage proposal that does not provoke a strike. The relation between the worker's expected income and the wage proposal is pictured in figure 7A.

Notes

1. To bring our comparative statics results of section 7.5 into sharp relief, we do not explicitly consider the government budget constraint. However, inclusion of this constraint would introduce no *conceptual* difficulties. We could think of a change in one government policy parameter to be financed through money or debt creation, whose feedback effects on the labor market could then in principle be considered. Alternatively, we could let a change in one parameter be matched by a counterveiling change in another parameter, and we could then amalgamate our comparative statics results accordingly.

2. Allowing the government to offer a different wage could not affect our conclusions, provided that the government wage is at least as large as the reservation wage, so that the government is able to attract the labor it requires.

3. Naturally, entrants may be expected to be less productive than insiders. A straightforward way of accounting for this in the production function would be to write $Q = \min[(L_I + \alpha \cdot L_E), K]$, where $0 < \alpha < 1$. In our analysis, however, we instead include the entrants' productivity shortfall $((1 - \alpha) \cdot L_E)$ in the costs of hiring and training.

4. These conditions are fullfilled in the solutions to a variety of bargaining models, both of the "sequential" and "axiomatic" varieties. (See, for example, the literature summarized in Sutton, 1986).

5. Of course, the lockout can serve other purposes as well, e.g., to enable the firm to avoid paying for labour services (of nonstrikers) that have become unprofitable.

6. This idea is related to the literature on "wars of attrition" (e.g., Fudenberg and Tirole, 1986). In our model, however, the players have perfect information about each other's costs, whereas in this literature they have imperfect information and each player grows increasingly pessimistic about his opponent's costs with the passage of time.

7. In the real world we often find that unions call out on strike only a fraction of the firm's workforce (e.g., workers in a limited number of occupations or a limited number of plants may be called out on strike). A potentially important reason for such behavior is (as suggested by our analysis below) that unions weigh the strike's harm to the firm against its harm to themselves through the depletion of strike funds.

8. We could equally well assume that the firm and the union have different subjective probabilities, so long as there is an inverse relation between each of these probabilities and the wage proposal W.

9. There are further bounds on w_L and w_B: They must be greater than or equal to the firm's profit-maximizing wage offer in the event that the union members lose or break their strike. It can be shown that this profit-maximizing offer satisfies the restrictions of g.

10. Recall that all insiders are alike. The union is assumed to pursue the same wage objectives as those of the individual insiders it represents, but—given its ability to threaten a strike—it can do so more effectively.

11. Note that the lockout threat is not the only conceivable response by the firm to the strike threat. Another is the threat of replacing all the strikers with new entrants. In practice, this replacement strategy is hardly ever followed. Presumably the reason is that the firing-hiring costs associated with this strategy are usually so high that lockouts, or no response at all, represent a smaller drain on firms' profits. President Reagan's replacement of air traffic controllers in 1982 is a rare exception. In this case, the availability of military personnel with the requisite skills meant that the associated firing-hiring costs were manageable. In the light of its rarity, we omit an analysis of the replacement strategy.

12. This simplifying assumption is not one of substance in the context of our analysis.

13. The firm (like the union) is assumed to have a zero rate of time discount. In stationary equilibrium, if the firm has an incentive to accept the wage proposal in the first period, then it will continue to do so in the second period. Thus, we need not consider the case of first-period acceptance and second-period rejection.

14. Observe that the union's decision regarding the proportion of strikers in the firm's workforce (a) is not relevant to the proposal-acceptance wage. Since the firm locks out all the nonstrikers, variations in the proportion of strikers have no effect on π^l.

15. Here we assume that the union members derive only a negligible proportion of their profit income from the firm for which they work or whose products they consume. In addition, they make the Nash equilibrium assumption that all other unions do not call strikes. Thus, their profit income is taken to be independent of their strike activity and equal to what they would earn in the absence of strikes.

16. The relative strength of these influences depends (among other things) on the magnitude of ρ' and g_1. The smaller ρ' (i.e., the stronger the impact of W_{CT}^l on ρ), the more U^S falls relative to U^b and the less credible the strike. The greater g_1 (i.e., the stronger the impact of W on w), the more U^b rises relative to U^S (since there is a greater chance of receiving w when the strike is broken than when it is observed) and the more credible the strike.

17. Note that if the credible-threat constraint is flatter than the proposal-acceptance constraint, the maximum wage is attained at $J = 0$. This is not an interesting case, and thus we do not pursue it. If there are multiple intersections between the two constraints, the union chooses either the one associated with the highest wage (whether the credible-threat constraint is steeper than the proposal-acceptance constraint at $J = 0$) or the one associated with $J = 0$. As indicated by the analysis below, these possibilities make no difference to our qualitative conclusions.

18. In particular, the former firm earns no current profit, while the latter generates some through the nonstrikers.

19. Recall that the union sets its first-period wage claim in (rational) anticipation of the size of J that it may receive in the second period. This is the way in which a change in J can affect W.

20. If $a = 1$, then the firm's profit is the same regardless of whether all its employees strike or whether some strike and the rest are locked out. Thus, the proposal-acceptance wage must be the same in both cases as well. Moreover, at $a = 1$, the strike fund payment J reaches its minimum level, J^l. Accordingly, in Figure 7.5 the proposal-acceptance constraints W_{PA}^l and W_{PA}^n meet at $J = J^l$.

21. As figure 7.5 happens to be drawn, W^n is above the $\pi^l = \pi^n$ line and thus the threats of strike and lockout occur together. In this case, the credible-threat constraint (W_{CT}) is binding and, given the strike fund payment J^l, the insider wage is $\hat{W}^l$. On the other hand, had the $\pi^l = \pi^n$ line passed above the intersection of the constraints W_{CT} and W_{PA}, then there would have been no lockout and therefore the insider wage would have been $\hat{W}^n$.

22. Recall that the government offers employment at the insider wage (W). An increase in rotating government employment shifts the R locus upward, since outsiders now face an increased probability of employment ($\theta = [L_G/(L_F + L_G)]$,

where L_F is total employment by firms). The R locus under rotating government employment is defined as follows:

$$U[(R + \sigma \cdot \pi) \cdot (1 - \tau), 1] + U[(W + \sigma \cdot \pi) \cdot (1 - \tau), 1]$$

$$= 2 \cdot \theta \cdot U[(W + \sigma \cdot \pi) \cdot (1 - \tau), 1] + 2 \cdot (1 - \theta) \cdot U[(B + \sigma \cdot \pi) \cdot (1 - \tau), 0].$$

23. Workers who break a strike receive w in both periods, whereas workers who observe a strike receive w only in the second period and only if the strike is lost.

24. By contrast, in the case of union bargaining under combined strike and lockout threats, this decision is irrelevant to wage determinations. No matter how many workers are called out on strike, the firm locks out the rest. Thus, variations in the number of potential strikers make no difference to the firm's expected profits or the union's strike fund payments, in the event of a strike.

8 Wage Rigidity, Union Activity, and Unemployment

Overview

This chapter, like the previous one, examines the way in which union strike threats affect labor market activity. However, we examine here a different rationale for strike threats. In addition, we also rationalize work-to-rule threats. Our analysis shows why insiders have an incentive to join unions that pose such threats and how these threats affect wages and unemployment.

In the previous chapter, the strike threat functioned as a "wage-preserving device," since we assumed that the strike was triggered by the firm's refusal to accept the union's wage demand. Moreover, once the strike was called, the firm made the decision whether to retain or lock out the remaining union members. In this context, the strike threat may be seen as an instrument to boost the union wage; the strike makes rejection of the union's wage proposal costly to the firm. The greater the profit forgone as result of the strike, the greater the maximum wage that the firm will accept.

In this chapter, we portray the strike threat as a "job preserving device," since we now assume that the strike is triggered by the firm's decision to fire union members in response to the union's wage claim. Furthermore, we assume that once the strike has been called, the firm makes the decision whether to hold the strikers' positions vacant or whether to replace the strikers by entrants. Here the strike threat is an instrument for providing job security, in the sense that the strike makes replacement of insiders by outsiders costly to the firm. The greater this cost, the fewer insiders will be replaced at any given wage.

Of course, this strike threat—like the one in the previous chapter—also serves to boost the wage, since the greater the union members' job security, the higher the wage the union will set. However, this channel of wage determination is different from that in the previous chapter, and thus the effect of the strike threat on the wage is different as well.

As we can see, a crucial difference between the sequence of decisions in this chapter and in the previous chapter lies in the firm's response to the union's wage decision. The difference concerns the way in which the responsibility for setting wages is divided between the firm and the union. The determinants of this division of responsibility have remained relatively unexplored in labor economics literature. Clearly, the division must depend on the relative market power of the union and the firm: If the union's monopoly power in the labor market is significantly larger than the firm's monopsony power, then the union will dominate the wage-setting process. Yet if the firm and union have comparable strength, then the firm may have more discretion in accepting or rejecting the union's wage proposal (as described in the previous chapter).

The previous chapter focused on the firm's direct input into the wage-setting process, whereas this chapter is concerned with the indirect influence the firm exerts on the wage through its employment decisions. Both effects are often encountered in practice: Firms usually have a significant say over the wages they pay, and, in addition, they are usually able to respond to wage negotiations by adjusting employment.

Both this chapter and the previous one suggest a simple reason why unions may come into existence: By permitting workers to coordinate the conditions under which they are available for work, unions may raise firms' labor turnover costs and thereby raise union members' expected income. This may happen because an increase in firms' turnover costs may enable enable workers to achieve either higher wages (as shown in chapter 7) or more job security at any given wage (as shown in this chapter) than they could have achieved individualistically. In either event, our analysis suggests that the exercise of union power may give rise to involuntary unemployment.

8.1 Introduction

Economists tend to approach the phenomenon of wage rigidity from two distinct perspectives. The first focuses on the variability of real wages relative to some other economic variable. For example, it has often been noted that real wages fluctuate less than employment over cyclical swings in macroeconomic activity. The second is concerned with the failure of real wages to clear the labor market. Here the underlying presumption is that "flexible" wages could bring labor demand and supply into equality, and thus the presence of involuntary unemployment becomes evidence of wage "rigidity."

Clearly the two perspectives bear no logical relation to one another. It is conceivable that real wages may fluctuate widely through time, but that involuntary unemployment nevertheless exists. Conversely there may be full employment while real wages remain constant. Although a number of unemployment theories incorporate both wage nonvariability and involuntary unemployment, it is nevertheless important to opt for either one or the other perspective in an analysis of wage rigidity.

This chapter concentrates exclusively on the second perspective, arguing that wage rigidity—of the sort mirrored in the existence of involuntary unemployment—may be rationalized in terms of the conflict of interest between established employees (the "insiders") and the unemployed workers (the "outsiders"). This approach also enables us to gain some basic insights into the macroeconomic role of labor unions.

The chapter is organized as follows. Section 8.2 tells the intuitive story underlying this version of the insider-outsider theory. Section 8.3 describes the macroeconomic equilibrium with wage rigidity when employees bargain individualistically over wages with their employers. Section 8.4 examines what happens to this macroeconomic equilibrium when insiders form unions and pose strike threats. Section 8.5 analyzes threats of work-to-rule, and section 8.6 is the epilogue.

8.2 The Underlying Story

In this chapter, as in chapter 3, we concentrate on the explicit costs of hiring, training, and firing. These costs generate economic rent, which may be divided between firms and their employees. In particular, the rent from the employment of insiders vis-à-vis entrants arises from the training and some firing costs. It may be measured by the difference between the maximum wage that the firm would be willing to pay its insiders (before finding it worthwhile to replace them with entrants) and the entrant wage. Similarly the rent from the employment of entrants arises from the hiring and some firing costs. We assume that all the turnover costs are firm-specific.

We assume that wages are determined through a bargaining process between each firm and its employees, whereas the employment decisions are made unilaterally by the firms. Each entrant goes through an "initiation period," whereupon he generates as much rent as an insider *and* his wage contract may be renegotiated. In effect, the entrants *becomes* an insider after this time period.

Moreover, we assume that insiders are able to capture at least some of their respective rent in the wage-bargaining process. Thus the insiders have an inherent advantage over the entrants. They can raise their wage (W_I) above the entrant wage (W_E); but so long as the $W_I - W_E$ differential does not exceed the rent of insiders vis-à-vis entrants, the firms have no incentive to replace the insiders by entrants.

Moreover, entrants may have access to economic rent as well. The reason is that once a worker has been hired, his position may become associated with "rent-related labor turnover costs" (described in chapter 4). For example, he may have the opportunity to engage in litigation if fired (thereby generating a firing cost of the sort analyzed in chapter 3), or he may have the ability to withhold "cooperation" from or to "harass" other workers (thereby creating cooperation and harassment differentials as described in chapter 5). The entrants may be able to capture some of the rent inherent in such turnover costs by driving the entrant wage above the reservation wage of the outsiders. Consequently, the outsiders would be willing to work at less than the entrant wage, but—on account of the rent-related turnover costs—the firms have no incentive to permit underbidding. Under these circumstance, the unemployment is involuntary.

Moreover, even if entrants have no market power, involuntary unemployment may nevertheless arise if workers have limited access to credit. The reason is straightforward. Since insiders are assumed to have more market power than entrants and since wages are renegotiated regularly, it follows that the insider wage exceeds the entrant wage. Given that entrants anticipate that they will become insiders in the future, their reservation wage must be inversely related to the insider wage. In fact, the greater the present value of insider wages that an entrant expects to receive, the lower his reservation wage will be. If the insider wage is sufficiently high, the entrants' reservation wage will be a negative number. However, if entrants are credit rationed (for the standard moral hazard and adverse selection reasons), then they might not be able to borrow enough to achieve their reservation wage. In that event, the entrants capture some economic rent even when they have no market power, and, as result, the outsiders are involuntarily unemployed.

Finally, as we have argued in chapter 4, involuntary unemployment can arise if insider wages reflect rent-related turnover costs and the difference between the insider wage and the outsider reservation wage exceeds the corresponding productivity differential. Then the outsiders unsuccessfully seek work at wages that would more than compensate the firm for their lower productivity vis-à-vis the insiders, but the firms would be unwilling to replace their insiders by outsiders on account of the rent-related turn-over costs. (See the discussion on pp. 8 and 73.)

Labor unions enter this picture in a simple way. Not only can unions strengthen insiders' bargaining power, not only can they amplify the costs of replacing an insider by an outsider, but they can also give the insiders an additional, potent set of rent-creating tools, such as the strike and work-to-rule. Thereby the unions may enable insiders to achieve much higher wages than they could have achieved in isolation.

But that is not all. Unions' wage demands depend not only on how much damage they are potentially able to inflict on firms ("union punch") but also on the "credibility" of their threats. A union that threatens to strike must be able to induce its members to observe the strike once it has been called. Union credibility depends on quite different things from union punch. For example, a rise in personal income-tax rates may reduce union credibility by reducing the return to a successful strike but have no effect on union punch. On the other hand, a rise in firms' payroll tax rates may increase the punch by amplifying the wage-cost increase but leave the credibility unchanged.

8.3 The Behavior of Individualistic Agents and the Macroeconomic Equilibrium

The economy is composed of firms, households, and a government. There are three goods: a consumption good, labor, and another factor of produc-tion—say, "capital." The firms produce the consumption good by means of capital (which they own) and labor. The households buy the consump-tion good and may provide labor services to the firms. These are the flows of purchases.

The expenditure flows are straightforward. The firms use their revenues to remunerate labor and distribute what is left over to the households. The households use their nonwage incomes and their wage incomes (if they are employed) or their unemployment benefits (if they are unemployed) to make consumption purchases from the firms and pay taxes to the govern-ment. The government collects taxes from the households in order to pay unemployment benefits. The reason for giving the government such a limited role in the model is that we are not going to analyze the effects of government policy in this chapter (in contrast to chapter 7, where a wide variety of government policy actions are investigated).

As noted, the firms make the hiring and firing decisions, and wages are set through bargaining between each firm and its employees. The time span involved in formulating and implementing the wage and employment decisions is assumed to be exogenously given and identical for all workers and firms. It corresponds to the time period of our analysis.

For simplicity, we consider only the behavior of economic agents under *stationary Nash equilibrium* conditions. In the context of our analysis, this means that (a) firms' investment outlays are zero, (b) firms' employment decisions are made under the assumption that wages are at optimal levels for the workers, and (c) workers' wage-setting decisions are made under the assumption that employment is optimal for the firms.

8.3.1 The Firms

The output of each firm is Q. K is its capital input. Two types of labor are available to the firm: entrant-labor, L_E, and insider-labor, L_I (both measured in terms of numbers of people). There is no retirement from or entry into the labor force during the period of analysis. For simplicity, we make the following assumption about the firm's factor availability and technologies:

A1 *The firm's supply of capital is fixed:*

$K = \bar{K},$

where $\bar{K}$ is a positive constant. The firm's current supply of insiders (L_I) is also fixed; yet it can obtain as many entrants (L_E) as it requires.

The firm does not have a deficient supply of entrants, because (as shown later) wages may be set so as to generate involuntary unemployment.

A2 *Insiders and entrants use the same amount of capital per head, but insiders are more productive than entrants:*

$$Q = \alpha \cdot L_E + L_I,$$
$$L_E + L_I = v \cdot K,$$

(1)

where the productivity of insiders is normalized to unity and the productivity of entrants is α;

$0 < \alpha < 1.$

(This depiction of technologies is particularly convenient since we aim to show how the behavior of insiders can give rise to involuntary unemployment quite independently of their influence on entrants' productivity and firms' capital-labor substitution.)

All insiders of the firm receive the same real wage (W_I) (see proposition 2 below) and all entrants receive the same real wage (W_E) as well. The firm's cost of hiring L'_E entrants is $H(L'_E)$ and its cost of firing L'_I insiders is $F(L'_I)$, where $H(0) = F(0) = 0$ and H', $F' > 0$. The firm seeks to maximize its cash flow, $CF = Q - [W_E \cdot L_E + W_I L_I] - H(L'_E)$ (i.e., its revenue minus its variable costs), where $L_E = L'_E$ (since all workers hired in the current time period remain entrants only during this time period) and $L_I \leqslant \bar{L}_I$. Since the firm's capital supply is fixed, this is equivalent to profit maximization.)

In equilibrium, no firing or hiring takes place and only insiders are employed, since insiders do not find it worthwhile to post wages that are sufficiently high to occasion their dismissal, nor do they retire voluntarily from their jobs. Under these circumstances, the firm's maximization problem (for a single time period) becomes

Maximize $CF = Q - W_I \cdot L_I$

subject to $L_I \geqslant Q,$ $v \cdot \bar{K} \geqslant Q.$

(2)

Whenever $(1 - W_I) > 0$, the firm has a positive cash flow, and thus its insider employment will be $L_I = v \cdot \bar{K} = \bar{L}$. On the other hand, if $(1 - W_I) < 0$, then $L_I = 0$.

8.3.2 The Workers

Each worker maximizes his utility subject to a budget constraint. His utility is a function of his consumption, C, and his labor, l. For simplicity, we make the following assumptions about the worker's decision-making:

A3 *For each worker, work (measured in units of time) is an on-off activity. When $l = 0$, he is unemployed; when $l = 1$, he has a full-time job. There is no part-time employment. No worker can work more than $l = 1$.*

A4 *Each worker's utility function may be expressed as $U = U(C, l)$, where $U_C > 0$ and $U_l < 0$. Utility is maximized over a single-period time horizon. All workers have identical preferences.*

A5 *Each worker's nonwage income is A, which is exogenous to his decision-making. An unemployed worker receives an unemployment benefit of B, which is also exogenous. All employed workers face a constant income tax rate of τ.*

A6 *Insiders capture all the available bilateral monopoly power.*

The last-mentioned assumption means that insiders are wage-setters. It is made for expositional simplicity only. The basic argument of this chapter requires only that insiders capture some of the bilateral monopoly power, and that the higher the maximum wage achievable by doing so, the higher the actual wage achieved.

A7 *There is perfect competition among the outsiders in the labor market.*

This assumption is natural enough in an economy characterized by involuntary unemployment.

In addition, we make a further assumption, which will be modified in sections 8.3 and 8.4 (where union activity is introduced):

A8 *In setting his wage, each insider behaves individualistically. In particular, his wage demands are not related to the firing or hiring of other workers.*

Since the unemployed are perfect competitors, they offer to work at their reservation wage, R. This is defined as the wage at which workers are indifferent between employment ($l = 1$) and unemployment ($l = 0$):

$$U\{R \cdot (1 - \tau) + A, 1\} = U\{B + A, 0\}, \tag{3}$$

where U is a household's utility and the time horizon covers one period.

We assume that the entrant wage (W_E) is set as a fixed markup over R, the size of the markup depending on entrants' borrowing constraints and the rent of entrants vis-à-vis outsiders.

Each insider sets his wage so as to maximize his utility. This means that the wage is set as high as possible subject to two constraints.

i. *the zero-cash-flow constraint*: the wage must not be so high that the firm achieves a negative cash flow (and consequently closes its operations), and

ii. *the firing-hiring constraint*: the wage must not be so high that it is in the firm's best interest to fire the insider and hire an outsider (at wage R) instead.

Let W_{ZC} and W_{FH} be the wages corresponding to these two constraints, respectively.

From the firm's maximization problem (2), it is apparent that in equilibrium

$$W_{ZC} = 1. \tag{4}$$

Furthermore, W_{FH} is the wage at which the cash flow generated by an insider ($1 - W_{FH}$) is equal to that generated by firing the insider and hiring an entrant $(\alpha - W_E - F(1) - H(1))$. Consequently

$$W_{FH} = W_E + [(1 - \alpha) + F(1) + H(1)]. \tag{5}$$

This condition indicates that the "wage spread" $(W_{FH} - W_E)$ is equal to the "productivity spread" $(1 - \alpha)$ plus the firing-hiring cost per worker $(F(1) + H(1))$.

Thus, the wage that the insider actually demands is

$$W_I = \min(W_{ZC}, W_{FH}). \tag{6}$$

$W_I = W_{FH}$ is the case with which this chapter is primarily concerned. It is interesting to note that here all three determinants of W_{FH}—the reservation wage, the productivity spread, and the firing-hiring costs—may be influenced by the insiders.

First, as shown in chapter 5, by being unfriendly to entrants, insiders are able to make the entrants' work more unpleasant than it otherwise would have been and thereby raise the wage at which the latter are willing to work. In practice, outsiders are commonly wary of underbidding the insiders. This behavior pattern is often given an ad hoc sociological explanation: "Social mores" keep outsiders from "stealing" the jobs from their employed comrades. Our line of argument, however, suggests that these mores may be traced to the entrants' anticipation of hostile insider reaction and that this reaction may follow from optimization behavior of insiders.

Second, insiders are usually responsible for training the entrants and thereby influence their productivity. Thus insiders may be able to raise their wage demands by threatening to conduct the firm's training programs inefficiently or even to disrupt them.

Observe that if $W_I = W_{FH}$, then not only do insiders generate a non-negative cash flow (i.e., $W_I \leq W_{ZC}$), but entrants do so as well: $\alpha - W_E > 0$. This implies a positive lower bound on the productivity of entrants. Unless this lower bound is exceeded, the entrants would be unable to compete with the insiders, and the insiders, knowing this, would raise their wage until the firm's profit were reduced to zero.

For this reason, firms have an incentive to supervise the training of entrants and ensure that workers are productive during their training period. In practice, firms may undertake on-the-job training (rather than job-unrelated training), not only because this type of training may be the most effective way of raising an entrants' productivity and because (in the case of firm-specific training) it reduces entrants' incentive to switch to other firms, but also to dampen the wage demands of the insiders.

Third, insiders are commonly able to affect their potential firing and hiring costs. Threatening litigation and insisting on lengthy and expensive firing and hiring procedures are ways of doing this.

In sum, to raise his wage, an insider may find it worthwhile to threaten to become a thoroughly disagreeable creature, as summarized in the following proposition:

PROPOSITION 1 *Under the assumptions above, whenever a firm has a positive cash flow, each of its insiders has an atomistic incentive to be maximally uncooperative toward entrants, to provide minimal training, and to make the process of firing and hiring as costly as possible.*

Moreover, our model of wage setting suggests an explanation for a commonly observed labor market phenomenon:

PROPOSITION 2 *If insiders behave atomistically (assumption A8) and firms differ with regard to their firing-hiring costs or their insider-entrant productivity differentials, then while there is equal pay for equal work within each firm (with positive cash flow), this is not so across such firms.*

An economy populated by the agents above may get stuck in a macroeconomic equilibrium with involuntary unemployment. If firms have positive cash flows, then the insider wage exceeds the entrant wage, which, in turn, exceeds the outsider reservation wage. Consequently the outsiders prefer employment to unemployment. Moreover, as indicated in section 8.2, the wage differentials W_I-W_E and W_I-R may exceed the associated productivity differentials on account of credit rationing or worker market power based on dispensable labor costs. In that event, the unemployment may be classified as involuntary. It is also persistent since, no matter what wage the outsiders offer to work for, they are either unable to gain job offers (for offers in excess of R) or have no incentive to accept these offers (for offers less than R).

PROPOSITION 3 *For an economy with agents described above, wages may be set so as to generate persistent involuntary unemployment.*

8.4 Union Activity: The Threat of Strike

Let "union activity" refer to any activity that workers perform in unison in order to achieve an outcome that they could not have achieved individually. Within the microeconomic context oulined above, we rationalize this form of cooperative behavior by showing that insiders, acting together, can each achieve a higher wage than they could have done on their own.

Ways of doing this can be inferred from section 8.3. With regard to firms with positive cash flows, unions may be able to stimulate insiders' wages relative to the wage achievable atomistically by (i) raising the entrant wage (through threats of organised harassment of entrants), (ii) diminishing entrant productivity (through organized training disruption), (iii) capturing a greater share of the economic rent (provided that they do not capture it all when bargaining atomistically), and (iv) raising the firms' firing-hiring costs. As the first three rationales are rather obvious, let us concentrate on the last one, which may be pursued by two very common union threats: the threat to strike and the threat to work-to-rule.

Our explanations for both threats have a single root: Both serve to make the productivity of insiders dependent on the firms' hiring and firing decisions and thereby make the hiring-firing process more expensive for firms than when workers behave atomistically. Clearly, this can be done only if employees collude—and that, in short, is this chapter's approach to unionization.

In order for the threat to operate in this manner, two conditions must be fulfilled:

A9 *All firms have positive cash flow (i.e., their zero-cash-flow constraints are not binding:* $W_I < W_{ZC}$).

(Whenever a firm's zero-cash-flow constraint is binding, changes in firing-hiring costs have no effect on the insider wage.)

A10 *The marginal firing and hiring costs (i.e., F' and H') are increasing functions of the number of workers fired and hired (i.e., F'', $H'' > 0$).*

Assumption A10 is not at variance with the occasional observation that, for firms with large personnel departments, firing and hiring costs per worker may fall with the number of workers fired and hired, over a particular range of workers. Clearly, falling average costs of firing and hiring are consistent with increasing marginal costs.

Provided that the revenues and costs of different firms are mutually independent, unions issuing strike and work-to-rule threats in our model will be firm-specific.

Workers have no incentive in our model to form unions covering more than one firm as long as firms act atomistically. Yet this incentive may arise in reaction to the organization of *employers*, in response to the organization of employees within individual firms. Indeed, this is commonly the order in which employees and employers have become organized in practice: Firm-specific unions have been followed by employers' associations, which, in turn, have been followed by industry-wide or even economy-wide unions.

This section is devoted to the *threat of strike*; the next is concerned with the threat of work-to-rule.

Let the threat of strike be interpreted as the following implicit contract that the union imposes on the firm:

Contract C1 If a firm retains all its union members, then none of them go on strike; yet if any of them are fired, then some (possibly all) of the remaining ones strike.

Incorporating this union activity in the theoretical frame work of section 8.3 broadens our analysis in three ways: (i) it raises the number of control variables in the hands of both the firm and the workers, (ii) it makes the analysis inherently intertemporal, and (iii) it requires an explicit representation of the firm's and its workers' behavior under uncertainty. These complications are not expendable baggage; they lie at the heart of the strike threat above.

In the model of section 8.3, the firm and its workers each have one control variable: The firm decides whether to replace insiders and the insiders set their wages. Under contract C1, by contrast, the interaction between workers and their firm may be viewed as a sequence of events pictured in figure 8.1. First, workers set their wages (decision W1). We

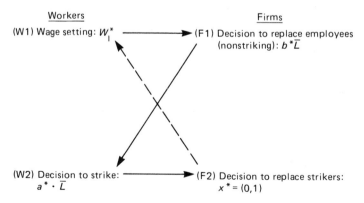

Figure 8.1
The sequence of wage-setting, strike, and employment decisions: W^* = the utility-maximizing wage; a^* = the utility-maximizing proportion of a firm's labor force that is on strike (given that the firm has replaced nonstrikers); b^* = the profit-maximizing proportion of a firm's labor force that is replaced; x^* = the profit-maximizing decision to replace $(x = 0)$ or retain $(x = 1)$ the strikers in a firm.

assume that all the members of a union demand the same wage. Second, in response, the firm decides whether to replace (nonstriking) insiders (decision F1). Third, if workers have indeed been replaced, the remaining insiders decide whether to strike (decision W2). Fourth, the firm decides whether to replace the strikers (decision F2).[1] Then, given (F1) and (F2), workers reset their wages and the process begins anew.

We study the Nash equilibrium of this process. In other words, the firm's employment decisions (with regard to strikers and nonstrikers) are exogenously given to the workers, and the workers' wage and strike decisions are exogenously given to the firm. At the equilibrium, the workers take into account employment decisions that maximize the firm's profits, and the firm takes into account wage and strike decisions that maximize the workers' utilities.

A union's strike activity and a firm's response to it are inherently intertemporal. Union members strike now in order to achieve something in the future. A firm's employment decisions are also forward-looking. Once the firm has precipitated a strike by firing some of its employees, there are three possible outcomes (in any given time period): (1) the union members win the strike, in which case all those who have been fired are rehired (at the insider wage); (2) the firm wins, in which case the fired workers irrevocably lose claim to their original jobs; and (3) the strike continues. Since the essence of the labor conflict can be captured in the context of two periods, let us assume that the workers and their firm have a two-period time horizon.

It lies in the nature of strike activity that its outcome is uncertain. A strike occurs only if the affected parties do not know how it will end. Thus, their subjective probabilities with regard to the possible outcomes become relevant to their strategies.

Let us now consider each of the decisions by the workers and their firm in turn. It is convenient to study these decisions in the reverse order from that which appears in figure 8.1.

8.4.1 Decision F2

Let δ^F be the firm's rate of time discount, ρ_ω^F its perceived probability that the workers will win the strike, and ρ_l^F its perceived probability that they will lose it. Assume that the firm is risk neutral and seeks to maximize the present value of its expected cash flow over two time periods.

If the firm decides to *hold all the strikers' positions vacant* (F2: $x = 1$), then this cash flow may be expressed as follows:

$$CF_{x=1} = \underbrace{[\alpha - W_E] \cdot b \cdot \overline{L} - H(b \cdot \overline{L}) - F(b \cdot \overline{L})}$$

first-period cash flow generated by the
entrants (net of firing-hiring costs)

$$+ \underbrace{(1 - a - b) \cdot \overline{L} \cdot [1 - W_I \cdot (1 + \delta^F)}$$

cash flow generated by the
nonstriking insiders

$$+ \underbrace{\delta^F \cdot \rho_\omega^F \cdot \{(1 - W_I) \cdot (a + b) \cdot \overline{L} - F(b \cdot \overline{L})\}}$$

additional second-period cash flow generated
if the strikers win

$$+ \underbrace{\delta^F \cdot \rho_l^F \cdot \{(1 - W_E) \cdot (a + b) \cdot \overline{L}\}}$$

additional second-period cash flow
generated if the strikers lose

$$+ \underbrace{\delta^F \cdot (1 - \rho_\omega^F - \rho_l^F) \cdot \{(1 - W_I) \cdot b \cdot \overline{L}\}}$$

additional second-period cash flow
generated if the strike continues

$$= (\alpha - W_E) \cdot b \cdot \overline{L} - (1 + \delta^F \cdot \rho_\omega^F) \cdot F(b \cdot \overline{L}) - H(b \cdot \overline{L})$$
$$+ (1 - W_I) \cdot \{\overline{L} \cdot (1 + \delta^F) - b \cdot \overline{L} - \alpha\overline{L} \cdot [1 + \delta^F \cdot (1 - \rho_\omega^F - \rho_l^F)]\}.$$

(7)

On the other hand, if the firm decides *to replace all the strikers* (F2: $x = 0$),
then $(a + b) \cdot \overline{L}$ workers enter the firm in the first time period, and, in the
second time period, these workers are fired if the strikers win or turn into
insiders otherwise. It can then be shown that the present value of the firm's
expected case flow is

$$CF_{x=0} = (\alpha - W_E) \cdot (a + b) \cdot \overline{L} - (1 + \delta^F \cdot \rho_\omega^F) \cdot F[(a + b) \cdot \overline{L}]$$
$$- H[(a + b) \cdot \overline{L}] + (1 - W_I) \cdot \overline{L} \cdot [1 - (a + b) \cdot (1 - \delta^F)].$$ (8)

A comparison of equations (7) and (8) leads to an interesting result: In
the Nash equilibrium, the decision (F2: $x = 0$)—to replace all strikers—is
never effective. The reason is that if the firm decides to replace its strikers,
it thereby makes the contract C1 ineffective: The workers lose their incentive to strike and the firm has no strikers to replace.

PROPOSITION 4 *With regard to the equilibrium (of the process summarized in
figure 8.1), if it is in the firm's best interests to replace all the strikers, then the*

workers have no incentive to use the strike threat in order to augment their wage demands.

To see why this is so, it is necessary to examine all the equilibrium decisions of the workers and their firm, given that the firm replaces all the strikers (and thus achieves a cash flow of $CF_{x=0}$).

In the first round of the strategic process of figure 8.1, the insiders begin by setting the wage in accordance with the firing-hiring constraint, given that $b = a = x = 0$. This constraint is not the same as that of section 8.3. Rather, it must be redefined to take into account the four instruments of workers and their firm, the two-period time horizon, and the uncertainty involved in posing the strike threat. At this constraint, the firm is indifferent between retaining all its insiders (who generate a cash flow of $[1 - W] \cdot (1 + \delta^F) \cdot \bar{L}$) and firing the optimal number of nonstriking employees ($b^* \cdot \bar{L}$) (given that all the strikers are replaced):

$$[1 - W_I] \cdot (1 + \delta^F) \cdot \bar{L} - CF_{x=0}(W_{FH}, b^*)$$

$$= [\alpha - W_E] \cdot (a + b^*) \cdot \bar{L} - (1 + \delta^F \cdot \rho^F_\omega) \cdot F[(a + b^*) \cdot \bar{L}]$$

$$\quad - H[(a + b^*) \cdot \bar{L}] - [1 - W_I] \cdot \bar{L} \cdot [(a + b^*)$$

$$\quad + \delta^F \cdot (1 - a - b^*)]$$

$$= 0, \tag{9}$$

where a and b are set equal to zero.

Then the firm finds the cash-flow maximizing number of nonstriking employees to be replaced (b^*):

$$\frac{\partial CF_{x=0}}{\partial b} = [\alpha - W_E] \cdot \bar{L} - [1 - W_I] \cdot \bar{L} \cdot (1 - \delta^F)$$

$$\quad - (1 + \delta^F \cdot \rho^F_\omega) \cdot F'[(a + b^*) \cdot \bar{L}] \cdot \bar{L} - H'[(a + b^*) \cdot \bar{L}] \cdot \bar{L} = 0,$$

for any values of W and a, determined by the workers. The second-order condition for optimality is satisfied if F'', $H'' > 0$, in accord with assumption A10.

In response, the insiders determine the wage-maximizing number of strikers (i.e., $a^* \cdot \bar{L}$); they do this by maximizing $CF_{x=0}$ with respect to a (because the greater the value of their firm's cash flow—given its decision to replace all strikers ($x = 0$)—the greater the value of their wage).

However [as equation (8) indicates], a marginal increase in the number of nonstrikers replaced ($b^* \cdot \bar{L}$) affects the firm's cash flow ($CF_{x=0}$) in the same way as a marginal increase in the number of strikers ($a^* \cdot \bar{L}$). Regardless of whether a marginal insider is fired or goes on strike, he is replaced by an entrant in the first period (and the associated firing-hiring costs are expended); in the second period, he is rehired if the strikers win, irrevocably loses his job if the strikers lose, and remains on strike if the strike continues.

Since the firm has already maximized its cash flow $CF_{x=0}$ with respect to b, a marginal increase in the number of nonstrikers replaced has no effect on this cash flow $(dCF_{x=0}(b^*)/da) = 0$, and consequently a marginal increase in the number of strikers (above zero, which is the initial level) leaves this cash flow unaffected as well. Thus, the remaining insiders choose not to go on strike.

In the second round of the strategic process, the insiders once again set the wage according to the firing-hiring constraint, but now given that $b = b^*$ and $a = x = 0$. Given this wage, the firm once again finds the cash-flow-maximizing number of nonstrikers to be replaced, and in this manner the process continues.

Note that in each successive round, insiders have no incentive to strike. Thus, they must lack this incentive at the Nash equilibrium—hence proposition 4.

Since the strike threat is not used when the firm replaces all the strikers, it is not necessary to consider this case further. Instead, we can restrict our attention to the case in which it is in the firm's best interests not to replace all the strikers (i.e., $x = 1$).

In this case, of course, the marginal effect on the cash flow ($CF_{x=1}$) of replacing nonstrikers ($b^* \cdot \bar{L}$) is not the same as the marginal effect of going on strike ($a^* \cdot \bar{L}$). This is spelled out by equation (7). When a nonstriker is replaced in the first period, an entrant takes his place; and this entrant is fired if the strikers win, but retains his job if the strikers lose or if the strike continues. On the other hand, when an insider goes on strike in the first period, no one takes his place, and thus no one is fired if the strikers lose and no one does the insider's work if the strike continues. Due to this distinction between the effect of striking and firing nonstrikers, insiders may have an incentive to strike (and thereby augment their wage) even after the firm has replaced a cash-flow-maximizing number of nonstrikers.

8.4.2 Decision F1

Given that the firm decides to retain the strikers ($x = 1$), there remains only one decision variable for the firm to set: b. The firm decides on how many of its nonstriking employees to replace by maximizing its cash flow, $CF_{x=1}$,

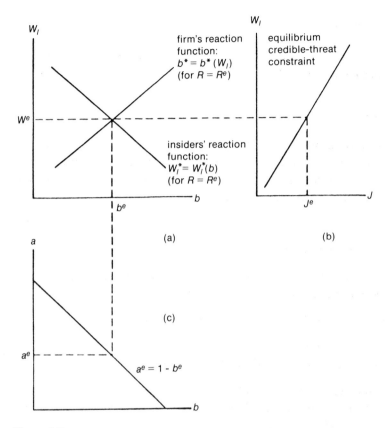

Figure 8.2
The Nash equilibrium under threat of strike.

with respect to b (for an exogenously given values of W_I and W_E):

$$\frac{\partial CF_{x=1}}{\partial b} = [(W_I - W_E) - (1 - \alpha)] \cdot \bar{L}$$

$$- H'(b^* \cdot \bar{L}) \cdot \bar{L} - (1 + \delta^F \cdot \rho_\omega^F) \cdot F'(b^* \cdot \bar{L}) \cdot \bar{L} = 0. \tag{10}$$

This equation is illustrated by the *firm's reaction function* $b^* = b^*(W_I)$ (which can be shown to have an unambiguously positive slope) in figure 8.2a.[2]

The fact that b^* may be positive in the Nash equilibrium does not mean that nonstriking insiders will actually be fired. In fact, the insiders set their wage so as to prevent this from happening. All that $b^* > 0$ implies is that *if* the firm were to fire any of its nonstriking insiders, it would be most profitable to fire $b^* \cdot \bar{L}$ of them.

8.4.3 Decision W2

By analogy with equation (9), the firing-hiring constraint that is relevant to the firm's employment decisions F1 and F2 (viz., $b \cdot \overline{L}$ and $x = 1$, respectively) is

$$[1 - W_I] \cdot (1 + \delta^F) \cdot \overline{L} - CF_{x=1} = 0.$$

From this equation it can be shown that $(dW_I/da) > 0$ (for given b, which is exogenous to the workers). Since the insiders seek to maximize their wage, they set a as high as possible. Recall that $a + b \leqslant 1$. Thus, the optimal level of a illustrated in figure 8.2c is

$$a^* = 1 - b^*. \tag{11}$$

This result may be summarized as follows:

PROPOSITION 5 *If it is in the firm's best interests to retain all its strikers, then all the insiders of the firm have an incentive to issue the strike threat of contract C1.*

In other words, contract C1 may be reworded as follows:

Contract C1′ If a firm retains *all* its insiders, then none of them go on strike; yet if any of them are fired, then *all* of the remaining ones strike.

The only union that can implement the above contract is a firm-specific union of maximium size. In other words, *insiders have an incentive to join unions each of which cover the entire work force of a firm.*

Once again, a positive value of a^* does not mean that workers actually go on strike. As noted, the insider wage is low enough to discourage firms from firing nonstrikers, and consequently the workers have no cause to strike (according the contract C1). A positive a^* simply means that if the firm were to fire $b^* \cdot \overline{L}$ nonstrikers (where $0 < b^* < 1$), $a^* \cdot \overline{L}$ of the insiders would have an incentive to strike.

8.4.4 Decision W1

Substituting equation (11) into (10), we obtain the insiders' wage-setting decision given the firm's employment decisions, $b \cdot \overline{L}$ and $x = 1$:

$$W_I^* = 1 - \frac{(\alpha - W_E) \cdot b \cdot \overline{L} - [1 + \delta^F \cdot \rho_\omega^F] \cdot F(b \cdot \overline{L}) - H(b \cdot \overline{L})}{\{b \cdot \overline{L} + (1 - b) \cdot \overline{L} \cdot [1 + \delta^F \cdot (1 - \rho_\omega^F \cdot \rho_I^F)]\}}. \tag{12}$$

This equation is illustrated by the *insiders' reaction function* $W_I^* = W_I^*(b)$ in figure 8.2a, which can be shown to have an unambiguously negative slope in the neighborhood of the Nash equilibrium: From equation (12) we obtain

$$\frac{dW_I}{db} = -\{[\alpha - W_E] \cdot \overline{L} + [1 - W_I] \cdot \overline{L} \cdot \delta^F \cdot (1 - \rho_\omega^F)$$

$$- (1 + \delta^F \cdot \rho_\omega^F) \cdot F'(b \cdot \overline{L}) - H'(b \cdot \overline{L})\}$$

$$\cdot \{[b \cdot \overline{L} + (1 - b) \cdot \overline{L} \cdot (1 + \delta^F \cdot (1 - \rho_\omega^F - \rho_I^F)]\}^{-1}.$$

From equation (10) it is apparent that, in the neighborhood of the Nash equilibrium, this expression reduces to

$$\frac{dW_I}{db} = -[1 - W_I] \cdot \overline{L} \cdot [1 + \delta^F \cdot (1 - \rho_w^F - \rho_I^F]$$

$$\cdot \{[b \cdot \overline{L} + (1 - b) \cdot \overline{L} \cdot (1 + \delta^F \cdot (1 - \rho_w^F - \rho_I^F))]\}^{-1} < 0.$$

8.4.5 The Nash Equilibrium

Thus far we have considered the decision-making of the firm and its insiders. It remains to analyse that of the outsiders and entrants. As noted in section 8.3, the outsiders are perfect competitors in the labor market, and thus they offer to work at their reservation wage, over which the entrant wage is marked up.

We assume that outsiders, like the insiders, have a two-period time horizon. In that case (unlike the single-period case) the reservation wage comes to depend on the insider wage. Let δ^H be the workers' rate of time discount and b^H be their perceived probability of being fired in the second period. The reservation wage relevant to our analysis of strike threat may be defined as

$$(1 + \delta^H) \cdot U[B + A, 0]$$

$$= U[R \cdot (1 - \tau) + A, 1] + \delta^H \cdot b^H \cdot U[B + A, 0]$$

$$+ \delta^H \cdot (1 - b^H) \cdot U[W_I \cdot (1 - \tau) + A, 1]. \tag{13}$$

The left-hand term is the utility from unemployment in both periods; the first right-hand term is the utility from employment as an entrant in the first period; and the second and third right-hand terms stand for the second-period utility from unemployment if fired and from employment as an insider if retained.

This implies that

$$R = R(W_I, B).$$
$$\quad\;\; (-) \; (+)$$
(13a)

In other words the higher the insider wage that the outsider anticipates in the future, the lower the entrant wage for which he is willing to work at present; the higher the benefit he receives when unemployed, the greater the reservation wage he requires to compensate him for accepting employment.

In the Nash equilibrium, firms and their insiders not only take each other's decisions as exogenously given, but also the reservation wage of the outsiders above. Substituting this reservation wage (13a) plus the appropriate entrant markup into the firm's and the insiders' reaction functions [equations (9) and (12), respectively], the Nash equilibrium may be characterized as the intersection of the corresponding reaction functions, as given by point (b^e, W_I^e) in figure 8.2a.

Provided that $b^e < 1$, a^e is positive, i.e., *the strike threat is ex ante desirable for each of the union members*. This means that, given the firm's employment decision F1 and F2, each union member can achieve a higher wage by issuing the strike threat of contract C1' than by forgoing this threat.

8.4.6 Strike Credibility

Yet in order for the strike threat to be effective, it must be credible; i.e., the *strike threat must be ex post desirable for each of the union members*. Once the firm has fired some of the nonstriking insiders, the remaining insiders—confronted with this *fait accompli*—must have an incentive to fulfil their strike threat. Clearly, such an incentive exists if and only if their ex post utility from striking exceeds their ex post utility from remaining on the job.

Recall that each worker's utility depends positively on consumption (which is purchased with the worker's income) and leisure. For simplicity, let the utility function be additively separable, normalize the utility from maximum leisure (viz. no employment: $l = 0$) to zero, and let the utility from minimum leisure (viz., employment: $l = 1$) be $-\Gamma$ (where Γ is a positive constant). Let ρ_w^H and ρ_l^H be the worker's (households) perceived probabilities of winning and losing the strike, respectively, and let b_1 be his perceived probability of being fired if he loses.

Suppose that if the worker does strike, then his only source of nonprofit income is a payment out of a strike fund. Let this payment be J (a positive constant) per time period. (Recall that his profit income is A, also a positive constant.)

Under these circumstances, the worker's ex post utility from striking (i.e., his utility, given that the firm has engaged in firing activity) is

$$U_1 = \underbrace{U[J + A]}_{\substack{\text{first-period} \\ \text{utility}}} + \underbrace{\delta^H \cdot \rho_w^H \cdot \{U[W \cdot (1 - \tau) + A] - \Gamma\}}_{\text{utility if strikers win}}$$

$$+ \underbrace{\delta^H \cdot \rho_l^H \cdot (1 - b_1) \cdot \{U[W \cdot (1 - \tau) + A] - \Gamma\}}_{\substack{\text{utility if strikers lose,} \\ \text{but are retained}}}$$

$$+ \delta^H \cdot \rho_l^H \cdot b_1 \cdot \underbrace{U[B + A]}_{\substack{\text{utility if strikers lose} \\ \text{and are fired}}}$$

$$+ \delta^H \cdot (1 - \rho_w^H - \rho_l^H) \cdot \underbrace{U[J + A]}_{\substack{\text{utility if strike} \\ \text{continues}}}$$

$$= U[J + A] \cdot \{1 - \delta_w^H \cdot (1 - \rho_w^H - \rho_l^H)\}$$

$$+ \{U[W_l \cdot (1 - \tau) + A - \Gamma\} \cdot \rho_w^H + \rho_l^H \cdot (1 - b_1)\} \cdot \delta^H$$

$$+ U[B + A] \cdot \rho_l^H \cdot b_1 \cdot \delta^H. \tag{14}$$

Let b_2 be the worker's perceived probability of being fired if he remains on the job.[3] Then his ex post utility from not striking is

$$U_2 = \underbrace{\{U[W_l \cdot (1 - \tau) + A] - \Gamma\}}_{\text{first period utility}} + \underbrace{\delta^H \cdot b_2 \cdot U[B + A]}_{\text{utility if fired}}$$

$$+ \underbrace{\delta^H (1 \cdot b_2) \cdot \{U[W_l \cdot (1 - \tau) + A] - \Gamma\}}_{\text{utility if retained}}$$

$$= \{U[W_l \cdot (1 - \tau) + A] - \Gamma\} \cdot \{1 + \delta^H \cdot (1 - b_2)\}$$

$$+ \delta^H \cdot b_2 \cdot U[B + A]. \tag{15}$$

As noted, the strike threat is credible if and only if $U_1 \geqslant U_2$, i.e.,

$$-\{U[W_l \cdot (1 - \tau) + A] - \Gamma - U[J + A]\} \cdot \{1 + \delta^H \cdot (1 - \rho_w^H - \rho_l^H)\}$$

$$-\{U[W_l \cdot (1 - \tau) + A] - \Gamma - U[B + A]\} \cdot \delta^H \cdot (\rho_l^H \cdot b_1 - b_2] \geqslant 0. \tag{16}$$

This condition may be called the "credible-threat constraint."[4]

It contains only two of the worker's decision variables: W_I and J. For any given value of W_I, there exists a minimum value of J for which condition (16) is satisfied as equality.[5] Since the strike fund can be augmented only at the expense of insider income (and therefore also insider consumption), this is indeed the utility-maximizing value of J. Condition (16) as equality is illustrated in figure 8.2b.

In equilibrium, the strike fund is not in fact changed and thus strike-fund contributions do not enter the insiders' utility maximization problems. The sole purpose of the strike fund in equilibrium is to establish a credible threat. Consequently, the optimal equilibrium strategy for insiders is to set their wage as high as the firing-hiring constraint (12) will allow and then to set J high enough so that the credible-threat constraint (16) is just satisfied. In this sense, condition (16) implies the optimal equilibrium size of the strike fund.

8.4.7 Macroeconomic Implications

Is the level of involuntary unemployment higher when insiders unionize to issue the strike threat than when they act atomistically? To make a valid comparison, consider two economies that are identical except that one is unionized in the sense above and the other is atomistic.

Assume that these economies have a fixed number of identical firms, each facing the same firing-hiring costs and insider-entrant productivity differential. There are also a fixed number of households with identical preferences over a two-period time horizon. Clearly, both economies have the same reservation wage [see equation (13)].

The firm's reaction function under atomistic wage setting is the same as that under the strike threat [equation (9)], except that the firm's perceived probability of strikers winning their strike (ρ_w^F) is obviously zero in the former case and generally positive in the latter. Similarly, the insiders' reaction function under atomistic wage setting [equation (5)] is the same as that under the strike threat [equation (10)], except that the proportion of strikers (a) and the insiders' perceived probabilities of winning and losing the strike (ρ_w^H and ρ_l^H, respectively) are zero in the former case and generally positive in the latter.

Substituting the expression for the reservation wage [equation (13)] into the firm's reaction function [equation (9)], we find that, for any given value of the insider wage, the firm's optimal firing under atomistic insider behavior ($b_{at} \cdot \bar{L}$) is less than that under the strike threat above ($b^* \cdot \bar{L}$) (*ceteris paribus*).[6] Thus, the firm's reaction function is lower (in b–W space)

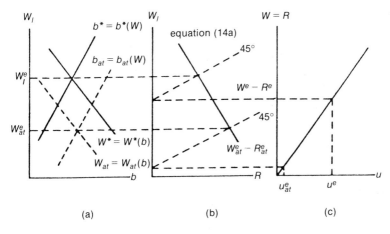

Figure 8.3
Involuntary unemployment under strike threat and atomistic wage setting.

for a nonunionized work force than for a unionised one, as shown in figure 8.3a.

Furthermore, substituting the expression for the reservation wage [equation (13)] into the insiders' reaction function [equation (12)], we find that, for any given value of firm firing ($b \cdot \bar{L}$), the insider wage is lower under atomistic than under union conditions (W_{at} and W_I^*, respectively). Thus, the insiders' reaction function is also lower in the former case than in the latter, as shown in figure 8.3a.

Consequently, an economy in which a fixed number of firms face atomistic insiders will display a lower insider wage (W_{at}^e in figure 8.3a) than the one (W_I^e) that emerges when all these firms face unions posing the strike threat (C1').

Recall that the reservation wage [equation (14)], illustrated in figure 8.3b, for a given value of b^H is inversely related to the insider wage. Thus, it is evident that the differential between the insider wage and the reservation wage must be larger under unionization ($W_I^e - R^e$) than under atomistic behavior ($W_{at}^e - R_{at}^e$). Assuming (as in section 8.2) that the amount of labor services offered by the outsiders depends positively on this differential (as pictured in figure 8.3c), we arrive at the following proposition:

PROPOSITION 6 *The level of involuntary unemployment and the level of the insider wage are greater* (ceteris paribus) *when all insiders in the economy unionise to issue the strike threat* (C1') *than when they set their wages atomistically.*

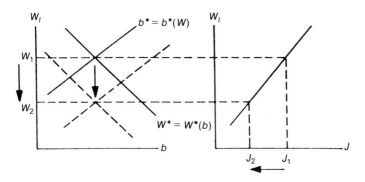

Figure 8.4
The effect of an increase in entrant productivity.

In Section 8.3 (proposition 3), involuntary unemployment was portrayed as a phenomenon that the insiders, setting their wages individually, impose on the outsiders. Now we find that insiders can augment their wage claims by forming unions to pose strike threats, and, as by-product, they raise the level of involuntary unemployment.

The macroeconomic implications of our union analysis may be clarified by various comparative static experiments.

Suppose that the productivity of entrants [relative to insiders (α)] rises exogenously. Then [by equation (9)], the cash-flow-maximizing number of nonstrikers to be fired ($b^* \cdot \overline{L}$) rises for every given insider wage and reservation wage; thus, the firm's reaction function (b^*) shifts to the right in $b-W$ space. In addition [by equations (12) and (13)], the utility-maximizing insider wage falls for every given value of b (as the reservation wage rises)—thus, the insiders' reaction function (W_I^*) shifts downward as well. However, the credible-threat constraint remains unchanged. These effects are shown in figure 8.4 and may be summarized as follows:

PROPOSITION 7 *When unions issue the strike threat (C1'), an increase in the productivity of entrants (α) leads to a reduction in the equilibrium levels of the insider wage and the strike fund.*

[With regard to the insider wage, this effect of entrant productivity is qualitatively the same as that in the world of atomistic wage setting—see equation (5).]

The effect of an increase in the firm's perceived probability that the strike will persist ($1 - \rho_w^F - \rho_I^F$) is pictured in figure 8.5. The firm's reac-

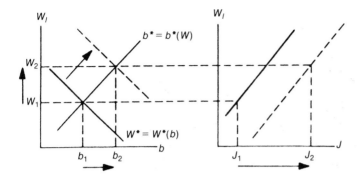

Figure 8.5
The effect of an increase in the firm's perceived probability that the strike will persist.

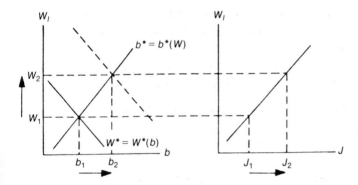

Figure 8.6
The effect of a lump-sum increase in firing or hiring costs.

tion function (b^*) remains unchanged; that of the insiders (W_I^*) shifts upward; and the credible-threat constraint shifts to the right.

PROPOSITION 8 *When unions issue the strike threat (C1'), an* increase in the firm's perceived probability that the strike will persist $(1 - \rho_w^F - \rho_l^F)$ *leads to a rise in the equilibrium levels of the insider wage and the strike fund.*

Figures 8.6 and 8.7 are concerned with the effects of an increase in firing or hiring costs, in lump-sum (F or H) and marginal (F' or H') terms, respectively. They illustrate the following comparative statics result:

PROPOSITION 9 *When unions issue the strike threat (C1'), both* a lump-sum and a marginal increase in the costs of firing or hiring *lead to a rise in the equilibrium levels of the insider wage and the strike fund.*

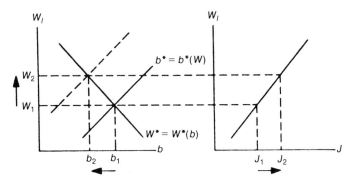

Figure 8.7
The effect of a marginal increase in firing or hiring costs.

(In the world of atomistic wage setting, a lump-sum increase in firing-hiring costs also raises the insider wage, but a marginal increase in these costs has no effect.)

It is also obvious that the macroeconomic consequences of a rise in the unemployment benefits (B) may be summarized as follows:

PROPOSITION 10 *A rise in unemployment benefits* (B) *raises the reservation wages and the insider wages. Under atomistic wage-setting, there is no effect on unemployment; under union wage-setting the unemployment effect is ambiguous.*

8.5 Union Activity: The Threat of Work-to-Rule

The threat of work-to-rule provides another rationale for unionization. Clearly, this threat can be operative only when firms are able to observe a particular *minimum effort level* that can be monitored and remunerated, but are unable remunerate workers in accordance with effort expended beyond this level. If this were not the case, there could be no "rule" that constitutes the basis of "work-to-rule," nor could there be any threat associated with doing so. The most common reason why firms may be unable to pay insiders in accordance with the above-minimum effort they expend is that they may be unable to observe such effort.

Accordingly, suppose that the monitoring of work effort is costly in the sense that a minimum effort level is readily observed (e.g., the presence of a worker interacting with a machine), whereas effort in excess of this level (e.g., the worker's degree of concentration, accuracy, or delicacy) can only be observed at prohibitive cost. Thus, the employer finds it worthwhile to

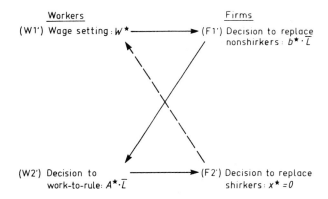

Figure 8.8
The sequence of wage-setting, work-to-rule, and employment decisions.

ascertain whether each of his workers provides minimum effort, but does not monitor the effort beyond that.[7]

In this context, consider the following implicit contract:

Contract C2 If all union members retain their jobs, then all of them will devote a particular, above-minimum level of effort to their jobs; yet if any of them are fired, then some (possibly all) of the remaining ones will work-to-rule (i.e., work at the minimum effort level).

If this contract is effective, then workers use effort as an "employer-disciplining device" (to preserve their jobs).

The interaction between workers and their employer under contract C2 is pictured in figure 8.8. First, workers set their wages (decision W1'). Second, the firm decides whether to replace any of its nonshirkers (i.e., workers providing an above-minimum level of effort) (decision F1'). Third, if workers have been replaced, the remaining insiders decide whether to work-to-rule (decision W2'). Fourth, the firm decides whether to replace the shirkers (decision F2'). We are concerned with the Nash equilibrium of this process.

In this setup, the threat of work-to-rule operates analogously to the threat of strike.

Let E be the above-minimum effort level that nonshirkers provide and let the minimal effort level be normalized to unity. Let us redefine ρ_w^F and ρ_l^F to be the firm's perceived probabilities that the shirkers will win and lose the work-to-rule confrontation (respectively).

Then, if the firm decides to *retain all the shirkers* (F2: $x = 1$), then its expected cash flow is

$$\hat{CF}_{x=1} = \underbrace{[\alpha \cdot E - W_E] \cdot b \cdot \overline{L} - H(b \cdot \overline{L}) - F(b \cdot \overline{L})}_{\substack{\text{first-period cash flow generated by the} \\ \text{entrants (net of firing-hiring costs)}}} + \underbrace{[1 - W_I] \cdot a \cdot \overline{L}}_{\substack{\text{first-period cash flow} \\ \text{generated by the shirkers}}}$$

$$+ \underbrace{(1 - a - b) \cdot \overline{L} \cdot [E - W_I] \cdot (1 + \delta^F)}_{\substack{\text{cash flow generated by} \\ \text{the nonshirking insiders}}}$$

$$+ \delta^F \cdot \rho_w^F \cdot \underbrace{\{[E - W_I] \cdot (a + b) \cdot \overline{L} - F(b \cdot \overline{L})\}}_{\substack{\text{second-period cash flow} \\ \text{generated if the shirkers win}}}$$

$$+ \delta^F \cdot \rho_l^F \cdot \underbrace{\{[E - W_I] \cdot (a + b) \cdot \overline{L}\}}_{\substack{\text{second-period cash flow} \\ \text{generated if the shirkers lose}}}$$

$$+ \delta^F \cdot (1 - \rho_w^F - \rho_l^F) \cdot \underbrace{\{[E - W_I] \cdot b \cdot \overline{L} + [1 - W_I] \cdot a \cdot \overline{L}\}}_{\substack{\text{second-period cash flow generated} \\ \text{if the work-to-rule confrontation continues}}}. \quad (18)$$

The firm's expected cash flow if it decides to *replace all the shirkers* (F2: $x = 0$) is defined analogously:

$$\hat{CF}_{x=0} = \underbrace{[\alpha \cdot E - W_E] \cdot (a + b) \cdot \overline{L} - H[(a + b) \cdot \overline{L}] - F[(a + b) \cdot \overline{L}]}_{\substack{\text{first-period cash flow generated by the entrants} \\ \text{(net of firing-hiring costs)}}}$$

$$+ \underbrace{(1 - a - b) \cdot \overline{L} \cdot [E - W_I] \cdot (1 + \delta^F)}_{\substack{\text{cash flow generated by} \\ \text{the nonshirking insiders}}}$$

$$+ \delta^F \cdot \rho_w^F \underbrace{\{[E - W_I] \cdot (a + b) \cdot \overline{L} - F[(a + b) \cdot \overline{L}]\}}_{\substack{\text{second-period cash flow generated} \\ \text{if the shirkers win}}}$$

$$+ \delta^F \cdot \rho_l^F \cdot \underbrace{\{[E - W_I] \cdot (a + b) \cdot \overline{L}\}}_{\substack{\text{second-period cash flow} \\ \text{generated if the shirkers lose}}}$$

$$+ \delta^F \cdot (1 - \rho_w^F - \rho_l^F) \cdot \underbrace{\{[E - W_I] \cdot (a + b) \cdot \overline{L}\}}_{\substack{\text{second-period cash flow} \\ \text{generated if the work-to-rule} \\ \text{confrontation continues}}}.$$

As for the case of a strike threat, it can be shown that, in the Nash equilibrium, the decision to replace all the shirkers is never effective (since then workers would lose their incentive to use the work-to-rule threat).

Now, if it is in the firm's interest to retain all shirkers (i.e., $\hat{C}F_{x=1} >$ $\hat{C}F_{x=0}$), then its reaction function is given by

$$\frac{\partial \hat{C}F_{x=1}}{\partial b} = [(W - W_E) - E \cdot (1 - \alpha)] \cdot \bar{L}$$

$$- H'(b^* \cdot L) \cdot L - (1 + \delta^F \cdot \rho_w^F) \cdot F'(b^* \cdot L) \cdot L = 0. \tag{19}$$

Thus, the firm's reaction function under the threat of work-to-rule is quite similar to that under the threat of strike [equation (10)].

The insider's reaction function however, is a different matter. As in the case of strike threat, the insider faces two constraints: a firing-hiring constraint and a credible-threat constraint.

The former constraint is

$$[E - W_I] \cdot (1 + \delta^F) \cdot \bar{L} - \hat{C}F_{x=1}(W, b^*)$$

$$= [E - W_I] \cdot \{a^* \cdot \bar{L} \cdot [1 + \delta^F (1 - \rho_w^F - \rho_I^F)] + b \cdot \bar{L}\}$$

$$- [1 - W_I] \cdot a^* \cdot \bar{L} \cdot \{1 + \delta^F \cdot (1 - \rho_w^F - \rho_I^F)\}$$

$$- [\alpha \cdot E - W_E] \cdot b \cdot \bar{L} + H(b \cdot \bar{L}) + (1 + \delta^F \rho_w^F) \cdot F(b \cdot \bar{L}) = 0. \tag{20}$$

By the appendix, the credible-threat constraint holds for all feasible values of W_I and E, and thus it may be ignored in what follows.

But how, it may be asked, can insiders give themselves the incentive to provide above-minimum effort? How can they prevent themselves from becoming free riders? One particularly plausible answer is that although the employer cannot monitor above-minimum effort of an insider, the insider's colleagues can usually do so. Workers are usually in a much better position to supervise each other than be supervised by their employer. Furthermore, workers in the present context have an incentive to alert their employer to any on-the-job shirking, since otherwise the employer would become aware of the existence of shirkers through comparing output and labor inputs, and then it would be in his best interests to fire insiders (i.e., the firing-hiring constraint would be violated). Each worker has an atomistic incentive to prevent this from happening.

The insider sets W_I and E so as to maximize utility subject to the firing-hiring constraint:

Maximize $(1 - \delta^H) \cdot \{U[W_1 \cdot (1 - \tau) + A] - \Gamma(E)\}$

(21)

subject to   (20)

Here the disutility of work (Γ) is taken to depend on the amount of effort (E) expended. We assume that U', $\Gamma > 0$, $U'' < 0$, and $\Gamma'' > 0$. [Since the insider's choice of (W, E) satisfies the firing-hiring constraint, he will not be replaced by the firm. His utility function is formulated accordingly. As above, the utility function is taken to be additively separable.]

As in the case of strike threat, it can be shown that, for any given level of E, $(dW_1/da) > 0$,[8] In other words, a rise in the proportion of insiders who work-to-rule (when nonshirkers have been fired) increases each worker's income (and thus consumption) without requiring increased effort. Hence, each worker has an incentive to join a union that covers the entire workforce of the firm. Once again, $a^* = 1 - b$.

For a given value of b, the solution to the insider's maximization problem (21) is pictured in figure 8.9.[9] Now suppose that b rises. As shown in figure 8.10, the firing-hiring constraint shifts downward and becomes flatter in $E-W$ space.[10] Thus there is an unambiguous drop in the insider wage (and E's direction of movement depends on the relative importance of the income and substitution effects). In sum, the insiders respond to a rise in b by reducing their wage; thus, the insiders' reaction function ($W^* = W^*(b)$) in figure 8.11 is downward-sloping. The firm's reaction function ($b^* = b^*W$) [equation (18)] is upward-sloping. The intersection of these two functions denotes the Nash equilibrium, given by (b^e, W^e) in figure 8.11.

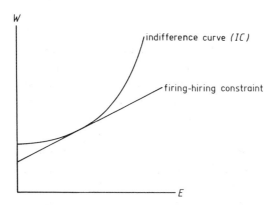

Figure 8.9
The insider's choice of wage and effort.

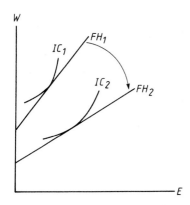

Figure 8.10
The insider's response to a rise in the firm's firing activity.

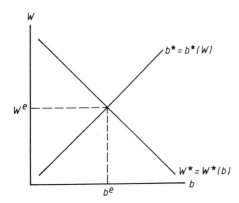

Figure 8.11
The Nash equilibrium under threat of work-to-rule.

As in the case of a strike threat, it can be shown that both the insider wage and the level of involuntary unemployment are higher when all the insiders in the economy unionize to issue a work-to-rule threat (C2) than when they set their wages atomistically. The effects of exogenous changes in entrant productivity, the firm's perceived probability that the strike will persist, and lump-sum and marginal firing-hiring costs are also qualitatively the same as in the case of strike threat (see proposition 8–10).

8.6 Epilogue

Wage rigidity is explained in this chapter as a consequence of the established workers ("insiders") exploiting the monopoly power that they obtain in wage-setting as a result of the costs of hiring and firing. The unemployed workers (the "outsiders") are unable to undercut the "monopoly wages" of the insiders, not only due to conceivably existing "social mores" against such attempts, but also because the firms would have no incentives to fire the insiders and hire the outsiders. Thus, although the resulting involuntary unemployment is a disequilibrium market phenomenon in the sense that excess supply for labor exists, there is no tendency for the situation to be rectified, as neither the firms nor the employed workers (possibly acting through unions) have an incentive to change their behavior.

Involuntary unemployment of this type exists even when workers bargain individualistically, although (as shown) unions serve to raise their members' wage levels and thereby the involuntary unemployment is amplified. In this vein, our analysis provides a rationale for the existence of unions and for their use of strike and work-to-rule threats, operating in the interests of the insiders and against those of the outsiders.

Appendix

The threat of work-to-rule is credible if and only if the insider's ex post utility from shirking exceeds his ex post utility from providing effort E. Let $\Gamma(E)$ be the disutility from providing E, and let $\Gamma(1)$ be the disutility from working-to-rule. Furthermore, redefine ρ_ω^H and ρ_l^H to be the worker's perceived probability of winning and losing the work-to-rule confrontation (respectively). Finally, redefine b_1 and b_2 to be his perceived probabilities of being fired when shirking and nonshirking (respectively). Then the ex post utility from working-to-rule is

$$\hat{U}_1 = \underbrace{U[W_1 - A] - \Gamma(1)}_{\text{first-period utility}} + \delta^H \cdot \rho_\omega^H \underbrace{\{U[W_1 + A] - \Gamma(1)\}}_{\text{utility if shirkers win}}$$

$$+ \delta^H \cdot \rho_l^H \cdot (1 - b_1) \cdot \underbrace{\{U[W_l + A] - \Gamma(E)\}}_{\substack{\text{utility if shirkers lose} \\ \text{but are retained}}} + \delta^H \cdot \rho_l^H \cdot \underbrace{b_1 U[B + A]}_{\substack{\text{utility if shirkers} \\ \text{lose and are fired}}}$$

$$+ \delta^H (1 - \rho_\omega^H - \rho_l^H) \cdot \underbrace{\{U[W_l + A] - \Gamma(1)\}}_{\substack{\text{utility if the work-to-rule} \\ \text{confrontation continues}}} . \qquad \text{(b1)}$$

The ex post utility from providing effort E is

$$\hat{U}_2 = \underbrace{U[W_l + A] - \Gamma(1)}_{\text{first-period utility}} + \underbrace{\delta^H b_2 \cdot U[B + A]}_{\substack{\text{utility if} \\ \text{fired}}}$$

$$+ \delta^H \cdot (1 - b_2) \cdot \underbrace{\{U[W_l + A] - \Gamma(E)\}}_{\text{utility if retained}} . \qquad \text{(b2)}$$

Thus, the credible-threat constraint is

$$\hat{U}_1 - \hat{U}_2 = \{U[W_l + A] - U[B + A]\} \cdot (b_2 - \rho_l^H - b_1)$$

$$+ [\Gamma(E) - \Gamma(1)] \cdot \{1 + \delta \cdot (1 - \rho_\omega^H - \rho_l^H)\}$$

$$+ \Gamma(E) \cdot \delta^H \cdot (b_2 - \rho_l^H \cdot b_1) \geqslant 0. \qquad \text{(b3)}$$

Since the firm is unable to observe effort above the minimum level, $b_1 = b_2$. Recalling that $W_l > B$ and that $E \geqslant 1$ (since firms can observe any level of effort less than or equal to unity), it is evident that the credible-threat constraint is always satisfied.

Notes

1. In our analysis, the firm is assumed either to hold *all* the strikers' positions vacant or to replace *all* the strikers by entrants. For expositional simplicity, we do not consider the intermediate possibilities, namely, that the firm replaces some, but not all, of its strikers.

2. Given assumption A10, the second-order condition for optimality is satisfied.

3. It might be argued that, should the firm decide to fire any of its insiders, it will fire $b^* \cdot \bar{L}$ of them, regardless of whether the insiders win or lose the strike (since that would be the most profitable firing strategy). Suppose that the firm chooses its insiders to be fired on a random basis, so that all insiders face an equal probability, b^*, of being fired. Then "rational" insiders would set their perceived probabilities of being fired equal to the actual probability: $b_1 = b_2 = b^*$.

However, this argument is not foolproof. Recall that we are concerned with the ex post (rather than ex ante) desirability of the strike threat. If the firm accepts contract C1, then $b^* \cdot \bar{L}$ is the cash-flow-maximizing firing decision. But it may decide to fire more or less than $b^* \cdot \bar{L}$ of its insiders in order to induce the insiders to abandon contract C1. (The firm's gain from scrapping contract C1 may exceed the opportunity cost of firing more or less than $b^* \cdot \overline{L}$ of the insiders.) It is this latter possibility that insiders guard against by establishing threat credibility. Consequently, it is not necessarily true that $b_1 = b_2 = b^*$ for the "rational" insider.

4. Since we aim to analyze the phenomenon of involuntary (rather than voluntary) unemployment, it is natural to assume that $U[W \cdot (1 - \tau) + A] - \Gamma > U[J + A]$, $U[B + A]$. In that case, the first right-hand term of equation (16) is unambiguously negative, and thus the credible threat constraint can be satisfied only if $\rho_t^H \cdot b_1 < b_2$; i.e., for given levels of W, J, and B, the worker has an ex post incentive to strike only if his expected probability of being fired is lower when he strikes than when he remains on the job. This is a straightforward implication of equations (14) and (15). The advantage of staying on the job over striking is that the former yields a higher current income (since $W_I > J$). The only countervailing advantage of striking can be the higher expected income in the future, but this is the case only if $\rho_t^H \cdot b_1 < b_2$.

5. For condition (15) expressed as equality,

$$\frac{dW_I}{dJ} = \frac{U'[J+A] \cdot [1 + \delta^H \cdot (1 - \rho_\omega^H - \rho_t^H)]}{U'[W \cdot (1-\tau) + A] \cdot [1 + \delta^H \cdot (1 - \rho_\omega^H - \rho_t^H) + \delta^H \cdot (\rho_t^H - b_1 \cdot b_2)]}. \tag{17}$$

We consider only the nondegenerate case in which this expression is positive. If the insider wage could be raised by reducing J, then workers would have an incentive to reduce the strike fund to zero.

6. For ease of comparison, we assume that, in determining the reservation wage [equation (13)], the outsiders' perceived probability of being fired in the second period (b^H) is the same under atomistic and unionized wage-setting. With regard to the firm's reaction function [equation (9)], given that $\rho_\omega^F = 0$ in the atomistic case but $\rho_\omega^F > 0$ in the unionized case and given that $(\partial^2 CF_{\tau=1} / \partial b^2) < 0$, it is evident that $b_{at} < b^*$ (ceteris paribus).

7. Of course, employers can always observe the average effort level of their workforce simply by comparing their output with their labor input; what they do not find worthwhile is to monitor above-minmium effort of individual employees.

8. With regard to equation (20),

$$\frac{dW_I}{da} = \frac{[1 + \delta^F \cdot (1 - \rho_\omega^F - \rho_t^F)] \cdot \overline{L} \cdot [E -]}{b \cdot \overline{L}} > 0.$$

9. The firing-hiring constraint is upward-sloping in $E-W$ space:

$$\frac{dW_I}{dE} = \frac{b \cdot \overline{L} \cdot (1 - \alpha) + a \cdot \overline{L} \cdot [1 + \delta^F \cdot (1 - \rho_\omega^F - \rho_t^F)]}{b \cdot \overline{L}} < 0.$$

10. The firing-hiring constraint shift downward, since (for any given E)

$$\frac{dW_I}{db} = -\frac{(E - 1) \cdot \overline{L} \cdot [1 + \delta^F \cdot (1 - \rho_\omega^F - \rho_t^F)]}{b \cdot \overline{L}}.$$

From (dW_I/dE), given in note 9, it is clear that the constraint also becomes flatter.

9 Union Activity and Unemployment Persistence

Overview

Thus far, we have been concerned with the microeconomic underpinnings of the insider-outsider theory and its static predictions regarding wage-employment determination, persistent involuntary unemployment, and union activity. In this chapter and the next, we turn to some dynamic macro implications of the theory. However, much work remains to be done in integrating our insider-outsider analysis of the labor market into a full-blown macro model.

We are primarily concerned with how the exercise of insider market power affects the "resilience" of a labor market, i.e. the labor market's ability to recover from a business downswing. We argue that unfavorable, unforeseen swings in employment and unemployment tend to be comparatively persistent (ceteris paribus) in economies with comparatively large labor turnover costs and powerful insiders. Thus, when there is a worldwide recession, these economies may experience more prolonged periods of stagnation than economies with comparatively small labor turnover costs and weak insiders. In this light, our analysis may provide one possible explanation of why the recession of the early 1980s was more protracted in Europe than in the United States.

We focus attention on random variations in labor demand around a constant mean. We suppose that after wage negotiations have taken place, an unforeseen reduction in labor demand occurs, so that firms dismiss some of their insiders. As result, the remaining insiders now face new circumstances: Given that the mean of the labor demand shocks is constant through time, the remaining insiders now enjoy greater job security at the previously negotiated wage. Consequently, in the next (future) round of wage negotiations, the insiders may raise their wages. This means that for any given future position of the labor demand curve, employment will be lower than it would have been in the absence of the wage increase. For this reason, the labor market may fail to recover fully from a transient, adverse shock; the exercise of market power by insiders has robed the labor market of "resilience."

Observe that this argument rests on two crucial assumptions, namely, (i) that the labor demand shocks be unforeseen by the wage negotiators and (ii) that the mean of the shocks remain stationary through time. For if the shocks were foreseen, then the wage may fall in response to an unfavorable shock, and thus no insiders may be dismissed. Furthermore, if the shocks were assumed to follow a random walk, then a drop in the insider workforce would not increase the job security of the remaining insiders. These assumptions are relaxed in the next chapter, where we shall investigate whether insiders can reduce labor market resilience under permanent, foreseen shocks.

Within the analytical context above, we inquire whether lack of resilience may in some situations be a blessing in disguise: If insiders are able to prolong the effects of transient adverse shocks, can they do the same for favorable shocks? For this purpose, we analyze labor market resilience in terms of two separate effects of insider power on unemployment:

(i) the "symmetric persistence effect," whereby the role of insiders in wage negotiations causes random labor demand shocks around a stationary mean to give rise to symmetric, persistent changes in unemployment, and

(ii) the "asymmetric persistence effect," whereby insiders' influence on wages causes random labor demand shocks around a stationary mean to lead to larger wage changes and smaller employment changes in the upswings than in the downswings.

The sense in which the first effect is symmetric is that favorable and unfavorable shocks in current labor demand have equal but opposite effects on future unemployment. In this case, lack of resilience is bad news in a slump but good news in a boom, since unfavorable and favorable shocks are perpetuated in the same way. By contrast, under the asymmetric persistence effect, the wage rise from a favorable labor demand shock is greater than the wage fall from an unfavorable shock of equal magnitude, and consequently employment rises less in the former case than it falls in the latter. Here, lack of resilience is bad news in a boom as well as a slump.

As in chapters 7 and 8, this chapter assumes that insiders exercise their influence over wages via firm-specific unions. Yet our arguments for the symmetric and asymmetric persistence effects could be made even when insiders bargain individualistically with their firms. The significance of our union analysis is that it permits us to treat wages as the outcome of a Nash bargain between unions and firms (in contrast to chapters 7 and 8, where unions are assumed to set wages unilaterally). Thus we can explore how variations in union power affect the workings of the labor market. In particular, whereas the previous two chapters focused on how the existence of unions affects the equilibrium levels of wages, employment, and unemployment, this chapter analyzes the relation between the degree of union power and the dynamic response of labor market activity to exogenous shocks.

Our analysis shows that the greater the labor turnover costs and the greater the bargaining strength of insider unions, the greater is the symmetric persistence effect. By contrast, asymmetric persistence effect is shown to depend on the conditions governing workers' entry into and exit from the union. In particular, the asymmetric persistence effect is present when the laid-off insiders have a greater chance of losing influence on wage determination than the newly hired entrants have a chance of gaining such influence. Then unfavorable labor demand shocks have a greater effect on union membership than favorable shocks. Consequently the unfavorable shocks change employment more than do the favorable shocks. The greater the asymmetry in the unions' entry and exit conditions, the stronger is the asymmetric persistence effect.

In this context, our analysis may help clarify some differences in the recent labor market experience of Europe and the United States. In particular, the symmetric persistence effect may help explain why the high levels of unemployment—arising out of the worldwide recession in the early 1980s—have lasted longer in Europe than in the United States, and why Europe has been less successful than the United States in creating new jobs. The asymmetric persistence effect, may provide one conceivable reason why European unemployment had a stronger upward trend in the 1970s and 1980s than did US unemployment, and why European unemployment appears to have been less responsive than US unemployment to demand stimuli in the 1980s.

9.1 Introduction

Among the most notable features of the American and European macroeconomic experiences in the 1970s and 1980s have been the pronounced differences in their wage, employment, and unemployment paths. The American economy appears to have been more "resilient" than most European economies, in the sense that the recovery from the worldwide recession of the late 1970s and early 1980s occurred sooner and took place more rapidly in the United States. The US unemployment rate peaked in late 1982 and fell sharply over the following five years, whereas the European unemployment rate rose inexorably through the first half of the 1980s. In the decade from 1975 to 1985, the United States created about 20 million new jobs, whereas in Europe employment remained stagnant in that period. During the recent recession, real product wages stayed roughly constant in the United States, but they rose steadily in Europe.

Several divergent explanations for the differences in resilience have been offered. New Classical Macroeconomies, focusing on errors in wage-price expectations and intertemporal substitution, cannot explain these differences. Yet it strains the imagination to interpret the extraordinary persistence and magnitude of European unemployment in terms of a stubbornness of expectational errors or a disinclination to work.

Keynesian economists often point to cross-country differences in fiscal and monetary policies.[1] This demand-side approach must be part of the explanation, since the European fiscal stance in the first half of the 1980s was contractionary, while that of the United States was expansionary. But the Keynesian empirical models have been generally unable to explain why the previous trade-offs between inflation and unemployment in Europe broke down in the 1980s—in particular, why the massive unemployment of the early 1980s was not accompanied by a more rapid process of disinflation.

According to the "excessive wage approach," the high unemployment and stagnant employment in Europe may be explained by the failure of real wages to adjust downward in response to the oil and commodity price shocks and the productivity slowdown in the later 1970s. This approach doubtlessly has some explanatory power. However, it does not explain why Europe displays more "wage rigidity" than the United States, and it does not account for the persistent unemployment and the stagnation of employment in Europe despite the fall in oil and commodity prices in the 1980s. The divergent real wage paths in in various countries have also been ascribed to differences in wage bargaining (e.g., differences in the degree of centralization in bargaining and in the productivity expectations of workers and firms), but such arguments have received little choice-theoretic foundation.

This chapter offers another approach. It suggests that cross-country differences in recovery rates may be due to differences in labor turnover costs and in the power of firm-specific unions. Our analysis shows how the influence of labor unions over wage contracts may make an economy less "resilient" in two senses: (i) unfavorable and favorable shocks in employment tend to persist symmetrically and (ii) such swings may give rise to "asymmetric persistence," manifested by a larger real wage impact from labor demand expansions than from contractions.

The idea underlying this chapter is quite simple. Consider a labor market containing firm-specific unions facing labor demand shocks that are transient (in the sense that the distribution of shocks has a constant mean and finite variance). After an adverse shock, firms reduce the size of their workforces (through dismissals or failure to replace retiring employees) and unemployment rises. The remaining insiders now face a different position than previously: Since they are smaller in number but face the same distribution of shocks, their chances of retaining their jobs have risen. Now, acting through their unions, they respond to this enhanced job security by driving up their wages. However, the unemployed workers cannot underbid on account of labor turnover costs. At the new higher wages, the firms will employ fewer workers (for any given new labor demand shock) than they would otherwise have done. In this way, unions help perpetuate the initial rise in unemployment. We shall explore how this unemployment persistence is related to the degree of union power and how unions may generate wage-unemployment ratchets.

A number of recent studies have presented various analytical frameworks in which unions (or, simply, workers with market power) may be responsible for unemployment persistence. Gottfries and Horn (1986) and Blanchard and Summers (1986, 1987) consider unemployment persistence in the context of a union whose members have uncertain employment prospects, whereas chapter 5 of this book deals with persistence due to labor turnover costs arising from the discrimination of "outsiders" by "insiders" through noncooperation and harassment activities of insiders (who may or may not be unionized). Horn (1983) shows how an expansion of the government sector leads to lower employment and higher wages in the private sector, but a subsequent government contraction leaves the private sector unable to absorb the laid-off workers in the public sector. Finally, Drazen (1985a) considers how unemployment persistence can occur through the attrition of human capital in a recession. Yet unlike the present chapter, these studies do not show how unemployment persistence is related to the degree of union power; nor do they explore how union activity may give rise to wage-unemployment ratchets.

In using the insider-outsider approach to explain union activity, we now distinguish between two types of insiders: union members and employed nonmembers. The union is taken to be firm-specific. For simplicity, we assume that all union members are employed. (As soon as a union member loses his job, he is assumed to leave the union or, at least, lose his influence in union wage-setting decisions.) The employed nonmembers receive the same wage as the union members, but the former have no influence on this wage.

We assume that the union members enjoy two advantages over the employed nonmembers:

(i) They exercise market power over their wage. In fact, the wage is taken to be the outcome of negotiations between the union and the firm, where the union takes only the interests of its members into account.

(ii) Employed nonmembers are fired before union members.

The second assumption is made largely for expositional simplicity. Assuming instead that employed nonmembers have a lower probability of being retained than members would not affect the qualitative conclusions of our analysis. Moreover, even making the assumption that the retention probabilities of the two groups of employees are identical would not affect our conclusions with regard to the symmetric persistence effect, but—as we shall see—it does imply that there would be no asymmetric persistence effect.

9.2 Wages, Employment, and Unemployment

To begin with, we focus on a single firm, some (or all) of whose insiders belong to a single union. Let work be a discrete activity, with each employee providing one unit of work. The firm's production function is $Q = \varepsilon \cdot f(L)$, $f' > 0$, $f'' < 0$, where Q is output, L is the number of employees (union members and employed non-members), and ε is a random variable with a time invariant distribution ($G(\varepsilon)$) with zero mean and finite variance.

We assume that, in each period, labor market decisions are made in two stages. First, the wage (W) is set before the realized value of ε is known [but with full information about $G(\varepsilon)$]. Second, the employment decision is made after ε is observed.

The wage is assumed to be the outcome of a Nash bargain between the firm and the union. The employment decision is assumed to be made unilaterally by the firm.

Consider the second stage of decision making first. Given the known values of W and ε, the firm sets employment so as to maximize its profit: $\varepsilon \cdot f(L) - W \cdot L$, which yields the labor demand equation

$$L = l(W/\varepsilon), \qquad l' < 0. \tag{1}$$

Now turn to the first stage of decision making. Suppose that the union members are risk-neutral and that each of them faces the same probability of being retained by the firm. Moreover, suppose that the union is run by a majority voting rule and that the majority of union members are employed. Thus, in the first stage of decision making, the union's objective is to maximize each union member's expected utility.

For simplicity, suppose that if the worker is employed in the current period, he experiences utility of $U(W)$, where $U' > 0$, $U'' < 0$;[2] yet if he is fired, then his utility is zero. Let σ be the incumbent insider's expected probability of being retained. Then the union's objective is $\sigma \cdot U(W)$ and its threat point is zero.

Let L^I be the number of union members in the current period and let $l(W/\hat{\varepsilon}) = L^I$. Then σ may be defined as

$$\sigma \equiv \int_{-\infty}^{\hat{\varepsilon}} [L/L^I] \cdot G(\varepsilon)\, d\varepsilon + \int_{\hat{\varepsilon}}^{\infty} G(\varepsilon)\, d\varepsilon. \tag{2a}$$

Note that if $l(W/\varepsilon) < L^I$, then current employment (L) falls short of the union membership (L^I). In that event, $(l(W/\varepsilon)/L^I)$ is a union member's retention probability, since we have assumed that the firm fires non-members before members.[3] By implication,

$$\sigma = \sigma(L^I, W), \tag{2b}$$
$$\quad\;\; (-)\;\; (-)$$

for any density $G(\varepsilon)$ that is strictly positive between a minimum and maximum value of ε.[4] (In other words, the more union members there are in the firm and the higher their wage, the lower is each union member's chance of being retained.)

The firm's objective in the wage bargain is to maximize its profit. If an agreement with the union is reached, whereby the wage W is accepted and no insiders are replaced by outsiders, the firm's expected profit is

$$\pi(W) = \int_{-\infty}^{\infty} \{\varepsilon \cdot f[l(W/\varepsilon)] - W \cdot l(W/\varepsilon)\} \cdot G(\varepsilon)\, d\varepsilon, \tag{3}$$

where we assume that π', $\pi'' < 0$.

Let T be the firm's turnover cost[5] (i.e., the cost of firing an insider and hiring an outsider instead), which we assume to be a constant. In general, the firm's cost of altering its workforce may be divided into two categories: (a) the cost of replacing current employees by outsiders and (b) the cost of expanding or contracting the workforce. Per employee, the former costs (which, as we have seen in chapters 4–6, may involve litigation costs, severance pay, a drop in the effort of the remaining employees, and costs due to insiders' cooperation and harassment activities) are usually much larger than the latter (pertaining to temporary layoff and subsequent recall). Our analysis focuses attention on the former costs (as a threat that the union uses in wage negotiation) and ignores the latter. Consequently, the labor demand equation (1) does not take the turnover cost T into account. Let R be the reservation wage (at which a worker is indifferent between employment and unemployment).[6] Then, for simplicity, we specify the firm's threat-point profit as $\pi = \pi(R + T)$. The $\pi(R + T)$ function may be interpreted as the profit that accrues when the insiders' positions are filled by outsiders. [We assume that $(R + T) > (0)$, so that the firm finds it more profitable to replace all its incumbents than to shut down its operations.]

Let $B = \pi(W) - \pi(R + T)$ be the firm's objective in wage negotiation and let $C = \sigma \cdot U(W)$ be the union's objective. Then the negotiated wage may be expressed as the solution to the following generalized Nash bargaining problem:

$$\max_{W} \Omega = B^a \cdot C^{1-a} \quad \text{subject to} \quad W \geqslant R, \quad \pi(W) \geqslant \pi(R + T),$$

$$\pi(W) \geqslant 0, \quad (4a)$$

where R and T are exogenously given to both negotiating parties, and the constant a $(0 < a < 1)$ measures the (exogenously given) bargaining strength of the firm relative to that of the union. Note that the turnover cost poses a threat to the firm, without which the union would have no bargaining power.

The first constraint of problem (4a) ensures that union members prefer employment to unemployment; the second and third constraints ensure that the firm has no incentive to replace its insiders by outsiders or to close down its operations, respectively. By (3), it is evident that the second constraint implies that

$$W \leqslant R + T. \quad (4b)$$

The first-order condition for an interior solution is

$$A = C_W + \delta \cdot (C/B) \cdot B_W = 0, \quad (4c)$$

where $\delta = a/(1 - a)$. From this condition, along with some restrictions on the density G and the production function f (see the appendix), we can show that the wage depends on the number of incumbent insiders (L^I) and on $(R + T)$ in the following way:

$$W = \phi(\underset{(-)}{L^I}, \underset{(+)}{R + T}), \quad (5a)$$

for values of W in the range

$$R \leqslant W \leqslant \min[R + T, \pi^{-1}(0)] = W^{\max}, \quad (5b)$$

[with $\pi^{-1}(0)$ given by (3)]. The larger the number of union members, the lower the retention probability, and thus the lower the wage is set. Also, the greater $(R + T)$, the lower the firm's threat-point profit, and the higher the wage.

Having analyzed wage formation, we now turn to the determinants of the firm's current incumbent workforce, L^I. Let r be the retirement rate (a positive constant), so that $r \cdot L^I_{-1}$ of last period's incumbent insiders retire. Let $h[(1 - r) \cdot (L_{-1} - L^I_{-1})]$ be the "entry-exit function," which describes how many of the firm's nonretired, employed nonmembers $[(1 - r) \cdot (L_{-1} - L^I_{-1})$ when $L_{-1} > L^I_{-1}]$ become union members or how many of the nonretired insiders who have been dismissed $[(1 - r) \cdot (L^I_{-1} - L_{-1})$ when $L_{-1} < L^I_{-1}]$ exit from the union. Then the current incumbent insider workforce is

$$L^I = (1 - r) \cdot L^I_{-1} + h[(1 - r) \cdot (L_{-1} - L^I_{-1})]. \tag{6}$$

The entry-exit function has the following properties:

$$h = 0 \quad \text{if} \quad L^I = L^I_{-1}, \tag{6a}$$

$$h = 1 \quad \text{if} \quad L_{-1} < L^I_{-1} \tag{6b}$$

(i.e., when incumbent insiders are dismissed, they lose their influence in wage determination, since—as noted—union behavior is determined by majority vote, with the majority consisting of the employed members), and

$$0 \leqslant h \leqslant 1 \quad \text{if} \quad L_{-1} > L^I_{-1}, \tag{6c}$$

(i.e., a fraction of the nonretired, employed nonmembers enter the union).[7]

Note two extreme cases. On the one hand, there is "free entry," where each of last period's employed nonmembers becomes a union member in the current period if he retains his job. Here, $h = 1$ for all $(L_{-1} - L^I_{-1})$, so that $L^I = (1 - r) \cdot L_{-1}$. On the other hand, there is the case of "no entry," where employed nonmembers have no opportunity of joining the union. Here $h = 0$ for $L_{-1} - L^I_{-1} \geqslant 0$, so that $L^I = (1 - r) \cdot L^I_{-1}$ over this range.

In short, our microeconomic model consists of the labor demand function (1) (pictured in figure 9.1a), the "wage setting function" [given by the conditions (5a) and (5b) and pictured in figure 9.1c], and entry-exit function (6) (pictured in figure 9.1d), which specifies the incumbent insider workforce. To move from this microeconomic model to a simple macroeconomic characterization of the labor market equilibrium, we make the following assumptions. First, we suppose that the labor market contains a fixed number of identical firms, union members, employed nonmembers,

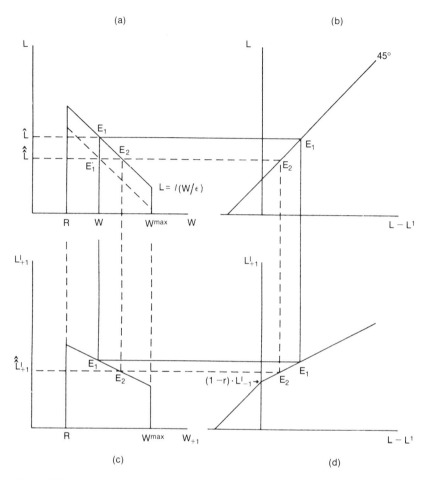

Figure 9.1
The labor market equilibrium and the unemployment persistence effect.

and outsiders. Then the wage-employment activity within an individual firm may be seen as a microcosm of that for the entire labor market. Second, we assume that the parameters of our model are such that, for any given value of ε, there exists a unique, stable, stationary equilibrium $(\hat{W}, \hat{L}, \hat{L}^I)$, for each firm, where $\hat{L}^I = \hat{L}^I_{+1}$ in the figure. Finally, we suppose that each realization of ε persists for long enough so that this equilibrium is reached. Such an equilibrium is illustrated by the points E_1 in figure 9.1.

9.3 The Influence of Union Power on Economic Resilience

We now show how the exercise of union power in wage bargaining may make the labor market less "resilient" in the face of cyclical swings in labor demand. We characterize this loss of resilience through two effects of unions on employment and unemployment:

a. By the "symmetric persistence effect," the union influences the wage in such a way that random variations in labor demand tend to create persistent, symmetric changes in unemployment. In particular, a temporary favorable shock in current labor demand leads to a fall in future unemployment, and a temporary unfavorable current shock leads to a rise in future unemployment. Furthermore, if the favorable and unfavorable shocks are of equal magnitude, the resulting changes in unemployment are of equal magnitude as well.

b. By the "asymmetric persistence effect," random variations in current labor demand have an asymmetric impact on future unemployment. In particular, the rise in future unemployment from an unfavorable current shock is larger than the fall in future unemployment from a favorable current shock of equal magnitude. Obversely, the rise in the future wage from the current unfavorable shock is larger than the fall in the future wage from the current favorable shock.

Consider the symmetric persistence effect first. Assume that given the level of ε, the initial equilibrium wage $(\hat{W})$ lies strictly between the upper and lower bounds given in condition (5b). Now consider what happens when there is a transient adverse shock to labor demand—generated by a fall in ε—after the current wage $\hat{W}$ has been negotiated. In other words, the labor demand curve in figure 9.1a shifts downward, so that for the current wage $(\hat{W})$, current employment $(\hat{L})$ is lower (as shown by point E'_1 in figure 9.1a). Assuming that $h > 0$ (so that the right-hand segment of the entry-exit function in figure 9.1c has a positive slope), the current incumbent insider workforce ($\hat{L}^I$) falls (as shown by point E_2 in figure 9.1c). Since a fall in the incumbent workforce (under the same distribution of employment shocks, ε, as before) raises each incumbent's retention probability, the union negotiates a higher wage. Thus, the wage rises above $\hat{W}$, as shown by point E_2 in figure 9.1c (where the new wage is less than W^{max}). The wage increase discourages the firm from employing as many workers as it would otherwise have done. Thus, for any given ε_{+1}, current employment will be lower than it would otherwise have been.

Given that the economy has n workers and m firms and that the negotiated wage (W) exceeds the reservation wage (R), the level of involuntary unemployment is $(n - m \cdot L)$. Then the argument above implies that once an employment slump occurs, the wage-setting activity of unions tends to make it persist, provided that $h > 0$ and $W < W^{max}$.[8,9]

Note that once the wage hits W^{max} [given by (5b)], the symmetric persistence effect disappears, in the sense that no further adverse shock in employment leads to a rise in the wage. (The reason is, of course, that if the union were to allow the wage to exceed this maximum level, the firm would respond by replacing the insiders by outsiders.) In other words, the unemployment persistence effect is bounded from above.[10]

We now consider how the magnitude of the symmetric persistence effect depends on *union entry conditions* (summarized by the function h). Clearly, entry conditions are relevant only when entry into the unions is actually taking place, i.e., only when $h > 0$ and $L > L^I$. Under these circumstances, the greater the opportunities for entry (i.e., the greater h), the more a given change in employment affects the magnitude of the insider workforce. Consequently, the greater is the symmetric persistence effect.

Next, we turn to the influence of *union bargaining power* on the symmetric persistent effect. In our analysis, a rise in such power is mirrored in (i) a fall in a (and hence δ) in (4c) (reflecting a fall in the bargaining strength of the firm relative to that of the union) and/or (ii) a rise in the firm's labor turnover cost, T.[11] It can be shown that each of these phenomena not only raises the wage (W), but makes the wage more responsive to changes in the incumbent insider workforce (L^I) [i.e., each increases the absolute value of ($\partial W / \partial L^I$) in (5a)] and thereby augments the symmetric persistence effect. This proposition is proved formally in the appendix; here we provide some intuitive interpretation.

The wage may be viewed as being set by a "Nashian arbitrator," whose objective function is a weighted average of that of the firm (B) and that of the union (C), as shown by the first-order condition (4c). This condition indicates that the arbitrator imposes a wage that makes the union's marginal gain from a wage increase (C_W) equal to the firm's associated marginal loss (B_W), appropriately normalized [by (C/B)]. When a fall in L^I raises the retention probability [as shown in equation (2b)], the union faces a larger marginal gain from a wage increase that heretoforce. Thus, the arbitrator raises the wage, making the union better off and the firm worse off.

But when the union's bargaining strength increases (i.e., falls), then the given drop in L^I calls forth a larger rise in W, because now the firm's loss from a wage increase is weighted less heavily in the arbitrator's objective function. Similarly, when the union raises the turnover cost T, it raises the firm's threat-point profit, and thus, once again, the arbitrator weights the firm's gain from a wage reduction less heavily. As above, the wage becomes less responsive to changes in L^I.

The larger the wage response to a given change in L^I, the flatter the W–L^I schedule in figure 9.1c. Thus, when there is an adverse employment shock (as shown in figure 9.1a) leading to a fall in the unionized workforce (in figures 9.1b and 9.1d), the resulting wage increase is larger than it would otherwise have been, and therefore the downturn in employment is amplified. In this way, a rise in union power strengthens the symmetric persistence effect.[12]

Figures 9.1 also indicate how union influence on wage bargaining may generate an "asymmetric persistence effect." In order for this effect to operate, it is necessary that there be less than "free entry" (i.e., $h < 1$) and that the random variations in labor demand be "large" relative to the incumbent insider workforce; i.e., adverse swings cause $L_{-1} < L_{-1}^I$ and favorable swings cause $L_{-1} > L_{-1}^I$.

To see this, observe that when $h < 1$, the left-hand branch of the entry-exit locus in figure 9.1d is steeper (45°) than the right-hand branch. In other words, the insiders who are dismissed all relinquish their influence on wage determination (since the union is assumed only to represent the interests of employed members), but the entrants who are hired do not all gain influence on wage determination (because when $h < 1$, some entrants do not promptly join the union). In other words, an unfavorable shock in current labor demand has a larger effect on the unionized insider workforce than a favorable shock has. Consequently, the increase in future wages and unemployment in response to a current unfavorable shock is larger than the fall in future wages and unemployment from a corresponding current favorable shock. This means that random variations in labor demand around a stationary mean lead to an downward trend in the unionized insider workforce and an upward trend in the wage and un-employment rates. A similar wage-employment ratchet may also arise from nonlinearities in the wage-setting function and the entry-exit function.

The greater union power (viz., the lower δ or the greater T) and the smaller h, the larger the ratchet effect, *ceteris paribus*. It is important to note that the presence of the ratchet effect does not imply that, over the course of successive business cycles, insider unions are able to drive wages upward without limit and thereby lead an ever larger proportion of the economy's workforce into unemployment. The reason is threefold. *First*, the ratchet effect is bounded from above by $W \leqslant W^{max}$, for otherwise the unions would give firms the incentive to replace insiders by outsiders. Once the wage reaches this upper limit, adverse labor demand shocks reduce employment while the wage remains rigid at W^{max}. *Second*, within this bound, unemployment rises secularly only if the random labor demand shocks have a stationary mean. If, on account of trend increases in labor productivity, the favorable shocks outweigh the unfavorable ones, then unemployment might not rise. And *third*, as union membership declines, the union's bargaining strength is likely to fall, and this brings downward pressure on the wage and on unemployment.

9.4 Concluding Remarks

Our analysis indicates that (a) unions' power over wages may, to some extent, hinder an economy in recovering from a recession and (b) the greater the unions' power (as reflected in their bargaining strength and the magnitude of labor turnover costs), the bleaker the economy's recovery prospects may become. In this light, the more widespread and intensive influence of unions in Europe than in the United States may help explain the drastically different product wage trajectories in these two parts of the world and Europe's comparative lack of success in reducing its unemployment after the recession of the early 1980s.

The same may be said of sectors within these economies. For example, unions play a comparative important role in wage determination of the steel and automobile industries in the United States, and it has been these industries that have witnessed relatively low employment rates.

It is worth noting that the symmetric persistence effect also works in reverse: Union wage setting tends to pertpetuate favorable random varia-tions in employment, and the stronger the unions are, the more pronounced this effect will be. Thus it may be argued that although a rise in union power has an adverse comparative static effect on the labor market—as shown above, it may lead to higher wages and lower employment—it also has a favorable dynamic influence after a business upswing, on account of the symmetric persistence effect.

This favorable dynamic effect is emphatically weaker in the presence of the asymmetric persistence effect. Here, union wage setting without concern for outsiders is doubly harmful, in that it leads to a persistent drop in employment in response to a business downswing and dissipates a business upswing through wage increases.

Observe that there is no intrinsic relation between the quantitative importance of the symmetric and the asymmetric persistence effects. The size of the former depends on the slopes of the labor demand function, the wage setting function, and the entry-exit function; the size of the latter depends on the degree of asymmetry in the entry-exit function (as well as on nonlinearities in the entry-exit function and the wage-setting function). Thus it is conceivable that a rise in union power may strengthen both effects or just one of them.

In this light, our analysis may provide a framework for explaining why unemployment rates in Europe and the United States have had an upward trend over the 1970s and most of the 1980s and why the US economy appears more "resilient" than many European economies. Our analysis also provides some microeconomic underpinning for the notion that European unemployment is more closely related to "excessive wages" than American unemployment. It also provides some microeconomic underpinning for the notion that European unemployment is more closely related to "excessive wages" than is American unemployment.

Appendix

The effect of the incumbent workforce on the wage: Rewriting (4c), $A = [\sigma \cdot U' + \sigma_l \cdot l' \cdot U] + \delta \cdot (\sigma \cdot U/B) \cdot \pi'(W) = 0$. In order for the second-order condition for optimality to be fulfilled, we need to assume that $[(\sigma_{ll} \cdot l'/\sigma_l) - (l''/l')]$ exceeds some negative critical value. For the sake of algebraic simplicity below, however, we suppose that $l'' = 0$, $\sigma_{ll} < 0$, and $\sigma_{lL} = 0$. These conditions may be derived by imposing the appropriate restrictions on the density G and the production function f.

$$(\partial W/\partial L')|_{A=C} = -A_L/A_W,$$

where

$$A_W = (\partial A/\partial W)$$

$$= -l' \cdot [\sigma \cdot U' + \sigma_{ll} \cdot l' \cdot U + \delta_1 \cdot \pi'(W) \cdot \sigma \cdot U/B]$$

$$+ \sigma \cdot U'' + \sigma_l \cdot l' \cdot U' + (\delta \cdot \sigma/B)$$

$$\cdot [\pi'(W) \cdot U' - (\pi'(W) \cdot U/B) - U \cdot \pi''(W)],$$

which must be negative in order for the second-order condition for optimality to be fulfilled. We assume that $\sigma_{ll} < 0$ to ensure this; furthermore, assuming $\sigma_{lL} = 0$ for simplicity,

$$A_L = (\partial A/\partial L^I) = \sigma_L \cdot [U' + (\delta \cdot U \cdot \pi'(W)/B)] < 0.$$

Thus, $(\partial W/\partial L^I)|_{A=0} < 0$.

The effect of $(R + T)$ on the wage:

$$[\partial W/\partial(R + T)]|_{A=0} = -A_{R+T}/A_W,$$

where

$$A_{R+T} = [\partial A/\partial(R + T)] = -\delta \cdot (\sigma \cdot Y/B^2) \cdot \pi'(W) \cdot [\partial B/\partial(R + T)] > 0.$$

Thus, $[\partial W/\partial(R + T)]|_{A=0} > 0$.

The effect of δ on the wage:

$$[\partial W/\partial \delta]|_{A=0} = -(\sigma \cdot U \cdot \pi'(W))/B \cdot A_W < 0.$$

The effect of T on the responsiveness of W to L^I: Note that

$$(A_W/A_L) = -l' + (\zeta/A_L) \equiv D,$$

where

$$\zeta = \sigma \cdot U'' + \sigma_l \cdot l' \cdot U' + (\delta \cdot \sigma/B) \cdot [\pi'(W) \cdot U' - (\pi'(W) \cdot U/B) - U \cdot \pi''(W)].$$

Then

$$\frac{\partial D}{\partial \delta} = \frac{\zeta_\delta \cdot A_L - A_{L\delta} \cdot \zeta}{(A_L)^2},$$

which is positive because

$$A_{L\delta} = \sigma_L \cdot \pi'(W) \cdot U/B > 0,$$

$$\zeta_\delta = (\pi'(W) \cdot \sigma/B^2) \cdot [U' \cdot B - \pi'(W) \cdot U] + (\sigma \cdot U \cdot \pi''(W)/B) < 0,$$

and thus

$$\zeta_\delta \cdot A_L - A_{L\delta} \cdot \zeta = \zeta_\delta \cdot [\sigma_L \cdot U' - \sigma'' \cdot l' \cdot U] - A_{L\delta} \cdot [\sigma \cdot U'' + \sigma_l \cdot l' \cdot U'] > 0.$$

Hence, $\partial[(\partial W/\partial L^I)|_{A=0}]/\partial \delta > 0$.

Notes

1. For a provocative recent account along these lines, see Fitoussi and Phelps (1987).

2. Note that the concavity of the utility function does not contradict our assumption of risk neutrality since W is not a random variable in our model.

3. If members and nonmembers had an equal chance of being fired, then the above retention probability would be (L/L^I).

4. We do not exclude the possibility that these minimum and maximum values of ε may be $-\infty$ and $+\infty$, respectively.

5. For microeconomic derivations of T, see chapters 4–6.

6. We assume all workers to have the same utility function and thus the same reservation wage.

7. How many of such workers join the union in the real world depends on laws, social norms, transactions costs, inertia in nonmembers' behavior—all of which lie beyond the influence of the union itself (and beyond the scope of this chapter).

8. Of course, insider market power is not the only conceivable rationale for such an effect. Other rationales include the depreciation of human and nonhuman capital during prolonged periods of unemployment and changes in workers' tastes and job search behavior over such periods (in particular, an increased preference for leisure relative to work and a loss of self-confidence in job search).

9. Observe that this result is superficially similar to that of Blanchard and Summers (1987). However, their unemployment persistence rests on a fundamentally different relation between wages and labor demand: In our model, unions may be responsible for "excessive" real wages and "deficient" employment due to production processes characterized by diminishing returns to labor; in their model, unions may give rise to excessive nominal wages, implying excessive product prices and thereby leading to deficient product demand and thus to a deficient derived demand for labor.

10. Observe furthermore that if $h < 1$ when $L_{-1} > L_{-1}^I$ and if adverse employment swings lead to shrinkage of the labor force while favorable swings lead to net hiring, then the unemployment persistence effect tends to be weaker in a boom than in a slump. Blanchard and Summers (1986) find empirical confirmation of this phenomenon.

11. Note that the degree of union power, as defined here, does not necessarily have anything to do with the degree of centralization in bargaining.

12. As the appendix shows, these are not the only channels whereby a fall in δ or a rise in T may influence the relation between W and L^I. Suffice it to say that the other channels pull in the same direction.

10   Long-Term Unemployment and Macroeconomic Policy

Overview

In the previous chapter we examined how the exercise of insider power could perpetuate the effects of labor demand shocks, create "unemployment persistence," and thereby reduce the labor market's "resilience" or ability to recover from disturbances. We noted that our analysis rested crucially on the assumption that the labor demand shocks are transient (with a constant mean) and unforeseen by the wage setters. This assumption is restrictive, particularly if we seek to provide a framework for understanding the recent unemployment experience of Europe and the United States. Although some of the supply- and demand-side shocks occurring in the initial phase of the recession beginning in 1979 could reasonably be considered surprises and perhaps did not significantly affect workers' long-term employment expectations, the same cannot be said of shocks occurring in the later phases of the recession. To explain the inexorable rise in European unemployment over many years and the briefer, but nevertheless protracted, period of high unemployment in the United States, it appears sensible to appeal to more than transient, unforeseen shocks.

One aim of this chapter is to respond to this problem. We inquire whether the exercise of insider power may generate unemployment persistence even when the labor demand shocks are permanent and foreseen. We show that this is indeed possible, particularly if the insiders have some influence on labor turnover costs and if firing decisions are governed by a seniority system.

Our argument is straightforward. When an unfavorable, foreseen shock occurs, the insider wage may respond little, if at all, because a wage drop is not in the interests of the majority of insiders. Consequently, workers are laid off. If these workers were to attempt to keep their jobs by offering to accept a lower wage, the remaining insiders could thwart them by manipulating the labor turnover costs (e.g., by refusing to cooperate with the underbidders or by harassing them). Yet when a favorable, foreseen shock occurs, then the insider wage may well respond.

As long as the insider wage is less than the reservation wage plus the labor turnover costs, the favorable shock creates economic rent, which the insiders may capture by raising their wage. In this manner, insiders' influence over their wage may give rise to asymmetric persistence of labor demand shocks.

This does not mean that insiders invariably raise their wage sufficiently in an upswing to prevent any increase in employment; nor does it mean that their wage never falls in a downswing. One reason is that the insiders never have the incentive to raise their wage above the level of the reservation wage plus the labor turnover costs, because otherwise it would be profitable for their firm to replace them by outsiders. Another reason is that when insiders and firms both have market power in wage determination, the insiders are unable to exploit all the rent from a favorable labor demand shock, and they may be only partially successful in keeping the wage from falling in the presence of an unfavorable shock.

The wage-employment response to labor demand shocks outlined above implies that there is no natural rate of unemployment, in the sense that the equilibrium level of unemployment is not uniquely determined by the tastes, technologies, and endowments of the agents in the economy. On the contrary, equilibrium unemployment depends on the size of the current insider workforce. The size of this workforce, in turn, is equal to the last period's insider workforce minus the number of workers who have quit or retired plus the number of the last period's entrants who have currently gained insider status. Labor demand shocks affect quits from and entries to the labor force and thereby affect equilibrium unemployment.

In addition to presenting an analysis of how wages and employment respond to labor demand variations, this chapter also examines how these variations may be generated through macroeconomic policies. In particular, we identify three channels whereby demand-management policies may shift the labor demand curve (in wage-employment space):

i. In the long run, increases in government expenditures on industrial infrastructure may raise the marginal product of labor directly and thereby shift the labor demand curve.

ii. In the medium run, expansionary demand-management policies may create incentives for the entry of new firms, thereby raising aggregate labor demand at any given real wage.

iii. In the short run, these policies may raise the rate of capital utilization. When workers are recalled to operate idle plant and equipment, the capital that is utilized is complementary with labor, and thus these policies indirectly raise the marginal product of labor.

Observe that all of these demand-side policies work on account of their supply-side effects. We show that demand-side policies that do not have such supply-side effects—say, policies that generate an elasticity-preserving shift in the product demand curve without affecting the number of firms or the marginal product of labor—leave the relation between aggregate labor demand and the real wage unchanged. By implication, the equilibrium levels of wages and employment in our analysis remain unchanged as well.

This chapter bears a simple double message: When insiders have some power in wage determination, then (i) there may be no natural rate of unemployment and (ii) both supply-side and demand-side policies may have lasting effects on the unemployment rate. However, our analysis implies that demand-side policies in the product market may be much less reliable, and operate through more complex channels, than the traditional Keynesians envisaged.

By "supply-side policies" we mean policy actions that have an immediate impact on an economy's production capability. "Demand-side policies" may be divided into two categories: (a) changes in public-sector employment and (b) policies that affect the labor market via other markets. Since the effects of the first policies on unemployment are trivial to analyze (though of considerable practical importance), we concentrate instead on the second. In particular, we focus attention on how demand management policies in the product market affect the labor market.

The Keynesian arguments for the long-term effectiveness of demand-side policies hinge on the assumption of either sluggish nominal wages or sluggish prices, or both. If nominal wages are sluggish, then an increase in product demand that raises the price level reduces the real wage and thereby stimulates labor demand. If prices are sluggish and firms are rationed in the product market, then an increase in product demand "spills over" into the labor market, thereby raising the demand for labor at any given real wage.

Although these effects may well be important in practice, we do not believe that they represent the only significant channels whereby product market shocks can be transmitted to the labor market. If sluggish nominal wages were the only channel, then real wages would always move counter-cyclically in response to demand shocks—which files in the face of much evidence of procyclical responses. The well-known weakness of the "sluggish price" argument is that it rests on the assumption that agents are price takers even though they face sales rations—which is implausible behavior.

In this chapter, by contrast, we examine the effectiveness of macro-economic policies when wages and prices are both flexible, in the sense that agents set them freely in response to policy changes. In this context, as we shall see, there are transmission mechanisms that permit both pro- and countercyclical movements of real wages.

We assume that pricing, production, and employment decisions are made by imperfectly competitive firms (taking wages as given) and that nominal wages are set by workers (who take the effect of wages on employment into account). (The substance of our argument would remain unchanged if nominal wages were determined through negotiations be-tween firms and workers.) The firms' decisions yield a relation between the real wage and aggregate labor demand—the "labor-demand relation," for short. The wage setters' only target variables are assumed to be the real wage and employment, and thus the wage setters in effect determine a point on the labor demand relation (i.e., a real wage and a level of employment).

As we have no quarrel with transmission mechanisms by way of changes in the real wage and concomitant movements along the labor demand relation, we concentrate here on the ways in which macroeconomic policies may affect wages and employment through shifts in the labor demand relation. We proceed in two steps. In section 10.1, we inquire how such policies change the relation between real wages and labor demand. In section 10.2, given a change in this relation, we examine how wages, employment, and unemployment are determined.

10.1 Transmission of Macroeconomic Policies to the Labor Market

We represent a firm's demand function by

$$P = P(Q, A), \qquad P_1 < 0, \quad P_2 > 0, \tag{1}$$

where P is the price, Q is product demand, and A is a shift parameter, which may be varied through demand management policies. Moreover, let the firm's production function be

$$Q = f(L), \qquad f_1 > 0 \quad f_{11} < 0, \tag{2}$$

where L is labor.

Suppose that each firm, when maximizing its profit subject to its product-demand function and production function, takes the nominal wage (W) as given, so that the real marginal value product of labor is equal to the real wage:

$$b \cdot f_1 = W/P, \tag{3}$$

where $b = (1 - (1/\varepsilon))$ and ε is the price elasticity of the firm's product-demand function.

Assuming (merely for simplicity) that there is a given number (M) of identical firms in the economy and that their product-demand functions are independent of one another, the aggregate labor-demand relation is

$$N = M \cdot L = M \cdot L(W/(b \cdot P)), \tag{4}$$

$$L = (f_1)^{-1} \quad \text{and} \quad L' < 0.$$

This simple condition tells us that, under the imperfectly competitive conditions outlined above, demand-management policies can shift the aggregate labor-demand relation [equation (4)] only if such policies are able to change one or more of the following three variables: (a) the number of firms in the economy (M), (b) the marginal product of labor (f_1), or (c) the price elasticity of product demand ($\varepsilon = 1/(1 - b)$).

It should be noted that the labor-demand relation does *not* depend directly on the shift parameter (A) of the product-demand functions. Thus, a policy that merely shifts the product-demand functions (without affecting any of the variables above) leaves the aggregate labor-demand relation unchanged.

Of the three variables above, the demand elasticity is probably not a reliable and systematic channel for the transmission of policy shocks from the product to the labor market. There do not appear to be compelling reasons to believe that this elasticity rises (falls) systematically whenever product demand rises (falls).

As for the other two channels of transmission, expansionary demand management policy may (a) create incentives for the entry of new firms (which in turn raises the demand for labor associated with any given real wage) and/or (b) raise the marginal product of labor—either *directly*, by government policies that augment the industrial infrastructure of the economy, or *indirectly*, when the policy leads to a rise in the use of factors that are complementary to labor or to a fall in the use of substitutes for labor.

The latter, indirect, effect on the marginal product of labor may have a significant role to play when there is excess capital capacity and the product-demand stimulus raises firms' rate of capital utilization. In that event, workers are simply recalled to operate unmanned machines and reestablish existing assembly lines. The point is that the plant and equipment that is brought into use in the course of cyclical upswings is usually complementary to labor, and this means that the rise in the capital utilization rate may occur without a reduction in the marginal product of labor.

In short, under flexible wages and prices set by imperfectly competitive agents, our analysis leads us to identify one short-run, one medium-run, and one long-run channel whereby these shocks may shift the aggregate labor-demand relation. The short-run channel involves a change in the rate of capital utilization; the medium-run channel operates through the entry and exit of firms; and the long-run channel works via the buildup and rundown of industrial infrastructure. (For a detailed analysis of these channels, see Lindbeck and Snower, 1987c.)

What are the policy implications of these lines of thought? First, the short-run transmission mechanism, involving changes in the rate of capital capacity utilization, is operative only as long as there is excess capital capacity—regardless of the rate of unemployment. Thus, demand-management policies may be able to raise employment at constant (or even rising) real wages when there is excess capacity, but be unable to do so at full capacity utilization. Second, the removal of barriers to the entry of firms may be an important ingredient in making demand-management policy effective. Third, changes in government expenditure on industrial infrastructure may have a much larger impact on the labor market, at least in a long-run perspective, than have spending changes on goods that are not complementary to labor (as in the case of tax reductions, increased transfer payments, or greater government purchases of consumer goods).

10.2 The Labor Market

Having examined the effect of demand-management policies on the relation between the real wage and aggregate labor demand, we now turn to the determination of a wage-employment point on this relation and to the associated level of unemployment.

In particular, we show that if insiders have some market power in the negotiations over nominal wages, then policy-induced shifts in the aggregate labor-demand relation may give rise to persistent changes in the level of unemployment. In this context, there is no natural rate of unemployment as commonly envisaged by natural rate theories. In other words, when wage-price expectations are correct, unemployment is not necessarily at a unique rate, determined exclusively by the tastes, technologies, and endowments of the agents in the economy.

Modifying the firm's marginal productivity condition (3) to include the employment of insiders L_I and entrants L_E, we obtain

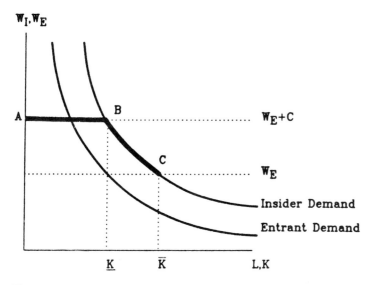

Figure 10.1
The firm's equilibria.

$$b \cdot f_i(L_I, L_E) = W_i/P, \qquad i = I, E, \tag{5}$$

where W_I and W_E are the nominal wages of insiders and entrants, respectively, and f_I and f_E are their marginal products adjusted for the relevant labor turnover costs. For instance, f_I could be the insiders' marginal product plus their marginal firing cost and f_E could be the entrants' marginal product minus their marginal hiring cost.

The labor-demand relations for insiders and entrants are illustrated by the downward-sloping curves in figure 10.1. In particular, let K be the firm's incumbent workforce and suppose that the insider wage is set so that the firm never has the incentive to replace incumbents by entrants. Thus the insider demand relation is $P \cdot b \cdot f_I(L_I, 0) = W_I$ and the entrant demand relation is $P \cdot b \cdot f_E(K, L_E) = W_E$.

Turning to wage determination, our analysis requires that the insider wage be the outcome of negotiations between each firm and its insiders (who may bargain collectively or individually), and that the insiders have some market power in these negotiations. Yet, merely for expositional simplicity, we assume that the insiders have complete market power in the determination of the nominal insider wage and that each insider sets his wage "individualistically" (taking the wages and employment of the other insiders as exogenously given), so that each insider views himself as the marginal employee in his firm.

Then the nominal insider wage W_I will be set as high as possible, subject to the constraint that the insider does not become unprofitable to the firm ($W_I \leqslant P \cdot b \cdot f_I(K, L_E)$) and that the insider is at least as profitable as the marginal entrant ($W_I \leqslant W_E + C$), where C is the nominal cost of replacing an insider by an entrant. (This cost enters the specification of the functions f_I and f_E.) In short,

$$W_I/P = \min[b \cdot f_I(K, L_E), (W_E/P) + (C/P)]. \tag{6a}$$

Assuming that the outsiders are perfect competitors for jobs, the entrant's real wage (W_E/P) is equal to the outsiders' real reservation wage (R), which is taken to be an exogenous constant:

$$W_E/P = R. \tag{6b}$$

Combining the employment equation (5) with the wage equations (6a) and (6b) yields the locus of microeconomic equilibrium points, given by the equilibrium insider wage associated with any incumbent workforce, as illustrated by the thick segment in figure 10.1.

Observe that if the incumbent workforce (K) is less than a critical value $\underline{K}$ (in figure 10.1), then the insider wage is set equal to the cost of replacing an insider by an entrant ($W_E + C$). Here the incumbent workforce is sufficiently small so that entrants are profitable to the firm ($P \cdot b \cdot f_E(K, 0) > W_E$) and thus each insider must ensure that he is at least as profitable as the marginal entrant. At the resulting insider wage ($W_I = W_E + C$), all the incumbents are retained and some entrants are hired.

Yet if the incumbent workforce is larger than that above, lying in the range, $\underline{K} \leqslant K \leqslant \overline{K}$ (in figure 10.1), then the insider wage is set equal to the marginal product (adjusted for firing costs) of the incumbent workforce. In this case, the incumbent workforce is sufficiently large so that entrants are not profitable to the firm ($P \cdot b \cdot f_E(K, 0) < W_E$) and consequently insiders can set their wage without reference to their replacement cost. At that wage ($W_I = P \cdot b \cdot f_I(K, 0)$), all the incumbents are retained and no entrants are hired. Note that the firm's workforce cannot exceed $\overline{K}$ for, at any higher employment level, the reservation wage (R_E) would exceed the marginal product (adjusted for turnover costs) of all workers.

Moving from the micro- to the macroeconomic level, we take the horizontal sum of each firm's equilibrium locus ABC (in figure 10.1) and thereby obtain the labor market equilibrium locus DEF (in figure 10.2). Suppose now that the aggregate incumbent workforce is K_1 (in figure 10.2); then the equilibrium insider wage is W_I^*. (The corresponding equilibrium point is denoted by e_1 in the figure). At this wage, all incumbents are

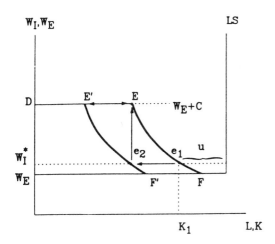

Figure 10.2
Labor market equilibria.

retained and no entrants are hired. Given the labor supply curve (*LS*) drawn in the figure, u workers remain unemployed.

10.3 Persistence of Policy Effects in the Labor Market

Let us now examine the effects of supply-side and demand-side macroeconomic policy shocks on the labor market above. We illustrate supply-side shocks (affecting the marginal product of labor) as shifts in the labor market equilibrium locus in figure 10.2.

Our economy's wage-employment response to these shocks depends on (a) whether the shock is foreseen by the wage setters, (b) whether insiders are able to exert some control over labor turnover costs, and (c) whether firing decisions are governed by a seniority system. These three conditions are important for the following reasons. First, it is obvious that the insider wage can respond only to shocks that are foreseen by the wage setters. (The previous chapter dealt with the repercussions of unforeseen shocks.) Second, insiders' influence over turnover costs may give them the ability to prevent underbidding by laid-off workers. They may do so by refusing to cooperate with the underbidders (thereby reducing their productivity), by creating a hostile work environment for the underbidders (thereby raising their reservation wage), or by threatening to strike or work-to-rule (see chapters 5, 7, and 8). Third, the existence of a seniority system permits the insiders to identify in advance the workers who will be laid off in response to a particular adverse shock and whose underbidding activities are to be thwarted. We assume that the seniority system specifies an order to dismissal, given the existing wage structure, but that firms are free to modify that order if the wages of senior employees rise relative to those of junior employees.

Let us consider the effects of supply-side shocks. Suppose that these shocks are anticipated in the wage decisions, that insiders can influence labor turnover costs, and that a seniority system exists. Let the initial labor market equilibrium be given by point e_1 in figure 10.2 (where the incumbent workforce lies in the range $\underline{K} \leqslant K \leqslant \bar{K}$). Thereupon an unfavorable supply-side shock occurs, which shifts the labor market equilibrium locus from DEF to $DE'F'$. The insider wage may fail to fall in response to this shock, even though workers are laid off.

To see this, observe that if the insider wage exceeds the reservation wage, the layoff candidates may attempt to retain their jobs by offering to worker for a lower wage. The remaining insiders have the following choice:

i. If they allow the layoff candidates to underbid, then their own wages will fall as well. For, if the remaining insiders refused to accept a wage cut, then the firms would fire them and retain the layoff candidates.

ii. If the remaining insiders prevent underbidding by the layoff candidates (through the appropriate manipulation of the labor turnover costs), they may be able to preserve their wages in the face of the adverse shock. In that event, the remaining insiders protect their positions by treating the underbidding layoff candidates in the same way as they treat the underbidding outsiders.

Clearly, the remaining insiders are better off under the second option. Thus, if this option is open to them, the adverse shock leads to a drop in employment at constant insider wages. The labor market equilibrium moves from point e_1 to e_2.[1] The reason is that if the workers to be laid off should try to keep their jobs by offering to work for a lower wage, the remaining insiders could prevent this from happening by manipulating the labor turnover costs (for example, by harrassing the underbidders.) Consequently, employment falls while insider wages remain unchanged.

Now suppose that, later on, a favorable supply-side shock occurs, shifting the labor market equilibrium locus back out to DEF. Now the insiders have the opportunity to raise their wage without fear of being displaced by other workers. As result, the insider wage rises and employment remains unchanged. The labor market equilibrium moves from point e_2 to point E.

As we can see, when the incumbent workforce lies in the range $\underline{K} \leqslant K \leqslant \bar{K}$, favorable and unfavorable supply-side shocks do not have symmetric effects on wages and employment: The unfavorable shock reduces employment, but the favorable shock does not increase employment. (If we instead assume that *both* insiders *and* firms have power over the insider wage, then the unfavorable shock reduces employment merely by more than the favorable shock increases it.)

In this manner, the exercise of insider power over wages can lead to "asymmetric persistence" of foreseen supply-side policy impulses. This asymmetric persistence disappears once the insider wage reaches the level $W_E + C$. The reason is that the insiders cannot raise their wage above this level, for otherwise they would be replaced by outsiders. At $W_I = W_E + C$, upward and downward shifts of the equilibrium locus lead to variations in employment at constant real wages. (This is illustrated by the arrows between equilibrium points E' and E in figure 10.2.)

Now turn to the effects of demand-side macroeconomic policies on the labor market, in the light of the discussion of the transmission mechanisms in section 10.1. We consider the three demand-side transmission mechanisms of section 10.1 in turn. First, some types of government investment in industrial infrastructure will raise the marginal product of labor and thereby shift the labor market equilibrium locus outward. Conversely, a rundown of infrastructure causes the locus to shift inward. The resulting effects on wages, employment, and unemployment are basically the same as the effects of the supply-side policies considered above.

Second, demand-side policies that lead to the entry of new firms serve to raise employment of entrant workers, who receive the reservation wage (provided that union agreements or government legislation do not prevent new firms from hiring labor at the reservation wage). After these workers turn into insiders, they receive the insider wage. (For instance, letting the firm in figure 10.1 be a new firm, $\underline{K}$ entrants are hired at wage W_E, and once they achieve insider status, their wage becomes $W_I = W_E + C$.)

Finally, consider demand-side policies that raise the marginal product of capital by increasing the rate of capital utilization. Assuming that the capital brought back into operation is complementary with labor, the insider and entrant labor demand curves (in contrast to those pictured in figure 10.1) may be upward sloping at cyclically low levels of capital capacity utilization and downward sloping only at full capacity utilization. Accordingly, the labor market equilibrium locus (in contrast to that pictured in figure 10.2) may have both upward- and downward-sloping portions. This means that the demand-side policies above can move the labor market equilibrium point along either an upward- or a downward-sloping labor market equilibrium locus (see Lindbeck and Snower, 1987c).

10.4 Concluding Remarks

Our analysis suggests that the entry and exit of firms may play an important long-term role in the transmission of product market shocks to the labor market. In this light, lower barriers to entry by firms in the United States than in Western Europe may help explain why US employment recovered more rapidly from the recession of the late 1970s and early 1980s than European employment did.

We also argue that demand management policies that have "supply-side" effects on labor productivity—for example, policies that stimulate the rate of capital utilization or expenditures on industrial infrastructure (such as that undertaken by Western governments in the 1950s)—may have a larger impact on employment than policies without such supply-side effects (such as the transfer payments that have commanded progressively larger portions of European government budgets in the postwar period).

Finally, our analysis suggests that aggregate supply shocks may affect the labor market more directly and speedily than most aggregate demand shocks do. In this light, it appears that the overall level of unemployment in Europe during the 1950s and 1960s may have been low partly on account of the steady stream of expansionary supply-side shocks (such as a falling real price of oil). By contrast, European unemployment may have been comparatively high since the mid-1970s because the contractionary supply-side influences (including the overshooting of product wages) may have been difficult to counteract through demand-management policies, particularly in the face of limited entry of firms and insufficient excess capital capacity.

Note

1. In this connection it is important to ask, If the senior workers are able to erect reentry barriers against the junior, laid-off workers, what keeps the senior workers from erecting these barriers against junior workers who have not been laid off? After all, under diminishing returns to labor, a fall in the number of junior workers would raise the marginal product of the incumbent workforce and thereby raise the wages of the senior workers. There are various reasons why senior workers may erect barriers against underbidders but not against colleagues who do not underbid. First, the erection of entry barriers may be costly to the senior workers (e.g., the activities of harassing, refusing to cooperate, and striking may all generate

disutility). The disutility from erecting entry barriers may well be nondecreasing, whereas the marginal utility of wage income may be decreasing. Consequently, the marginal benefit from foiling underbidders may exceed the marginal benefit from ousting colleagues who do not underbid, but the associated marginal costs may be the same. Moreover, this may hold true for a broad range of wages if we suppose —in line with recent developments in the theory of choice by Kahneman and Tversky (1986, for example)—that the utility gain from a wage increase is substantially greater than the utility loss from a wage decrease, even if these wage changes are very small. Second, the senior insiders' disutility from erecting entry barriers may depend on whether these workers perceive that they have been provoked. For example, it may be less distasteful to harass an underbidder than to do so to a colleague who does not threaten one's own income.

11   Predictions and
        Policy Implications

Economic theories have one or more of the following three purposes: (i) to provide an understanding of why particular economic phenomena occur, (ii) to generate conditional predictions, and (iii) to suggest policy prescriptions. With regard to the first purpose, the primary aim of the insider-outsider theory is to provide an understanding of how labor turnover costs may give rise to insider power and how the exercise of this power, in turn, affects wages, employment, and unemployment. Most of this book has been devoted to this task. We now turn to the other two purposes. Section 11.1 is a brief overview of some of the theory's main predictions; section 11.2 deals with policy implications.

11.1 Predictions

The worth of a theory may be measured not only by its ability to explain what it was designed to explain, but also by the light it sheds on economic phenomena lying beyond the theory's primary objective. The insider-outsider theory was originally designed to explain the existence of involuntary unemployment in market economies and, in particular, the failure to underbid prevailing wages in the presence of such employment. Let us now consider some predictions that are not intrinsically related to this objective. For the sake of brevity, our discussion will be informal.

11.1.1 Persistence of Temporary Shocks in Labor Demand

The insider-outsider theory implies that temporary labor demand shocks (i.e., temporary shifts of the labor demand curve in real wage/employment space) may have persistent effects on wages, employment, and unemployment. We call this phenomenon "effect persistence," for short. Broadly speaking, the theory predicts that effect persistence will be comparatively pronounced in countries with comparatively large labor turnover costs and strong unions, provided that these unions are not much concerned about the employment prospects of the unemployed workers. Thereby the theory offers a conceivable explanation of why the worldwide recessions of the 1970s and 1980s had more protracted after-effects in Europe than in the United States.

The phenomenon of effect persistence is absent from most other theories of labor market activity. For instance, in the standard model of perfect competition in the labor market, temporary shocks have only a temporary effect on the wage and employment levels. After a shock occurs, there is a new point of intersection between the labor demand and supply curves; and when the shock is reversed, the intersection point returns to its original position. In models with endogenous capital formation, a temporary shock may affect the stocks of physical and human capital, and consequently it may generate longer-run shifts of the labor demand and supply curves. However, when the shocks last only a few years and when they give rise to factor price adjustments and capital-labor substitution, it is difficult to imagine that these longer-run shifts could be very significant impacts on employment and unemployment.

Nor do employment and unemployment effects of temporary shocks persist in the traditional models of monopolistic and imperfectly competitive behavior in the labor market. For example, in the "monopoly union" model (where the union sets the wage so as to maximize its objective function subject to the labor demand curve), a temporary shift of the labor demand curve may, of course, lead the union to choose a new wage, associated with a new level of employment; but this response lasts only for as long as the shock does. This is also the case in the wage bargaining models (where the wage is the outcome of a bargain between the union and the firms, while employment is set subsequently by the firms alone) and the wage-employment bargaining models (in which the union and the firms bargain over wages and employment simultaneously). Temporary shocks also have only temporary employment effects in the standard efficiency wage theories. A shock to the production function or the productivity-wage relation may induce the firm to offer a new wage-employment combination; but once the shock is over, the initial equilibrium is reestablished.

The insider-outsider theory offers a different picture. Here temporary shocks may have persistent effects on wages and employment, due to a combination of two factors:

i. the shocks may affect the size of firms' insider workforces and

ii. a change in the size of these workforces may influence the insiders' future objectives in wage negotiations.

A firm's insider workforce, like its capital stock, is a state variable that can be changed only gradually. The rate at which the insider workforce can be augmented depends on the time required to turn entrants into insiders (analogous to the time between orders and deliveries of capital goods). The rate at which this workforce is reduced depends on the quit and retirement rate (analogous to the capital depreciation rate) and the labor turnover costs (perhaps analogous to the price differential between first-hand and second-hand capital goods). Just like investment at any point in time has persistent effects on the size of the capital stock, temporary labor demand shocks may have persistent effects on the insider workforce.

Furthermore, a change in the insider workforce may affect the insiders' future wage demands. These wage demands, in turn, influence the firm's future employment decisions. In this manner, the insiders' power in wage setting may serve to perpetuate temporary labor demand shocks. Chapter 9 showed how this may happen when the shocks are unforeseen by the wage setters, whereas chapter 10 dealt with foreseen shocks.

When the shocks are *unforeseen*, the insiders clearly do not have the opportunity to adjust their wages in response to these shocks. Thus, as we have seen in chapter 9, when an adverse shock occurs, some insiders are dismissed. However, if their remaining colleagues expect the underlying distribution of shocks to remain unchanged, they now perceive themselves to have greater job security than heretofore. Consequently, in the next round of wage negotiations, these remaining insiders may demand a higher wage. If they do, then the wage rise will discourage future employment, even though the adverse shock may have passed by then. The obverse holds when a favorable shock occurs.

Observe that if the labor demand curve and the insiders' wage-setting rule is symmetric around the long-run equilibrium wage-employment point, then current favorable and unfavorable shocks affect future employment in the same way. To be precise, the future employment rise from a current favorable shock is just as large as the future employment fall from a current unfavorable shock of equal magnitude. In this sense, there is "*symmetric* persistence" of the effects of temporary labor demand shocks on employment.

When the shocks are *foreseen* by the insiders, the persistence effects may arise from another source: the asymmetric response of insiders' wage claims to upward and downward shifts of the labor demand curve. There are many conceivable reasons for this asymmetry.

First, as we have shown in chapter 10, an asymmetric wage response may occur when firing decisions are governed by a seniority system and when some labor turnover costs can be manipulated by the insiders. Under these circumstances, the senior insiders may be able to protect themselves from a foreseen, adverse shock by preventing laid-off junior workers from regaining their jobs through underbidding. As we have discussed in chapter 5, the senior workers may do this by, for example, threatening to harass underbidders or by refusing to cooperate with them in the process of production. As result, the adverse shock may lead to a significant drop in employment, but to little, if any, fall in the insider wage. However, once the shock disappears (so that the labor demand curve shifts out to its original position), the remaining insiders may be able to raise their wages without facing the threat of dismissal. In that event, there is a significant rise in the wage, while the rise in employment is muted.

Clearly, the degree of asymmetry in the insiders' wage response depends on the speed with which laid-off incumbents lose their insider status. For example, suppose that the insiders who remain employed after the adverse shock regard the laid-off incumbents as "near-insiders." Then, once the shock disappears, the remaining insiders may be reluctant to raise their wages sufficiently to prevent the laid-off incumbents from regaining their jobs. By implication, the asymmetry in the insiders' wage response will be weakened. If the shock is prolonged, however, the laid-off incumbents are unlikely to be viewed as "near-insiders."

Second, even in the absence of seniority and manipulable turnover costs, there may be an asymmetric wage response to positive and negative shocks due to asymmetric risks faced by the insiders in upswings and downswings. In an anticipated upswing, the insiders face no employment risk. Provided that nominal wages do not increase by more than their marginal revenue product, they are certain to retain their jobs, because they know the magnitude of the favorable shock. Consequently, the insiders have an incentive to demand higher wages without reducing their job security. By contrast, in an anticipated downswing, the insiders may face significant employment risk, because—in the absence of a comprehensive seniority system, covering all the occupations and geographic locations of the firm's workforce—each individual insider will be uncertain about whether he will be retained at the previous wage. Generally, insiders will respond to this employment risk not by reducing their wages sufficiently to preserve their job security (which is the opposite of what they do in an upswing), but rather by accepting a limited wage reduction together with a reduction in job security.

Third, an asymmetric wage response may occur in the special case when a labor union, dominated by insiders, has kinked indifference curves.[1] When employment falls short of the insider membership, the indifference curves may be downward-sloping in wage-employment space (reflecting the union's willingness to trade off wages for employment). However, when employment exceeds membership, the indifference curves may be rather flat (reflecting insiders' lack of concern about outsiders' interests). Now suppose that an adverse shock occurs that reduces employment—at the original wage—below union membership. In response, the union may allow some reduction in both the wage and insider employment and, with it, a drop in union membership. Yet once the labor demand curve shifts outward to its original position, the new, smaller union may no longer be interested in fully reversing the drop in membership. The insiders who were laid off are now outsiders, and the remaining insiders may exploit the outward shift of the labor curve by driving their wages up.

It is important to note, however, that the practical significance of this "membership effect" can be limited by countervailing influences that may be at least as strong: Not only may unions regard recently laid-off incumbents as "near-insiders" (along the lines discussed above), but union leaders may also regard a rise in membership as an advantage per se, since it raises membership fees and perhaps also the prestige and political power of the union.

Be that as it may, an asymmetric wage response to favorable and unfavorable shocks means that the effects of these shocks on employment persist in an asymmetric way. In particular, current favorable shocks tend to have a stronger effect on the future wage and a weaker effect on future employment than do current unfavorable shocks. In this sense, there is "asymmetric persistence" of the effects of temporary labor demand shocks on employment.

Observe that in our discussion above, the persistent effects of shocks arise entirely from the influence of insiders on wage setting. In this context, our analysis suggests that there may be *symmetric* persistence in response to *unforeseen* shocks, while there may be *asymmetric* persistence in response to *foreseen* shocks. Furthermore, it can be shown that the greater the labor turnover costs, the more persistent the effects of temporary shocks on wages and employment tend to be.

Yet insider influence on wage setting is clearly not the only conceivable source of effect persistence. Another source, as we have seen in chapter 9, comprises "insider membership rules," namely, the rules determining how many of the entrants become insiders, and how fast they do so, as well as rules governing how many insiders become outsiders after having lost employment, and how fast they do so. Understandably, these rules generate symmetric persistence when the entry-exit conditions are symmetric, and asymmetric persistence when (as in chapter 9) the entry-exit conditions are asymmetric.

11.1.2 Variability in Employment

Our discussion of effect persistence—whether symmetric or asymmetric—is relevant to pronounced and prolonged labor market shocks, i.e., shocks that are large enough and last long enough to make it worthwhile for firms to fire workers in the downswings and possibly rehire them in subsequent upswings. Yet if instead the shocks are mild and short-lived, then firms may have an incentive to hoard labor during downswings and bring this labor back into regular use during the upswings. In that event, the shocks will clearly not have persistent effects on employment; in fact, for labor that is hoarded, they have no employment effects at all.

Let us define "ordinary business cycles" to be a succession of such mild and short-lived downswings and upswings. To study labor hoarding under ordinary business cycles, it is necessary to extend our formal analysis of the previous chapters to cover intertemporal optimization problems of firms facing labor turnover costs. We assume that insider wages do not rise so much in an upswing as to make it unprofitable for firms to bring hoarded labor back into use. (There are many conceivable rationales for this assumption: wage contracts may be renegotiated only periodically; insiders may only have limited market power; or insiders may be up against their "relative profitability constraint," described in chapters 1 and 5). Firms' employment decisions are designed to maximize the present value of their profits, taking account of the labor turnover costs and the cyclic variations in the marginal revenue product of labor. The firms face a trade-off between the present value of expected labor turnover costs and the present value of profit gained through prompt employment adjustments.

Under these circumstances, it can be shown that the greater a country's labor turnover costs, *ceteris paribus*, the more labor will be hoarded over ordinary business cycles—and consequently the more stable its employment path and the lower the average level of unemployment may be over these cycles. In figure 11.1A, the solid line depicts the employment trajectory of a country with small turnover costs, whereas the broken line illustrates the employment trajectory of a country with large turnover costs.

Employment

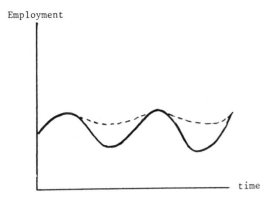

Figure 11.1A
Employment variability under ordinary business cycles.

Employment

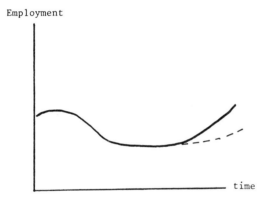

Figure 11.1B
Employment paths after a severe recession.

We wish to argue that, in the 1950s and early 1960s, many OECD countries may have experienced "ordinary business cycles." By contrast, however, in the worldwide recession of the late 1970s and early 1980s, these countries may have experienced a "pronounced and prolonged" adverse shock. This may be a reason why countries with high labor turnover costs stopped hoarding labor once the severity of the recession became evident. As we have discussed in the previous section, the insider-outsider theory suggests that the greater a country's labor turnover costs, *ceteris paribus*, the more persistent the employment effects of such a severe adverse shock—and consequently the higher the average level of unemployment in the wake of this shock. In figure 11.1B, the solid line depicts the postrecession employment path of a country with small turnover costs, whereas the broken line pictures this path for a country with large turnover costs.

The dynamic considerations above strengthen this conclusion. When a severe recession is followed by an upturn of uncertain magnitude and duration—such as the one starting in 1982—then countries with large labor turnover costs may be comparatively slow to raise their employment not only on account of the labor acquisition costs that this would involve, but also due to the expected future dismissal costs that would accrue were the upturn to turn out to be transient.

Juxtaposing these two types of shock, we are led to the following prediction: Countries with comparatively high labor turnover costs may be characterized by comparatively stable employment paths and comparatively low average levels of unemployment under ordinary business cycles; but these same countries may experience comparatively high levels of unemployment in the aftermath of a pronounced and prolonged adverse shock.

This argument may help explain

• why US employment was more variable than European employment in the 1950s and early 1960s and

• why the average rate of unemployment was significantly higher in the United States than in Europe in the 1950s and early 1960s, but significantly lower in the 1970s and 1980s.

11.1.3 Dual Labor Markets

"Dual labor markets" have been defined in different ways by different authors. What the various definitions have in common is that they focus on wage and job discrimination: Workers of comparable skills are better paid and have more job security in the "primary (formal) sector" than in the "secondary (informal) sector." We wish to concentrate on the following four features of dual labor markets:

i. Both the unemployed and the secondary-sector workers would prefer to be employed in the primary sector, but are unable to find jobs there.

ii. The retention probability of incumbent workers is greater in the primary than in the secondary sector.

iii. Employment is more variable in the secondary sector, accounting for more than a proportionate share of the employment increase in an ordinary cyclical upswing and of the employment decrease in a corresponding downswing.

iv. Firms in the primary sector have more extensive job ladders, and there may also be a tendency to fill the upper echelons of these ladders through internal promotion rather than through outside hiring.

By extending the formal analysis in the previous chapters, an insider-outsider rationale for these features can be derived. For this purpose, it is natural to distinguish between the primary and secondary sectors on the basis of labor turnover costs. In the primary sector, these turnover costs are high, wage contracts are generally covered by job security legislation, wage bargaining is frequently institutionalized, and consequently incumbent employees have significant market power. In the secondary sector, turnover costs are low, wages tend to be set through informal agreements, and workers have little (if any) market power.

In the light of this interpretation, the primary sector may be viewed as the proper focus of the insider-outsider theory, whereas the secondary sector may be covered by the traditional competitive theory of labor markets. Since the previous chapters focused on the insider-outsider theory, we assumed that workers are either unemployed or employed in what we have just defined as the primary sector. By contrast, we now assume that they have another choice: employment in the secondary sector. Accordingly, "insiders" are the incumbent employees in the primary sector, whereas "outsiders" now fall into two categories: the unemployed and the employees in the secondary sector.

In this context, our first two features of dual labor markets—namely, that outsiders would prefer to be insiders and that insiders have a higher retention probability than their counterparts in the secondary sector—follow straightforwardly from the basic premises of the insider-outsider theory (especially the notion that rent-related turnover costs permit insiders to enjoy more favorable conditions of work than those available to unemployed workers and secondary-sector employees.) Under deterministic conditions (such as those considered in chapters 3, 5, 7, and 8), the insiders may aim for the maximum wage compatible with complete job security.[2] Under stochastic conditions (such as those considered in chapters 6 and 9), the insiders face a trade-off between the wage and job security, and they generally choose both higher wages and more job security than they could have achieved in the absence of the turnover costs. As for the incumbent employees in the secondary sector, their positions are not protected by turnover costs, and consequently their wages and retention probabilities may be expected to be less than those of the insiders in the primary sector.

Our feature (iii) of dual labor markets—namely, that employment in the secondary sector is more variable than that of the industrial sector, over the course of ordinary business cycles—may be rationalized in two ways. First, by our argument on employment variability in section 11.1.2, firms in the primary sector may engage in more "intertemporal smoothing" of employment over ordinary business cycles than do firms in the secondary sector, due to the differences in labor turnover costs. Second, the insiders—through their influence on their wages—may reinforce this tendency. If the insiders in the primary sector are able to achieve more job security than the incumbents in the secondary sector and if, in addition, entrants to the primary sector become insiders during an ordinary cyclic upswing, then primary-sector employment—comprising both insiders *and* entrants—will be more stable than secondary-sector employment. The shorter the time span within which entrants turn into insiders (i.e., the shorter the period over which recently hired employees are exposed to competitive pressures), *ceteris paribus*, the more stable the employment in the primary sector can be expected to be.

Finally, let us address our feature (iv) of dual labor markets—namely, that firms in the primary sector may have more extensive job hierarchies than do firms in the secondary sector, and that firms in the primary sector might be more reliant on internal promotion than are firms in the secondary sector. For this purpose, we need to extend our previous models to take account of *different types of insiders*. In practice, the distinction between "insiders" and "entrants" in the primary sector is generally one of degree rather than of kind. The longer the span of time over which a worker remains employed at a particular firm, the greater the costs of replacing him and the greater his bargaining strength tends to be (possibly up to some limit). The reasons for this are various: workers' legal rights, their influence over other workers, their ability to cooperate with colleagues and trainees, their power within their unions, and their opportunities to damage their firms, as well as feelings of loyalty and commitment between management and long-term employees—all these features tend to become more pronounced with the length of employer-employee association. Thus, as an employee rises through progressive stages of "insiderness," he may be able to negotiate employment contracts that provide progressively higher wages and greater degrees of job security. This, in short, is the idea underlying the insider-outsider rationale for wage scales and seniority systems.

Of course, labor turnover costs provide only one of the many conceivable criteria whereby the primary and dual labor markets (characterized by the features above) may be distinguished from one another. For example, in the context of the efficiency wage theory, the ability to monitor productivity serves as the main distinguishing criterion: Productivity in the primary sector is monitored imperfectly, and thus each firm there offers a wage that minimizes the efficiency wage; by contrast, productivity in the secondary sector may be monitored more accurately, and thus workers there receive approximately their marginal revenue products. Thereby the efficiency wage theory provides an alternative rationale for our features (i) and (iv) of dual labor markets: In order to encourage effort and to attract and retain high-ability employees, it may be in the firms' interests to offer wages in excess of the secondary-sector wage and to allow these wages and job security to rise with job tenure. Furthermore, features (ii) and (iii) may be explained by those versions of the efficiency wage theory in which firms' wage offers are designed to discourage workers from quitting.

There are, however, some obvious conceptual distinctions to be made between the insider-outsider and the efficiency-wage explanations of dual labor markets. For example, in the insider-outsider setup, the different features of the primary and secondary sectors depend, at least in part, on employees' opportunities for cooperating with and harassing one another. They also depend on employees' effort response to changes in job security, as well as on the degree of unionization. These factors are not important in the efficiency-wage setup, where the focus is on monitoring technologies and the productivity response to wage offers.

It is well to keep in mind, however, that the sharp distinction between the primary and secondary sectors is made primarily for simplicity. In practice, the difference is one of degree, and the insider-outsider theory may capture this difference through gradations in labor turnover costs, while the efficiency wage theory may do so through gradations in monitoring and in the responsiveness of productivity to wages.

11.1.4 Unemployment: Its Level, Duration, and Composition

Since the insider-outsider theory focuses on wage determination and labor demand in the primary sector, it cannot provide a comprehensive account of unemployment without some extra assumptions about (a) the aggregate labor supply and (b) the labor demand in the secondary sector. Chapters 3–6, which dealt formally with involuntary unemployment, tackled these assumptions in a particularly simple way: The labor supply was assumed to be exogenously given and the secondary sector was assumed absent. These were simplifications appropriate to the main purpose of these chapters, namely, to portray involuntary unemployment as job discrimination and to explain how such unemployment can arise from the exercise of insider power.

However, once we seek to explain the *level of unemployment*, these simplifications are no longer harmless. Accordingly, let us now consider the following more general—and plausible—assumptions:

a. The slope of the aggregate labor supply curve (in wage-employment space) is greater than that of the aggregate labor demand curve; i.e., it is either upward sloping or has a flatter downward slope than the labor demand curve. Consequently, a rise in the wage is associated with a rise in excess labor supply (or a fall in the excess labor demand).

b. There exists a secondary sector where wages and employment are determined competitively (i.e., they are given by the intersections of the demand and supply curves for labor in that sector).

The second assumption implies that, in equilibrium, the marginal outsider must be indifferent between working in the secondary sector and remaining unemployed. The nonmarginal, unemployed workers are without jobs because they *choose* not to work for the wage prevailing in the secondary sector. There are various reasons why they may do so. For example:

• Due to adverse selection or moral hazard, accepting a job in the secondary sector may reduce a worker's chances of gaining employment in the primary sector.

• Some workers may be able to search more effectively for primary-sector employment when they are unemployed rather than employed in the secondary sector. (Thus, some of the unemployed may queue for primary-sector jobs for the same reason as they do for urban-sector jobs in the Harris-Todaro model.)

• Independently of his chances of gaining employment in the primary sector, a workers tastes across employment and unemployment may be such that he prefers unemployment to secondary-sector employment, although he may of course prefer primary-sector employment to unemployment. For instance, people with specialized education or specific training may be reluctant to take jobs that do not permit them to use their specific skills, and thus they may have a high reservation wage for work in the secondary sector. (An unemployed school teacher may be unwilling to work as a street vendor, even if he could thereby earn more than his previous teacher's salary.)

The insider-outsider theory is not meant to describe the division of workers between secondary-sector employment and unemployment. It can, however, shed light on why workers may be involuntarily unemployed in the context of the dual labor market above. According to our notion of involuntary unemployment, amplified in chapters 3–5, workers are involuntarily unemployed when they are out of work because they face a more limited choice set—in terms of labor services supplied and wage received —than the insiders (in the primary sectors) do. This applies regardless of whether or not these workers refuse jobs in the secondary sector. The point at issue is that if these unemployed outsiders had the opportunity to work under the same conditions as the insiders, they would be willing to perform the insiders' work for less than the prevailing insider wage. But, on account of the rent-related turnover costs, they lack this opportunity. This is the sense in which involuntary unemployment can arise despite the existence of a market-clearing secondary sector.

Similarly, workers who accept jobs in the secondary sector may face "job discrimination," in the sense that they are unable to find work in the primary sector even though they are willing to work under the same terms as the insiders. This is the insider-outsider interpretation of a phenomenon that is often called "disguised unemployment," as distinguished from "open unemployment" (which we have discussed above). The theory suggests that disguised and open unemployment are similar problems, being two alternative consequences of discrimination in the labor market.

Given assumptions (a) and (b) above, the insider-outsider theory yields various qualitative predictions concerning the level of unemployment. In the simple models presented in this book, we have seen that the insider wage is inversely related to the size of the initial incumbent workforce and positively related to the magnitude of labor turnover costs and/or the bargaining strength of the insiders (which may depend, in part, on the degree to which the insiders are unionized). Moreover, a rise in the insider wage may be expected to lead to a rise in the level of unemployment, not only because labor demand in the primary sector may be inversely related to the insider wage, but also because a rise in the insider wage may induce workers to leave employment in the secondary sector and become unemployed. The reason for the latter (supply-side) effect is this: When the primary-sector wage increases relative to the secondary-sector wage, more workers may choose not to work in the secondary sector, because (as noted in our previous discussion) they now perhaps have a greater need to avoid adverse productivity signals and to search intensively for primary-sector jobs.

Furthermore, as we have seen in section 11.1.1, as well as chapters 9 and 10, the larger the labor turnover costs and the more powerful the insiders, the more persistent the effects of temporary labor demand shocks on the insider wage and the level of employment will tend to be. The argument above suggests that this persistence can be expected to generate persistence in unemployment as well.

In studying the causes of unemployment, it may be instructive to decompose a change in the unemployment rate into (i) a change in the rate of *inflow* into the pool of unemployed workers and (ii) a change in the rate of *outflow* from that pool. During the recessions of the 1970s and 1980s, the rise in unemployment in many European countries appears to have come about mainly through a fall in the outflow rate from the unemployment pool, rather than from a rise in the inflow rate.

The traditional Keynesian theory does not explain such asymmetric movements in the inflow and outflow rates. According to Keynesian principles, we would expect a fall in aggregate demand to induce some firms to lay off employees (thereby raising the inflow rate into the unemployment pool) and other firms to reduce their hiring (thereby reducing the outflow rate from that pool). There is no obvious reason, within that theoretical framework, why the latter tendency should significantly dominate the former.

The insider-outsider theory, by contrast, may help shed some light on this asymmetry. On account of labor turnover costs, firms may find it much cheaper to reduce their workforces through reductions in their hiring relative to their quits and retirements rather than through dismissals. Thus, in a moderate business downturn, or in the early stages of a severe one, firms may respond mainly by hiring fewer entrants than heretofore. Provided that the rate of voluntary exit from the labor force (due to retirement, the "discouraged worker effect," intertemporal substitution of labor supply, and so on) does not respond significantly to the downturn, the reduction in hiring implies a drop in the outflow rate from the unemployment pool. Furthermore, provided that the rate of voluntary entry to the labor force (by school leavers, people quitting the household sector, immigrants) also is not very responsive to the downturn, the absence of significant firing activity means that the inflow rate to the unemployment pool does not rise markedly. In short, the rise in unemployment is due more to a fall in the outflow rate than to rise in the inflow rate.

By contrast, the insider-outsider theory predicts that the inflow rate will rise in a severe business downturn. The reason is that, under these conditions, firms may wish to reduce their workforces faster than their employees' quit and retirement rates will allow, and consequently they may have an incentive to fire some of their insiders.

Turning to the *duration of unemployment*, the insider-outsider theory suggests some reasons why unemployment spells are much longer in some countries than in others, even after normalizing for differences in present and past unemployment rates. In the early 1980s, unemployment spells lasted, on average, 3–4 months in the United States, but were close to 1 year in Europe. At that time, the proportion of people continuously out of work for more than a year was typically 30–50% (of the total number of unemployed) in European countries, but it was well under 15% in the United States. These differences deserve special policy attention, since unemployment may become a particularly serious social problem once people's unemployment spells last a long time. It is perhaps mainly after lengthy unemployment spells that people's skills, as well as their attitudes to work, deteriorate.

As we have seen, the insider-outsider theory predicts that insiders' chances of retaining their existing jobs are generally much greater than the outsiders' chances of finding new jobs. This implies that unemployment is distributed unequally among workers. The greater the labor turnover costs and the greater the bargaining strength of insiders, the more unequal the distribution of unemployment spells is predicted to be.

Further mileage can be gained from the theory by allowing for different degrees of "outsiderness." The simplest way of doing this is to disaggregate the outsiders into short-term and long-term unemployed. It may be argued that, in general, the short-term unemployed tend to be closer substitutes for the current insiders than are the long-term unemployed. Not only is it reasonable to suppose that the short-term unemployed suffer from less skill attrition and obsolescence than do the long-term unemployed, but they tend also to have closer personal ties to the current insiders and thus are less likely to be the brunt of insiders' rent-creating activities (e.g., harassment or withdrawal of cooperation). For these reasons, the short–term unemployed may have a better chance of gaining employment than that facing the long-term unemployed. This is a possible rationalization of the evidence that workers' probability of finding jobs falls with their duration of unemployment.

It is, of course, easy to adduce other rationalizations as well. For instance, according to some variants of the efficiency wage theory, the length of unemployment spells may be used as a screening device for worker productivity. Moreover, in some models of job search, workers infer their probabilities of employment from the length of their unemployment spells and thus the long-term unemployed may become "discouraged" and withdraw from the labor force. Workers who have been unemployed for prolonged periods may also be subject to various psychological pressures, eroding their self-confidence and raising their preference for unemployment as a way of life. In contrast to these varius explanations, the insider-outsider theory emphasizes the size of labor turnover costs as determinant of inequality in the distribution of unemployment spells.

Finally, turning to the *composition of unemployment*, the insider-outsider theory offers an explanation for the comparatively high unemployment rates among youth, the female population, and various minority groups. The theory predicts that unemployment rates will be comparatively high for people with comparatively little stability in their work records—quite apart from the obvious reason that the more frequently people change their jobs, the more likely they are to be "frictionally" unemployed (i.e., in transit between one job and the next). The frequent job changes by young people may be attributed to their limited information about their job opportunities and about their abilities to match their skills and interests with the employers' needs. Women frequently exit from the workforce to care for their children or to accompany their husbands on job relocation. Some minority and immigrant workers may have a preference for temporary jobs and may also have limited information about job opportunities. Such people become outsiders more frequently than the average worker. According to the insider-outsider theory, outsiders have a lower chance of employment than insiders, and for this reason the theory predicts that youth, female, and some minority unemployment rates will be comparatively high. The greater the labor turnover costs and the stronger insiders' bargaining power, *ceteris paribus*, the more these unemployment rates are predicted to diverge from the average.

11.1.5 The Phillips Curve

The role that the insider-outsider theory attributes to incumbent workers also has implications for the Phillips curve. This relation—whether the original inflation-unemployment trade-off or the reinterpretation as product supply curve—is generally seen to reflect aggregate demand and supply conditions in the overall labor market. The insider-outsider theory, by contrast, maintains that conditions *inside* the individual firms are also relevant to the Phillips curve. In particular, the theory highlights intra-firm determinants such as

- the size of their incumbent workforces,
- the magnitude of their labor turnover costs,
- the bargaining strength of their incumbents,
- the speed with which entrants become insiders, and
- the speed with which insiders lose their power after leaving employment.

This emphasis on the labor market within each firm—rather than just on conditions external to the firm—reflects the basic assumption of the insider-outsider theory that the outsiders are disenfranchised in the process of wage determination and that the insiders are concerned primarily with their own wages and job security.

However, it is important to emphasize that the insider-outsider theory does *not* imply that the relation between wages and employment depends *only* on conditions inside the firms. Rather, it suggests that these intrafirm conditions have a role to play *in addition* to the "external" labor market conditions, such as the level of unemployment. This is so for several reasons.

First, although firms' internal conditions may be important to the wage-employment trade-off in the primary sector, external conditions may be dominant in the secondary sector (where wages are determined competitively). Thus the relative macroeconomic importance of internal versus external conditions depends on the pervasiveness of labor turnover costs, which underlie our distinction between the primary and secondary sectors. For example, the broader the coverage of union wage agreements and of job security legislation, and the greater the insiders' opportunities to engage in rent-creating activities, the more important we would expect the intrafirm conditions to become.

Second, the relative importance of internal versus external conditions depends on what we have called "insider membership rules." The longer the transition times between outsider and insider status (*ceteris paribus*), the stronger the influence of outsiders on wage and employment determination. In particular, the longer it takes for workers to lose their insider status (i.e., their influence in wage negotiations) after becoming unemployed (*ceteris paribus*), the more say the unemployed have in wage negotiations and the more important external labor market conditions may be expected to become. Thus, in countries where a small number of unions represent the interests of large population segments, the level of unemployment may play a particularly important role in wage determination. Furthermore, assuming that entrants receive their reservation wage,[3] the longer it takes for entrants to become insiders (*ceteris paribus*), the larger the proportion of entrants in firms' total workforces, and consequently the greater the influence of external conditions (as reflected in the entrants' reservation wage).

Third, external labor market conditions may affect insider wages in the primary sector due to the firms' influence on wage negotiations. Since insider wages are generally the outcome of negotiations in which both insiders and their firms have some say, these wages reflect both the insiders' and firms' objectives. The latter objectives, in turn, reflect external conditions in a straightforward way: The greater the ratio of vacancies to unemployment in the overall labor market, the lower is a firm's probability of attracting, motivating, and retaining all the labor it demands at any given wage—consequently, the higher is its profit-maximizing wage offer (*ceteris paribus*).

Fourth, the unemployed workers can also affect insiders' objectives in wage negotiations, since they are able to influence the insiders' bargaining positions within their firms. This can happen in a variety of ways. We have encountered one example in chapter 5, where insiders set their wage to remain at least as profitable as potential entrants, whose wage is equal to the outsiders' reservation wage. Thus, if a rise in the unemployment rate reduces this reservation wage, there will be a fall in the maximum wage that insiders can obtain without being replaced by outsiders.

Another way in which the unemployed may affect insider wages is by influencing the insiders' chances of finding new employment in case of dismissal. In particular, the greater the unemployment rate (*ceteris paribus*), the lower an insider's reemployment probability in case he should lose his current job. Consequently, the more importance insiders may be expected to attach to job security, and thus the more moderate their wage claims may turn out to be. Here it is the insiders' fear of losing their jobs—rather than the unemployed workers' ability to bid down wages, as emphasized in the conventional interpretations of the Phillips curve—that is responsible for downward pressure exerted by the unemployment rate on wages.

Moreover, the shorter the unemployment spells, the more substitutable outsiders and insiders may be expected to be. As we have discussed in the previous section, one reason is that short unemployment spells may mean little attrition of skills and work attitudes, and another is that the short spells imply little interruption of interpersonal relations between insiders and outsiders. Consequently, our analysis supports the hypothesis that the short-term unemployment rate has a larger influence on the wage-employment trade-off than the long-term unemployment rate. (Layard and Nickell, 1986, and Nickell, 1987, provide empirical support for this hypothesis.)

For these various reasons, the insider-outsider theory suggests that *both* internal conditions within the firms *and* the external conditions of the aggregate labor market are relevant to the wage-employment trade-off. The same reasons also help explain why, in the context of our theory, secular increases in the labor force do not necessarily lead to secular rises in unemployment. Historically, labor force growth has characteristically been accompanied by growth in productivity (associated with techno-logical progress) and growth in product demand (associated with the popu-lation growth), which tend to raise the demand for labor. Moreover, by showing how external labor market conditions affect insiders wages—especially via insiders' fear of losing their jobs and via firms' objectives in wage negotiations—our theory suggests why insiders have not exploited the secular rise in productivity and product demand by driving up their own wages at the expense of steady increases in the unemployment rate. In short, the theory is an "insider-outsider theory," not just an "insider theory," and it generates a variety of conditional predictions concerning the relative importance of the internal and external conditions above.

11.1.6 Interindustry Wage Structure

The apparent stability of the interindustry wage structure across occupa-tions, age groups, durations of job tenure, and countries has received renewed interest among economists. Industries that pay comparatively high wages to blue collar workers tend to be same as those that pay comparatively high wages to their white collar workers. The same tends to be true for a variety of occupational groups.[4] The regularity is also appa-rent for young and old workers and for workers with long and short job tenure,[5] which appears to imply that wage differences among industries cannot be fully explained by differences in human capital or in seniority. There also appears to be a close correlation among industry earnings of countries with markedly different labor market institutions (such as the United States, the United Kingdom, France, Germany, Sweden, and Korea).

Turning from the stability of the interindustry wage structure to its determinants, a few tentative empirical generalizations can be made. Industries that pay comparatively high wages tend to be characterized by high profits,[6] high concentration ratios in the product markets,[7] high capital-labor ratios,[8] and high union density.[9]

Various attempts have been made to explain this evidence. For example, according to the perfectly competitive theory of labor markets, interindustry wage differences among workers with identical measurable characteristics must be due to unmeasured differences in job attributes or in labor quality. Yet it is obviously beyond the scope of this theory to explain why interindustry wage structure is related to interindustry differences in concentration ratios and union density. Nor does the perfectly competitive theory explain why quit rates are comparatively low in the high-wage industries.[10] (If the industries that pay comparatively high wages are compensating their workers for onerous jobs or high abilities, then it is not clear why these workers should be comparatively disinclined to leave their jobs.)

Another approach is to try to understand the interindustry wage structure in terms of a competitive labor market model that is modified by adjustment costs. According to this approach, industries whose products are in rising demand are the ones that earn comparatively high profits and pay comparatively high wages. In this way, they encourage the entry of new firms and attract workers from industries whose products are in falling demand. This process is gradual and continues for as long as interindustry demands are changing. In this context, the stability of the interindustry wage structure across occupations, countries, age groups, and durations of job tenure may be viewed as the outcome of gradual, dynamic, free-market responses to changes in the composition of demand. The relation between wages and marginal profits across industries may be rationalized in this way as well. Note, however, that this approach does not predict wage differentials across industries with equal marginal profits and unequal average profits. Moreover, this theory, like the perfectly competitive approach, is not designed to explain how interindustry wage differentials are related to interindustry differences in concentration ratios and union density.

A quite different explanation of the interindustry wage structure is offered by the efficiency wage theory, which focuses on interindustry differences in the relation between wages (on the one hand) and productivity and quit-related costs (on the other). In particular, industries that pay comparatively high wages are the ones that, according to the theory, are comparatively successful in eliciting work effort and reducing quits.[11]

However, since the theory assumes wages to be set in accordance with firms' profit-maximizing principles, it cannot explain the relation between wages and union density. Nor does the theory appear to have been successful in explaining the relation between wages and profits across industries.

The insider-outsider theory offers another possible explanation of interindustry wage structure, one that does not share the particular drawbacks above and that appears to be complementary to the efficiency wage theory. As we have seen, the insider-outsider theory depicts insider wages as the outcome of a bargaining process whereby firms and their insiders share the economic rent from insider employment. In a Nash bargaining context (such as that of chapter 9), the amount of rent that the insiders capture is positively related to how much the firm stands to lose in the event of a "disagreement" (which may be characterized by a strike, work-to-rule actions, the replacement of insiders by new entrants, or other forms of industrial conflict). It can be shown that, under quite general conditions, the greater the profit, the concentration ratio, the capital-labor ratio, and the union density of an industry, the more firms stand to lose from a breakdown in wage negotiations with their insiders—and by implication, the higher the wages that these industries are prepared to pay (see Lindbeck and Snower, 1987d).

Beyond that, the theory suggests a further hypothesis (as yet untested) concerning interindustry wage structure: The industries that have comparatively high labor turnover costs tend to pay comparatively high wages (*ceteris paribus*). The reason, of course, is that the greater these costs, the greater the rent from insider employment and, given the relative bargaining strengths of firms and their insiders, the higher the wage that the insiders will be able to achieve.

These considerations may shed some light on why the industries that offer high pay to workers in one occupation tend also to offer high pay to workers in other occupations: The high-wage industries may be particularly vulnerable to the exercise of insider power. For example, industries that earn comparatively high profits tend to have a comparatively high stake in avoiding labor conflict among workers of *all* the relevant occupational groups. The same may be said of workers of different ages and different lengths of job tenure. Finally, the insider-outsider theory suggests that the similarity of interindustry wage structures in different countries may be due in part to similarities in the interindustry structures of labor turnover costs, particularly training.

11.2 Policy Implications

In the face of substantial unemployment and high labor turnover costs, what can governments do to stimulate employment and reduce unemployment? Little work has been done thus far on exploring the policy implications of the insider-outsider theory, and accordingly, our brief remarks here must be considered tentative.

Sections 11.2.1 and 11.2.2 will deal with what we shall call "structural labor market policies," namely, government policies that are designed to change the structure of institutions, laws, and contractual agreements with a view to creating greater equality of opportunity in the labor market. Section 11.2.3 will discuss the relative desirability of these policies vis-à-vis demand management and supply-side policies.

It is convenient to divide the structural policies into two groups:

i. policies to diminish insider power, which we shall call "power-reducing policies" for short, and

ii. policies to "enfranchise" outsiders in the wage negotiation process, to be called "enfranchising policies."

The former policies are designed to limit the preferential treatment insiders receive in the labor market. They may do this by reducing firms' costs of firing insiders or by reducing insiders' opportunities for engaging in rent-creating activities. The latter policies are aimed at inducing firms to hire more outsiders. For example, laws to reduce severance payments belong to the former group, whereas tax incentives for profit-sharing schemes belong to the latter.

Although both sets of policies are meant to reduce labor turnover costs, weaken the position of the insiders, and give the outsiders greater job opportunity, they achieve these ends through different means. Power-reducing policies aim to give insiders less economic rent to exploit; in the process, more outsiders may well be hired, but that is a by-product—rather than a proximate effect—of these policies. Enfranchising policies are designed to reduce firms' cost of hiring outsiders and thereby give more workers insider status—without necessarily weakening the positions of the previous incumbents.

11.2.1 Structural Policies: Reducing Insider Power

Power-reducing policies can take many forms. On the one hand, they may involve dismantling some existing job-security legislation, such as laws to reduce severance pay or to simplify firing procedures. On the other hand, they may cover legislation to reduce union power, such as legal restrictions on strikes and picketing.

The case for these policies is worth close attention. When insiders use their power to discourage firms from hiring outsiders, then there is a case of egalitarian fairness to be made in favor of policies that reduce the legal protection and rent-creating opportunities associated with insiders' jobs. A macroeconomic case can be made as well, since a reduction in the insiders' bargaining power may lead to a fall in unemployment and to a rise in production.

Clearly, the strength of this case depends on the degree to which insiders take outsiders' interests into account. To make our argument as clearly and simply as possible, the formal models of this book have all assumed that insiders are *completely* unconcerned about outsiders. In practice, however, insiders may have various self-interested motives not to ignore the outsiders' interests. For example, when there are increasing returns to labor or complementarities among heterogeneous workers to be exploited, the insiders may forgo rent-creating activities in order to induce their firm to expand employment, thereby raising the marginal revenue product of the incumbent workforce and giving the insiders an opportunity to achieve a higher wage. The insiders also have an incentive to encourage hiring of outsiders when union bargaining strength is strongly related to the size of union membership. Obviously, the greater the degree to which the insiders represent the interests of the unemployed, the less effective (and the less essential) power-reducing policies can be expected to be in equalizing worker incomes and stimulating macroeconomic activity.

The case for power-reducing policies also depends on "insider membership rules," determining the requirements for entry to and exit from insider status. The larger the proportion of entrants to become insiders within a specified period of time, the less opportunity do firms have to take advantage of the differential between insider and entrant wages, and consequently the more bite power-reducing policies can be expected to have. Furthermore, the larger the proportion of laid-off workers who lose their insider status within a specified period, the less the interests of the laid-off workers are represented by the current insiders, and the greater the potential impact of these policies.

It is important, though obvious, to note that power-reducing policies are usually not Pareto-improving. Rather, they tend raise the outsiders' chances of employment at the cost of reducing the insiders' real wages and job security. Thus, when a government attempts to implement these policies, it is likely run into all the various social and political difficulties that characteristically arise when there are conflicts of interest over income distribution and vested interest groups are stripped of some power. (However, the greater an insider's risk of becoming an outsider in the future, the greater his own incentive to take the interests of outsiders into account.)

This is a potentially important deficiency—one that other policies to stimulate employment may not share, or share in lesser measure. For instance, demand-management policies—*if* they are effective in raising the demand for labor—may be easier to implement, since they may make the outsiders better off without necessarily making the insiders worse off. We shall return to the effectiveness of demand management, which was also analyzed in chapter 10.

11.2.2 Structural Policies: "Enfranchising" Outsiders

One of the central messages of the insider-outsider theory is that outsiders are disenfranchised in the wage negotiation process. Not only are they absent from the negotiations, but the existence of large labor turnover costs may rob them of much indirect influence on these negotiations as well. In this context, we now turn to enfranchising policies, which aim to bring more workers into the employment pool and thereby give more people a voice in the wage negotiations.

The case for enfranchising policies, like that for power-reducing policies, clearly depends on the degree to which insiders take outsiders' interests into account, and on the stringency of insider membership rules. Obviously, the more insiders stand to lose from expanding employment, the greater their rent-creating activities are likely to be, and the greater the scope for the enfranchising policies. Similarly, the longer it takes for entrants to become insiders and the faster laid-off insiders become outsiders, the greater the number of workers disenfranchised in the wage negotiation process, and the more effective these policies may become.

Enfranchising policies are many and varied. First, there are *profit-sharing schemes* of labor remuneration, whereby workers receive part of their pay as a share of firms' profits. Governments could promote such schemes through a variety of tax incentives. These schemes do not necessaritly affect the cost of firing insiders, but they do make the hiring of new recruits cheaper. By reducing the marginal cost of hiring entrants, these schemes may induce existing firms—and new ones—to hire outsiders, who will then presumably have some say in future wage negotiations. In this manner, the insider-outsider theory lends some support to Weitzman's (1984,

1987) assertion that profit-sharing schemes can help fight unemployment.

The theory does, however, point attention to some potential difficulties in stimulating employment through profit-sharing schemes. Unless sufficient profit is shared, these schemes—like the power-reducing policies—may not be Pareto-improving: They may raise outsiders' chances of employment at the cost of reducing insiders' wage incomes. In that event, the insiders may engage in a variety of rent-creating activities in order to discourage firms from hiring new recruits under the profit-sharing schemes. Thus, the employment gains from adopting these schemes may be limited. In particular, the gains depend on the net impact of two countervailing influences: The direct effect of the schemes is to reduce the marginal cost of hiring new workers, the indirect effect may be to induce insiders to engage in rent-creating activities that (among other things) raise the marginal cost of hiring.

In order for profit-sharing schemes to receive the insiders' cooperation, enough profit must be shared to more than compensate the insiders for the loss of market power from rent-creating activities. Even then, as we have seen in chapter 5, these schemes may be unable to prevent some forms of rent-creation—e.g., harassment of entrants by insiders—because firms may be unable to monitor some rent-creating activities accurately and objectively. Two-tier wage systems, whereby incumbent workers receive at least their previous remuneration level while new recruits receive permanently less, may be time-inconsistent since firms may find it profitable to replace the incumbents by the recruits once the latter have acquired the necessary skills.

It is also well to remember that profit-sharing schemes *do* impose costs on all workers participating in them. For example, these schemes generally impose risk on the employees (since the receipt of profit is uncertain) and, for reasons of adverse selection and moral hazard, the employees may be unable to avoid the cost of risk-bearing through insurance contracts. In addition, the employees may find it necessary to bear costs of monitoring managers' profit-accounting practices. Moreover, managers may wish to avoid a system of compensation that requires such monitoring by employees, possibly through their unions. The potential difficulties above should not, however, obscure the real possibility that profit-sharing schemes might actually work well, under certain circumstances, in dealing with labor market problems of the insider-outsider variety.

Second, the governments may be able to encourage *apprenticeship systems* and thereby lengthen what previous chapters have termed the "initiation period," i.e., the time span that elapses before a newly hired worker is able to renegotiate his wage, to acquire the productive skills and rent-creating abilities of an insider, and to satisfy any union membership rules. What apprenticeship systems often do is to extend the period covered by entrants' wage contracts. Whereas profit-sharing schemes aim to enfranchise outsiders by reducing firms' per period marginal cost of hiring, apprenticeship systems do so by giving firms a longer span of time in which to take advantage of the differential between insiders' and entrants' wage claims.

Third, *vocational training programs*—subsidized or run by the government—might help "enfranchise" outsiders. These programs are meant to make outsiders potentially more profitable to firms, without directly affecting the productive and rent-creating skills of the insiders. Clearly, the effectiveness of these vocational training programs depends on the relative importance of general skills and firm-specific skills in overall worker productivity. If firm-specific skills predominate, then these programs cannot be of much help to outsiders.

Of course, if general skills predominate and if vocational training programs actually manage to improve these skills, then the level of unemployment will fall, albeit for not entirely conventional reasons. In particular, the training programs would raise the entrant demand curve and—if the entrant wage does not rise in proportion—firms would undertake new hiring. The new recruits would eventually join the ranks of the insiders, and the new, larger group of insiders would set their wages with a view to retaining their jobs. Thus, unemployment may remain permanently lower.

Furthermore, it is conceivable that insiders may seek to protect their positions by varying the training that entrants receive. In particular, an outsider may be considered involuntarily unemployed if his potential productivity depends on training received by insiders and if these insiders maintain their wages and job security by providing deficient training. But barring this possibility, the outsider does not face discrimination in the labor market, and consequently the vocational training programs are not compensating for such discrimination. They may, however, be rectifying unequal educational opportunities. These are important issues for a government to confront before deciding whether to provide training that firms have no incentive to provide themselves.

Fourth, *job-sharing programs* during recessions are a particularly straightforward way of enfranchising workers in the wage negotiation process, provided that these programs are not implemented in such a way as to increase firms' labor costs per hour. By providing tax incentives for such programs, governments may be ensure that insider status is given to more workers, all of whom have a vested interest in negotiating their wages with their own job security in mind.

Aside from the various well-known objections to job sharing (which we do not follow up here), it is well to observe that this policy is generally not Pareto-improving either. If the policy is implemented solely with regard to new hires, then the gainers are the outsiders who now have parttime work, while the losers are the incumbents whose real income may fall as a result of the expansion of the insider workforce. Thus, insiders may resist the implementation of these programs by engaging in various rent-creating activities.

Finally, *reducing barriers to the entry of new firms* may be a particularly effective way of enfranchising outsiders. New firms generally have no insiders, though with the passage of time their employees may eventually become insiders. Consequently, new firms may be in an especially good position to create employment opportunities.

The market power of incumbent firms, much like that of incumbent workers, may be responsible for involuntary unemployment in an insider-outsider setting. Just as incumbent workers may find it in their interest to erect entry barriers (in the form of labor turnover costs) against potential job holders, so incumbent firms may have an incentive to erect entry barriers against new firms. This can be a serious practical obstacle to expanding employment, since the creation of new firms is frequently cited as an important source of new jobs in countries emerging from a recession. In countries with comparatively high barriers to firm entry, the existing firms may be hampered by the rent-creating activities of their insiders, while new firms (which have no insiders) have difficulty getting started. Evidence that such entry barriers tend to be higher in Europe than in the United States may help explain why Europe has been less successful than the United States in creating new jobs in the 1970s and 1980s.

Thus, government policies to reduce entry barriers may be a potentially important contribution to reducing unemployment. These policies can come in many forms. For example, government regulations governing the creation of new firms can be dismantled; financial institutions can be given incentives to reduce credit restrictions on new firms; the systems of profit taxes, income taxes, capital gains, and wealth taxes can be changed to put new firms at less of a disadvantage vis-à-vis the incumbent firms. Finally, government measures to reduce the industrial, occupational, and geographic coverage of union wage agreements may also encourage the entry of new firms, since these agreements determine the degree to which new firms are legally bound to pay insider wages. This last point may be particularly important since new firms tend to be especially hard hit by hiring and firing costs: These firms tend to have comparatively few workers close to retirement age, and consequently they are in a poor position to reduce their workforces through natural attrition.

11.2.3 Demand Management, Supply-Side Policies, and Structural Policies

What does the insider-outsider theory tell us about the relative desirability of using demand management, supply-side policies, and structural policies in dealing with unemployment and stagnation arising from the exercise of insider power? To fix ideas, we take demand management policies to be ones that work primarily through their influence on aggregate product demand; supply-side policies are aimed at expanding the economy's production possibility frontier; and structural policies are the power-reducing and enfranchising policies that we have discussed above. For simplicity, let us consider the relative effectiveness of these policies in the context of a particularly simple insider-outsider model (e.g., see chapter 10): We assume that the insiders periodically set their nominal wages (either individual-istically or through unions); entrants receive their reservation wages, which (for expositional simplicity) are exogenously given in real terms; and firms make the employment, production, and pricing decisions.

In this context, there are at least two routes whereby demand management can raise employment and production: (a) It can raise the price level before the insiders have a chance to adjust their nominal wages, thereby reducing the real product wage and inducing firms to hire more workers, or (b) it can give firms the incentive to expand employment at any given real wage. Route (a) involves a movement along a downward-sloping labor demand curve, whereas route (b) involves either an outward shift of that curve or a movement along a horizontal segment of the labor demand curve.

It may be tempting to argue that the effects of demand management under route (a) are only temporary, i.e., that they last for only as long as it takes insiders to adjust their nominal wages. Yet, in the context of the insider-outsider theory, this is not necessarily the case. The employment increase, induced by the fall in the real wage, can lead to an expansion of the insider workforce in the future, which, in turn, may keep the future insider wage lower than it would otherwise have been, and thereby stimulate future employment. In this manner, the employment effects of demand management under route (a) may persist through time.

However, it is doubtful that route (a) tells the whole story, for if it did, aggregate product demand and the real wage would always move in opposite directions. Thus, let us turn to route (b). As we have shown in chapter 10, if firms have unused machines and unmanned assembly lines when a business upswing starts, it may be possible to raise output without reducing the marginal product of labor. Furthermore, if the hoarded labor is insufficient to put this idle capital capacity into use, then there may be new hiring without a fall in the product wage rate. Then the labor demand curve will be flat as long as the idle capital is available. Besides, if the labor demand curve is downward-sloping, a rise in government product demand may shift this curve outward by encouraging the entry of new firms or by raising the marginal product of labor (say, through investment in industrial infrastructure).

In short, demand management policies are effective in shifting the labor demand curve insofar as they have "supply-side" effects! Supply-side policies, of course, work quite straightforwardly: They simply shift the labor demand curve by raising the marginal product of labor.

How does such a labor demand shift affect wages and employment in our insider-outsider framework? This question was addressed in section 11.1.1, where we showed that the persistent wage-employment effects of labor demand shocks may be either "symmetric" or "asymmetric." The policy implications of these two types of persistence are radically different.

In countries where there is strong symmetric persistence, but weak asymmetric persistence, there may be a strong case in favor of expansionary demand management and supply-side policies—provided, of course, that these policies have a significant impact on employment. In fact, the case for such policies may be much stronger than the traditional Keynesian and Neoclassical theories would suggest, because a current policy shock does not merely raise current employment, but—due to the consequent expansion of the insider workforce—may raise future employment as well.

By contrast, in countries where there is strong asymmetric persistence, expansionary demand management and supply-side policies may not be very effective. Although contractionary policies may reduce employment, expansionary ones may do little to increase it. Rather, the impact of the expansionary policies may be largely dissipated in wage increases. Under these circumstances, structural policies (as defined above) may be necessary to reduce the degree of asymmetric persistence. Not only may these policies stimulate employment in their own right, but they may also create labor market conditions that make demand management and supply-side policies more effective.

These considerations might suggest that a combination of expansionary demand management policies and wage controls may be an effective means of stimulating employment. In particular, the demand expansion may shift the labor demand curve outward while the wage controls may prevent the insiders from exploiting this outward shift. Although this is indeed a theoretical possibility, we are doubtful of its practical feasibility. Past experience tells us that wage controls tend eventually to result in wage explosions and distorted wage rates among different categories of workers.

The insider-outsider theory is still in its infancy, and much work remains to be done. Among other things, it would be particularly important (a) to provide an integrated analysis of the "formal" and "informal" sectors of the labor market, (b) to incorporate into the theory an analysis of labor supply decisions, covering households' allocation of time among leisure, "formal-sector" work, and "informal-sector" work, (c) to explore the intertemporal implications of our analysis for wage and employment decisions, (d) to integrate our labor market analysis in an explicit macroeconomic model, and (e) to analyze the effectiveness of government policies in this context.

Nevertheless, the broad drift of the theory is clear: It is concerned about equality of opportunity in the labor market. It shows that outsiders may not have the opportunity to participate in the labor market on equal terms with the insiders, not only on account of job security legislation, but also because insiders may have strong incentives to engage in discriminatory activities. The discrimination does not arise because the insiders are malicious. Quite the contrary, they may prefer to have the outsiders "in"— provided that their own jobs and wages are not threatened in the process. In fact, however, insiders' jobs and wages *are* threatened, and this is why the discrimination occurs, and why involuntary unemployment may arise.

Notes

1. See, for example, Lockwood and Manning (1987) and Carruth and Oswald (1987).

2. There are, of course, circumstances under which insiders cannot achieve complete job security even under deterministic conditions. For example, in section 11.1.1 we argued that insiders may lose their jobs in a foreseen downswing either when senior workers can manipulate labor turnover costs or when insider unions are willing to accept job reductions in return for wage increases. Yet even under these circumstances, it may well be true that, for a downswing of given magnitude, insiders have a higher average probability of retaining their jobs than their counterparts in the secondary sector.

3. In practice, of course, the entrant wage need not always be equal to the outsiders' reservation wage. Insiders may use their market power to drive up not only their own wages, but those of the entrants as well. This may be an effective way for insiders to restrict entry to the firm's workforce and thereby (under diminishing returns to labor) raise the insider marginal product and the insider wage. But even under these circumstances the entrant and insider wages will be related to the outsiders' reservation wage, because the insiders wish to avoid making entrant and insider wage claims that induce the firm to replace the insiders by outsiders instead.

4. See, for example, Dickens and Katz (1986a).

5. See Krueger and Summers (1986, 1988).

6. See, for example, Dickens and Katz (1986b), Blanchflower, Oswald, and Garrett (1987), and Pugel (1980).

7. See, for example, Dickens and Katz (1986b), Kwoka (1983), and Mishel (1982).

8. See, for example, Dickens and Katz (1986b) and Lawrence and Lawrence (1985).

9. See, for example, Dickens and Katz (1986b) and Podgursky (1986).

10. See Pencavel (1970).

11. See Krueger and Summers (1988).

References

Akerlof, G. A., 1970, The Market for Lemons, Qualitative Uncertainty and the Market Mechanism, *Quarterly Journal of Economics*, 84, 488–500.

Akerlof, G. A., 1982, Labour Contracts as Partial Gift Exchange, *Quarterly Journal of Economics*, 97, 543–569.

Akerlof, G. A., and Miyazaki, H., 1980, The Implicit Contract Theory of Unemployment Meets the Wage Bill Argument, *Review of Economic Studies*, 47(2), 321–338.

Akerlof, G. A., and Yellen, J. L., 1985, A Near-Rational Model of the Business Cycle, with Wage and Price Intertia, *Quarterly Journal of Economics*, 100, 823–838.

Alchian, A. A., 1970, Information Costs, Pricing and Resource Unemployment, in E. Phelps et al. (1979), 27–52.

Alchian, A. A., and Demsetz, H., 1972, Production, Information Costs and Economic Organization, *American Economic Review*, 62, 777–795.

Alogoskoufis, G., and Manning, A., On the Persistence of Unemployment, *Economic Policy*, forthcoming.

Aoki, M., 1980, A Model of the Firm as a Stockholder-Employee Cooperative Game, *American Economic Review*, 70(4), 600–610.

Arrow, K., 1963, Uncertainty and the Welfare Economics of Medical Care, *American Economic Review*, 53.

Ashenfelter, O., and Johnson, G. E., 1969, Bargaining Theory, Trade Unions and Industrial Strike Activity, *American Economic Review*, 59(1), 35–49.

Azariadis, C., 1975, Implicit Contracts and Underemployment Equilibria, *Journal of Political Economy*, 83, 1183–1202.

Azariadis, C., and Stiglitz, J. E., 1983, Implicit Contracts and Fixed Price Equilibria, *Quarterly Journal of Economics*, 98, 1–22.

Bailey, M. N., 1974, Wages and Employment under Certain Demands, *Review of Economic Studies*, 41, 37–50.

Barro, R. J., 1972, A Theory of Monopolistic Price Adjustment, *Review of Economic Studies*, 39(1), 17−26.

Barro, R. J., 1976, Rational Expectations and the Role of Monetary Policy, *Journal of Monetary Economics*, 2(1), 1−32.

Barro, R. J., and Grossman, H. I., 1976, *Money, Employment and Inflation* (Cambridge, Cambridge University Press).

Begg, D., Insider Out: Counterintuitive Properties of a Dynamic Game in an Insider-Outsider Framework, mimeo.

Benassy, J. P., 1975, Neo-Keynesian Disequilibrium in a Monetary Economy, *Review of Economic Studies*, 42, 502−523.

Benassy, J. P., 1977, A Neo-Keynesian Model of Price and Quantity Determination in Disequilibrium, in G. Schwodiauer, ed., *Equilibrium and Disequilibrium in Economic Theory* (Dordrecht, Reidel).

Bishop, R. L., 1964, A Zeuthen-Hicks Model of the Bargaining Process, *Econometrica*, 411−417.

Blanchard, O., and Kiyotaki, N., 1987, Monopolistic Competition and the Effects of Aggregate Demand, *American Economic Review*, 77(4), 647−666.

Blanchard, O., and Summers, L., 1986, Hysteresis and the European Unemployment Problem, *NBER Macroeconomics Annual*, Vol. 1 (Cambridge, MA, MIT Press), 15−17.

Blanchard, O., and Summers, L., 1987, Hysteresis in Unemployment, *European Economic Review*, 31, 1/2, 288−295.

Blanchflower, D. G., Oswald, A. J., and Garrett, M. D., 1987, Insider Power in Wage Determination, Part II, mimeo, Centre for Labour Economics, London School of Economics.

Blinder, A. S., 1980, Inventories in the Keynesian Macro Model, *Kyklos*.

Blinder, A. S., 1981, Inventories and the Structure of Macro Models, *American Economic Review*, 7(2), 11−16.

Brown, C., Gilroy, C., and Kohen, A., 1982, The Effect of the Minimum Wage on Employment and Unemployment, *Journal of Economic Literature*, 20, 487−528.

Brunner, K., Cukierman, A., and Meltzer, A. H., 1980, Stagflation, Persistent Unemployment and the Permanence of Economic Shocks, *Journal of Monetary Economics*, 6, 467−492.

Bulow, J., and Summers, L., 1986, A Theory of Dual Labor Markets with Application to Industrial Policy, Discrimination and Keynesian Unemployment, *Journal of Labor Economics*, 4, 377−414.

Calmfors, L., and Horn, H., 1985, Classical Unemployment, Accommodation and the Adjustment of Real Wages, *Scandinavian Journal of Economics*, 87, 234−261.

Calvo, G. A., 1979, Quasi-Walrasian Theory of Unemployment, *American Economic Review*, 69, No. 2, 102–107.

Calvo, G. A., and Wellisz, S., 1978, Supervision, Loss of Control, and the Optimum Size of the Firm, *Journal of Political Economy*, 86, 943–952.

Carlton, D. W., 1978, Market Behaviour with Demand Uncertainty and Price Inflexibility, *American Economic Review*, 68(4), 571–587.

Carlton, D. W., 1979, Contracts, Price Rigidity and Market Equilibrium, Journal of *Political Economy*, 87(5), 1034–1062.

Carruth, A. A., and Oswald, A. J., 1987, On Union Preferences and Labor Market Models: Insiders and Outsiders, *Economic Journal*, 97, 431–445.

Chamberlain, E. H., 1933, *The Theory of Monopolistic Competition* (Cambridge, MA, Harvard University Press).

Corden, A. M., 1981, Taxation, Real Wage Rigidity and Employment, *Economic Journal*, 91, 309–330.

Cross, J. G., 1965, A Theory of the Bargaining Process, *American Economic Review*, 66–94.

Diamond, P., 1982, Aggregate Demand Management in Search Equilibrium, *Journal of Political Economy*, 86, 943–952.

Dickens, W., and Katz, L., 1986a, Industry and Occupational Wage Patterns and Theories of Wage Determination, mimeo.

Dickens, W., and Katz, L., 1986b, Inter-Industry Wage Differences and Industry Characteristics, in K. Lang and J. Leonard eds., *Unemployment and the Structure of Labour Markets* (Oxford, Basil Blackwell).

Dixon, H., 1987, An Imperfectly Competitive Model with Walrasian Features, *Oxford Economic Papers*, 39(1), 134–160.

Doeringer, P. B., and Piore, M. J., 1971, *Internal Labor Markets and Manpower Analysis* (Lexington, MA, Heath).

Drazen, A., 1985a, Cyclical Determinants of the Natural Level of Economic Activity, *International Economic Review*, 26, No. 2, 387–397.

Drazen, A., 1985b, Involuntary Unemployment and Aggregate Demand Spillovers in an Optimum Search Model, mimeo.

Dreze, J., 1975, Existence of an Equilibrium under Price Rigidity and Employment, *Economic Journal*, 91, 309–330.

Ehrenberg, R. G., 1971, Heterogenous Labour, the Internal Labour Market, and the Dynamics of the Employment-Hours Decision, *Journal of Economic Theory*, 85–104.

Epstein, L., 1982, Competitive Dynamics in the Adjustment-Cost Model of the Firm, *Journal of Economic Theory*, 27.

Farber, H. S., 1978, Bargaining Theory, Wage Outcomes, and the Occurrence of Strikes, *American Economic Review*, 68(3), 262–271.

Fitoussi, J.-P., and Phelps, E. S., 1987, *The Slump in Europe: Reconstructing Open Economy Theory* (Oxford, Basil Blackwell).

Flanagan, R. J., 1973, The US Phillips Curve and International Unemployment Rate Differentials, *American Economic Review*, 63, 114–131.

Friedman, M., 1968, The Role of Monetary Policy, *American Economic Review*, 58, 1–17.

Friedman, M., 1976, *Price Theory* (Chicago, Aldine).

Fudenberg, D., and Tirole, J., 1986, A Theory of Exit in Duopoly, *Econometrica*, 54(4), 943–960.

Gordon, D. F., 1974, A Neoclassical Theory of Keynesian Unemployment, *Economic Inquiry*, 12, 431–459.

Gordon, R. J., 1972, Wage-Price Controls and the Shifting Phillips Curve, *Brookings Papers on Economic Activity*, 2, 385–421.

Gottfries, N., and Horn, H., 1986, Wage Formation and the Persistence of Unemployment, *Economic Journal*, 97, 877–884.

Gramlich, E., 1976, Impact of Minimum Wages on Other Wages, Employment and Family Incomes, *Brookings Papers on Economic Activity*, 2, 409–451.

Gregory, R. G., 1986, Wages Policy and Unemployment in Australia, *Economica*, 53, 553–574.

Gronau, R., 1971, Information and Frictional Unemployment, *American Economic Review*, 61, 290–301.

Grossman, S., and Hart, O., 1981, Implicit Contracts, Moral Hazard and Unemployment, *American Economic Review*, 61, 301–307.

Grossman, S., and Hart, O., 1983, Implicit Contracts under Asymmetric Information, *Quarterly Journal of Economics*, 98, 1223–1256.

Grossman, S., and Weiss, L., 1982, Heterogeneous Information and the Theory of the Business Cycle, *Journal of Political Economy*, 90, 699–727.

Guash, J. L., and Weiss, A., 1980, Wages and Sorting Mechanisms in Competitive Markets with Asymmetric Information: A Theory of Testing, *Review of Economic Studies*, 47, 653–664.

Gylfason, T., and Lindbeck, A., 1984, Union Rivalry and Wages: An Oligopolistic Approach, *Economica*, 51, 129–139.

Hall, R. E., 1975, The Rigidity of Wages and the Persistence of Unemployment, *Brookings Papers on Economic Activity*, 2, 301–335.

Harris, J., and Todare, M., 1970, Migration, Unemployment and Development: A Two-Sector Analysis, *American Economic Review*, 126–143.

Harsanyi, H. C., 1956, Approaches to the Bargaining Problem before and after the Theory of Games, *Econometrica*, 144–157.

Hart, O. D., 1982, A Model of Imperfect Competition with Keynesian Features, *Quarterly Journal of Economics*, 97, 109–138.

Hart, O. D., 1983, Optimal Labour Contracts under Asymmetric Information: An Introduction, *Review of Economic Studies*, 50, 3–36.

Hayes, B., 1984, Unions and Strikes with Asymmetric Information, *Journal of Labor Economics*, 57–83.

Horn, H., 1983, Imperfect Competition in Models of Wage Formation and International Trade, PhD dissertation, Monograph No. 15 (Institute for International Economic Studies, University of Stockholm).

Kahneman, D., and Tversky, A., 1979, The Prospect Theory: An Analysis of Decision under Risk, *Econometrica*, 47, 263–291.

Keynes, J. M., 1936, *The General Theory of Employment, Interest and Money* (London, Macmillan).

Krueger, A. B., and Summers, L. H., 1986, Reflections on the Inter-Industry Wage Structure, in K. Lang and J. Leonard, eds., *Unemployment and the Structure of Labor Markets* (Oxford, Basil Blackwell).

Krueger, A. B., and Summers, L. H., 1988, Efficiency Wages and the Inter-Industry Wage Structure, *Econometrica*, 56, 259–294.

Kwoka, J., 1983, Monopoly, Plant and Union Effects on Worker Wages, *Industrial and Labor Relations Review*, 36, 251–257.

Lawrence, C., and Lawrence, R., 1985, Relative Wages in US Manufacturing: An Endgame International, *Brookings Papers on Economic Activity*, 47–106.

Layard, R., and Nickell, S., 1985, The Causes of British Unemployment, *National Institute Economic Review*.

Layard, R., and Nickell, S., 1986, The Performance of the British Labour Market, London School of Economics, Centre for Labour Economics Discussion Paper No. 250.

Lazear, E., 1981, Agency, Earnings Profiles, Productivity and Hours Restrictions, *American Economic Review*, 71, 606–620.

Leontief, W., 1946, The Pure Theory of the Guaranteed Annual Wage Contract, *Journal of Political Economy*, 54, 76–79.

Lindbeck, A., 1963, *A Study in Monetary Analysis* (Stockholm, Almquist and Wiksell).

Lindbeck, A., and Snower, D. J., 1984a, Involuntary Unemployment as an Insider-Outsider Dilemma, Seminar Paper No. 282, Institute for International Economic Studies, University of Stockholm; revised version in W. Beckerman, ed., *Wage Rigidity and Unemployment* (Duckworth), 1986, 97−125.

Lindbeck, A., and Snower, D. J., 1984b, Strikes, Lock-Outs and Fiscal Policy, Seminar Paper No. 309, Institute for International Economic Studies, University of Stockholm and Discussion Paper No. 178 (Birkbeck College, London); revised version: Strikes and Lock-Out Threats and Fiscal Policy, *Oxford Economic Papers*, 39, December 1987, 760−784.

Lindbeck, A., and Snower, D. J., 1984c, Labor Turnover, Insider Morale and Involuntary Unemployment, Seminar Paper No. 310, Institute for International Economic Studies, University of Stockholm; revised version: Job Security, Work Incentives, and Unemployment, *Scandinavian Journal of Economics*, forthcoming.

Lindbeck, A., and Snower, D. J., 1985a, Cooperation, Harassment, and Involuntary Unemployment, Seminar Paper No. 321, Institute for International Economic Studies, University of Stockholm; revised version: *American Economic Review*, 78(1), March 1988, 167−188.

Lindbeck, A., and Snower, D. J., 1985b, Explanations of Unemployment, *Oxford Review of Economic Policy*, 1(2), Spring 1985, 34−69.

Lindbeck, A., and Snower, D. J., 1986, Wage Setting, Unemployment and Insider-Outsider Relations, *American Economic Review Proceedings*, 76, May 1986, 235−239.

Lindbeck, A., and Snower, D. J., 1987a, Union Activity, Unemployment Persistence, and Wage-Employment Ratchets, *European Economic Review Proceedings*, 31, 1986, 157−167.

Lindbeck, A., and Snower, D. J., 1987b, Efficiency Wages versus Insiders and Outsiders, *European Economic Review Proceedings*, 31, 407−416.

Lindbeck, A., and Snower, D. J., 1987c, Transmission Mechanisms from the Product to the Labor Market, Institute for International Economic Studies, Seminar Paper No. 403, University of Stockholm.

Lindbeck, A., and Snower, D. J., 1987d, Inter-industry Wage Structure and Insider Power, mimeo.

Lockwood, B., and Manning, A., Dynamic Wage-Employment Bargains with Endogenous Membership, mimeo.

Lovell, M. C., 1972, The Minimum Wage, Teenage Unemployment and the Business Cycle, *Western Economic Journal*, 10, 414−427.

Lucas, R. E., 1972, Expectations and the Neutrality of Money, *Journal of Economic Theory*, 4(2), 103−124.

Lucas, R. E., 1973, Some International Evidence on Output-Inflation Trade-Offs, *American Economic Review*, 63, 326−334.

Lucas, R. E., 1976, Econometric Policy Evaluation: A Critique, in K. Brunner, ed., *The Phillips Curve and Labour Markets*, supplement to the *Journal of Monetary Economics*, 1, 19–46.

Lucas, R. E., and Rapping, L. A., 1970, Real Wages, Employment and Inflation, in E. Phelps et al. (1979), 257–305.

MaCurdy, T. E., and Pencavel, J. H., 1982, Testing between Competing Models of Wage and Employment Determination in Unionized Markets, Stanford University, mimeo.

Malcomson, J. M., 1981, Unemployment and the Efficiency Wage Hypothesis, *Economic Journal*, 91, 848–866.

Malinvaud, E., 1977, *The Theory of Unemployment Reconsidered* (Oxford, Basil Blackwell).

Mankiw, N. G., 1985, Small Menu Costs and Large Business Cycles: A Macro-economic Model of Monopoly, *Quarterly Journal of Economics*, 100, 529–539.

Manning, A., 1987, An Integration of Trade Union Models in a Sequential Bargaining Framework, *Economic Journal*, 97(385), 121–139.

Marshak, J., and Radner, R., 1972, *Economic Theory of Teams* (New Haven, Yale University Press).

Maurice, S. C., 1974, Monopsony and the Effects of an Externally Imposed Minimum Wage, *Southern Economic Journal*, 41, 283–287.

McCall, J. J., 1970, Economics of Information and Job Search, *Quarterly Journal of Economics*, 84, 113–126.

McCallum, B. T., 1980, Rational Expectations and Macroeconomic Stabilisation Policy: An Overview, *Journal of Money, Credit and Banking*, 12(4), 716–746.

McDonald, I. M., and Solow, R. M., 1981, Wage Bargaining and Employment, *American Economic Review*, 71, 896–908.

Mincer, J., 1976, Unemployment Effects of Minimum Wages, *Journal of Political Economy*, 84, 87–105.

Mishel, L., 1982, Product Markets, Establishment Size and Wage Determination, *Industrial Relations Research Association Series*, Proceedings, 447–454.

Mitchell, D. J. B., 1985, Explanations of Wage Inflexibilities: Institutions and Incentives, Working Paper, No. 80, UCLA.

Moore, D. T., 1971, Unemployment Effects of Minimum Wages on Teenage Unemployment Rates, *Journal of Political Economy*, 79, 897–903.

Mortensen, D. T., 1970, Job Search, the Duration of Unemployment and the Phillips Curve, *American Economic Review*, 60, 847–861.

Mortensen, D. T., 1973, Generalised Costs of Adjustment and Dynamic Factor Demand Theory, *Econometrica*, 41.

Mortensen, D. T., 1988, The Persistence and Indeterminacy of Unemployment in Search Equilibrium, *Scandinavian Journal of Economics*, forthcoming.

Muellbauer, J., and Portes, R., 1978, Macroeconomic Models with Quantity Rationing, *Economic Journal*, 88, 788–821.

Muth, J. F., 1961, Rational Expectations and the Theory of Price Movements, *Econometrica*, 29, 315–335.

Nalebuff, B. J., and Stiglitz, J. E., 1985, Quality and Prices, *Quarterly Journal of Economics*, forthcoming.

Negishi, T., 1977, Existence of an Underemployment Equilibrium, in G. Schodiauer, ed., *Equilibrium and Disequilibrium in Economic Theory* (Boston, Reidel).

Nickell, S. J., 1978, Fixed Costs, Employment and Labour Demand over the Cycle, *Economica*.

Nickell, S. J., 1982, A Bargaining Model of the Phillips Curve, London School of Economics, Centre for Labor Economics, Discussion Paper.

Nickell, S. J., 1986, Dynamic Models of Labour Demand, in O. Ashenfelter and R. Layard, eds., *Handbook of Labor Economics* (Amsterdam, North-Holland).

Nickell, S. J., 1987, Why Is Wage Inflation in Britain So High?, *Oxford Bulletin of Economics and Statistics*, 49(1).

Nickell, S. J., and Andrews, M., 1983, Unions, Real Wages and Employment in Britain, 1951–79, *Oxford Economic Papers*, 35, 183–206.

Nickell, S. J., and Wadhwani, S., 1987, Insider Forces and Wage Determination, London School of Economics, mimeo.

Oi, W., 1962, Labor as a Quasi-Fixed Factor of Production, *Journal of Political Economy*, 538–555.

Okun, A. M., 1975, Inflation: Its Mechanics and Welfare Cost, *Brookings Papers on Economic Activity*, 2, 351–401.

Okun, A. M., 1981, *Prices and Quantities* (Washington, DC, The Brookings Institution).

Oswald, A. J., 1982, The Microeconomic Theory of the Trade Union, *Economic Journal*, 92, 576–595.

Oswald, A. J., 1985, The Economic Theory of Trade Unions: An Introductory Survey, *Scandinavian Journal of Economics*, 87(2), 160–193.

Parsons, D. O., 1973, Quit Rates over Time: A Search and Information Approach, *American Economic Review*, 63, 390–401.

Pencavel, J., 1970, *An Analysis of the Quit Rate in American Manufacturing Industry* (Princeton, Industrial Relations Section).

Perry, G. L., 1980, Inflation in Theory and Practice, *Brookings Papers on Economic Activity*, 1, 207–241.

Phelps, E., 1967, Phillips Curves, Expectations of Inflation, and Optimal Unemployment over Time, *Economica*, 34, 254–281.

Phelps, E., 1970a, Money Wage Dynamics and Labour Market Equilibrium, in E. Phelps et al. (1979), 124–166.

Phelps, E., 1970b, Introduction: the New Microeconomics in Employment and Inflation Theory, in E. Phelps et al. (1979).

Phelps, E., et al., 1979, *Microeconomic Foundation of Employment and Inflation Theory* (New York, Norton).

Podgursky, M., 1986, Unions, Establishment Size, and Intro-Industry Threat Effects, *Industrial and Labor Relations Review*, 39.

Pugel, T., 1980, Profitability, Concentration and the Inter-industry Variation in Wages, *Review of Economics and Statistics*, 62, 248–253.

Ragan, J. F., 1977, Minimum Wages and the Youth Labour Market, *Review of Economics and Statistics*, 59, 129–136.

Reder, M., and Neumann, G. R., 1980, Conflict and Contract: The Case of Strikes, *Journal of Political Economy*, 867–886.

Salop, S. C., 1979, A Model of the Natural Rate of Unemployment, *American Economic Review*, 69(1), 117–125.

Sargent, T. J., 1976, A Classical Macroeconomic Model for the United States, *Journal of Political Economy*, 84, 207–237.

Sargent, T. J., and Wallace, N., 1975, Rational Expectations, the Optimal Monetary Instrument and the Optimal Money Supply Rule, *Journal of Political Economy*, 83(2), 241–254.

Shaked, S., and Sutton, J., 1984, Involuntary Unemployment as a Perfect Equilibrium in a Bargaining Model, *Econometrica*, 52, 1351–1364.

Shapiro, C., and Stiglitz, J. E., 1984, Equilibrium Unemployment as a Worker Discipline Device, *American Economic Review*, 74(3), 433–444.

Shestinski, E., and Weiss, Y., 1977, Inflation and Costs of Price Adjustment, *Review of Economic Studies*, 44, 287–303.

Shiller, R. J., 1978, Rational Expectations and the Dynamic Structure of Macroeconomic Models, *Journal of Monetary Economics*, 4, 1–44.

Simon, H. A., 1979, Rational Decision Making in Business Organisations, *American Economic Review*, 69, 493–513.

Siven, C. H., 1974, Consumption, Supply of Labour and Search Activity in an Intertemporal Perspective, *Scandinavian Journal of Economics*, 7(1), 44–61.

Snower, D. J. 1983a, Imperfect Competition, Underemployment and Crowding-Out, *Oxford Economic Papers*, 35, 245–270.

Snower, D. J., 1983b, Search, Flexible Wages and Involuntary Unemployment, Discussion Paper No. 132, Birkbeck College, University of London.

Solow, R., 1985, Insiders and Outsiders in Wage Determination, *Scandinavian Journal of Economics*, 87(2), 143–159.

Stigler, G., 1946, The Economics of Minimum Wages Legislation, *American Economic Review*, 36, 358–365.

Stiglitz, J. E., 1974, The Efficiency Wage Hypothesis, Surplus Labour and the Distribution of Income in LDC's, *Oxford Economic Papers*, 28, 185–207.

Stiglitz, J. E., 1985, Equilibrium Wage Distributions, *Economic Journal*, 95, No. 379, 595–618.

Stiglitz, J. E., and Weiss, A., 1981, Credit Rationing in Markets with Imperfect Information, *American Economic Review*, 71, 393–410.

Sutton, J., 1986, Non-Cooperative Bargaining Theory: An Introduction, *Review of Economic Studies*, 53(5), 709–724.

Wachter, M. L., 1976, Some Problems in Wage Stabilisation, *American Economic Review*, 66, 65–71.

Walters, A. A., 1971, Consistent Expectations, Distributed Lags and the Quantity Theory, *Economic Journal*, 81, 273–281.

Weiss, A., 1980, Job Queues and Layoffs in Labour Markets with Flexible Wages, *Journal of Political Economy*, 88, 526–538.

Weiss, Y., 1972, On the Optimal Pattern of Labour Supply, *Economic Journal*, 82, 1293–1315.

Weitzman, M. L., 1982, Increasing Returns and the Foundations of Unemployment Theory, *Economic Journal*, 92, 787–804.

Weitzman, M. L., 1984, *The Share Economy* (Cambridge, MA, Harvard University Press).

Weitzman, M. L., 1987, Steady State Unemployment under Profit Sharing, *Economic Journal*, 97(385), 86–105.

Welch, F., 1974, Minimum Wage Legislation in the United States, *Economic Inquiry*, 12(3), 285–318.

Williamson, O. E., Wachter, M. L., and Harris, J. E., 1975, Understanding the Employment Relation: The Analysis of Idiosyncratic Exchange, *Bell Journal of Economics*, 6, 250–278.

Name Index

Subject Index